SUPER WORKING MOM'S HANDBOOK

Roseann Hirsch

WARNER BOOKS
A Warner Communications Company

Produced by Ultra Communications Inc.

Illustrations by Rose Mary Slader
Design and Art Direction by Jonette Jakobson Designs Unlimited
Contributor and Research Editor: Diana Childress

Warner Books, 666 Fifth Avenue, New York, NY 10103
A Warner Communications Company

Printed in the United States of America
First Printing: January 1986
10 9 8 7 6 5 4 3 2 1

Library of Congress Cataloging in Publication Data

Hirsch, Roseann C.
Super working mom's handbook.

1. Child rearing—Handbooks, manuals, etc.
2. Mothers—Employment—handbooks, manuals, etc.
I. Title.
HQ772.H55 1986 649'.1 85-8985
ISBN 0-446-38073-3 (U.S.A.) (pbk.)
0-446-38074-1 (Canada) (pbk.)

TO

Brian, Nicky, and Jonathan, who make being a mother pretty terrific.

Barry, who loves me when I'm not so super.

Connie, the starmaker . . .

Table of Contents

CHILD CARE

COPING

EDUCATION

FOOD

HEALTH

HOUSEKEEPING

JOB NOTES

JUST FOR YOU

SAFETY

SINGLE MOMS

TRAVEL

TION

eeds a little explaining: *You* are a super working mom *already*: You a family—and some of you are doing it without the help of a mate. super than that?

Don't wo… don't look like the working women you see photographed in magazines. Or if your living room sometimes resembles the Salvation Army drop-off center, or if your children go to school in wrinkled jeans. You are not supposed to be perfect—you are only supposed to get through the days in the best possible way that you can. And that's what the *Super Working Mom's Handbook* is all about. It is a book to help you handle those million and one details that make your life so very complicated and busy.

This book is broken down into sections like Coping, Child Care, Housekeeping and many more. In each of them you'll find helpful tips and ideas to make your life easier. Each article is self-contained, so you can read it quickly and find the information you need fast. It is not a book to be read all at once—you'll find you'll come back to it again and again. Use it as a reference. Consult it in an emergency. Curl up with it in a quiet moment—(should one come along). Just remember that there are millions of women out there like you struggling to get through the days and get it all done. You are not alone.

CHILD CARE

Guidelines for Going Back to Work

How old should my child be before I return to my job? Every working mother worries about this, especially if she has taken an extended maternity leave or left work altogether to stay home "while the kids are young." But there is no simple answer, for it depends largely on your child's individual personality and development and on all the circumstances surrounding your return to work. Ideally, you should plan to start working when your child is at the right developmental stage and when your working will not require major changes in his life.

Developmental guidelines can help give you an idea of what to expect at different ages, but it's important to remember that at any age change is stressful. By choosing a relatively tranquil time in his life—not, for example, directly after other stressful events such as a divorce or a death in the family—you can increase your chances of a successful adjustment.

Three to Eight Months Moms who definitely plan to return to work will find the transition easier if the stay-at-home does not exceed eight months, for infants usually begin to be fearful of strangers some time around their eighth month. Within three or four months after birth, babies are generally sleeping through the night and feeding on reasonably regular schedules; moms have recovered their strength and energy (and maybe even their figures) and have had time to choose a caretaker and accustom the baby to her handling.

Eight to Thirty Months Strong negative reactions to changes in child-care arrangements, and sometimes even to familiar sitters, are common among babies between eight and twelve months and toddlers between eighteen and thirty months—ages when separation anxiety often peaks. Returning to work at these critical times will be more difficult but need not be disastrous if the adjustments the child needs to make are introduced as gradually as possible. The new sitter should get to know your baby well beforehand, and their time together should be increased little by little; established routines should be strictly honored and regressions sympathetically tolerated; and your own absences should be kept to what is essential. He will need your undivided attention for ten or fifteen minutes before you leave in the morning and just after you come home, and you should plan as much additional quality time together as you can reasonably fit in.

Three to Five Years Most children take readily to nursery school at two-and-a-half or three years of age. They look forward to playing with their peers and to all the stimulating activities nursery schools offer. But since starting pre-school is in itself a big adjustment to make, it's wise to see that your child is comfortable with the new routine before setting out to work. As with younger children, a gradual transition is best.

Six to Twelve Years Moms who have left work to stay home with young children usually find that the simplest time to rejoin the work force is when the youngest starts school. For many families it makes the most sense economically. It's easiest on the child, too, for he is now in school much of the workday and deeply involved with his own friends and interests. A regular schedule of after-school activities can be planned to keep him busy and cared for until your return.

Older children are often so capable of looking after their own physical needs that it is easy to forget how great their emotional and psychological needs still are. Even teenagers can be distressed when good old dependable at-home mom leaves the kitchen for an office. Keeping in touch with their needs and concerns is as vital as hiring a baby-sitter would be for an infant. Parental involvement and attention are still important. Fortunately, now much of it can be accomplished with written messages, phone calls, and evening "dates" you will both enjoy.

What to Know About Hiring Someone to Care for Your Child

Choosing a caretaker for your child is one of the most important decisions you'll have to make as a working mother, but it need not be the most difficult. Intuition and common sense will be your best guides.

You might begin by thinking of the qualities you will look for. Remember, your sitter will be taking care of your child during her early, formative years. You will want someone who is cheerful, patient, energetic, experienced with small children, mature enough to handle any emergencies, and self-assured enough to cope with temper tantrums or wheedling. She must be loving, kind, and warmhearted. You will need her to be calm and easygoing but also dependable and punctual. Because your child will be learning constantly from her, you want someone able to help her learn to talk, to read to her, to answer her questions. How do you snare this paragon?

Looking for Likely Prospects

Neighborhood sources are often the best: Other mothers and their caretakers, relatives, neighbors, and friends may know of someone looking for employment. References and recommendations are easy to come by, and you can learn a lot about the person before you set up an interview.

Baby-sitting agencies are also an excellent source, because they do the initial screening for you. They check references and training, and give you a list of applicants. You will need to assess the reliability of the agency as well as check the references for yourself and interview the candidates.

Newspaper advertising in local newspapers can get the largest response. You will have to screen the applicants very carefully, but if you keep at it, you may find just the person you want.

Firming Up Your Expectations

Figure out the hours you will need your caretaker. Take into account your commuting time and whether you would like her to stay late one day a week to give you and your husband an evening out. Think of what chores you expect from her in addition to child care. Do you want her to do the laundry, buy the groceries, prepare the evening meal (regularly or occasionally), take clothes to the dry cleaners, do light housework? Consider, too, what kind of activities you want her to provide for your child. If you value fresh air and sunshine for your child, will she take her regularly to the playground? Will she help your child meet and learn to get along with other children? Do you need her to take your child to music lessons or other activities? Will she welcome your child's friends to your house and take your child to their homes for play dates? Think of any personal habits you would find it difficult to tolerate, such as smoking if you and your husband are nonsmokers.

Conducting the Interview

Find out ahead of time as much as you can about the applicant—age, experience, education, references (check these before the interview). Schedule the interview at a time your husband can be there and your child is awake and not hungry or tired, for you will want to know their reactions to her, too.

The interview should accomplish three things:

1. Make your expectations clear to the applicant.
2. Let both you and her know whether your child-raising philosophies agree. Have a list of questions ready to determine whether her views on feeding, discipline, toilet training, television, freedom to explore the environment, closely reflect your own. Ask, for example, if she thinks a baby should be picked up when it cries? Should you tell a child "no" when she reaches for something breakable, or move it out of her reach? How would she deal with a temper tantrum at the supermarket?
3. Reveal how you react to each other personally. You, your husband, and your child will react favorably or unfavorably to her personality. Don't lightly dismiss any instinctive negative reactions, for it is difficult to develop and maintain a trusting relationship with someone you don't like.

A final word: When you have made your choice, allow for a shake-down time. Have your caretaker start working for you *before* you return to work. It will help all of you to get acquainted and make the transition easier for you and your child.

Key Questions to Ask a Prospective Baby-Sitter

When interviewing a potential baby-sitter for your child, include questions that will elicit her values and attitudes toward child-raising. You are not looking for right or wrong answers, but whether her views reflect your own closely enough for you to entrust your child to her. Focus on key issues. Here are some sample questions you can adapt to fit your own needs—and some acceptable and unacceptable answers.

***1.* What do you do if a child cries when her mother leaves?**
Acceptable: Soothe and reassure her that her mother will return, distract her by suggesting other activities, read to her
Unacceptable: Go to another room and let her cry it out. Tell her that if she cries, her mother won't come back. Give her candy.

***2.* At what age do you think a child should be toilet-trained?**
Acceptable: When she is ready. Sometime between two and three.
Unacceptable: I start my babies on the potty as soon as they can sit up. When she is one. (Or any answer suggesting that precocity is important or that a specific deadline must be met.)

***3.* In what circumstances do you think a child should be spanked?**
Acceptable: None; I don't believe children learn from spanking.
Unacceptable: If she hits another child—children need to be taught not to hit. If she deliberately misbehaves.

***4.* How do you teach a toddler not to touch breakables?**
Acceptable: Keep them out of reach. Explain, "This is something that breaks very easily. We need to put it away where it will be safe," and remove the object.
Unacceptable: Shout, "No!" when she reaches for them. Slap her hands.

***5.* What would you do if my child bit another child at the playground?**
Acceptable: Tell her she may not bite anyone and take her home. Have her sit by me on a bench for a while, then watch her closely when she goes back to play with the other children and distract her if disagreements arise.
Unacceptable: Bite her back. Tell her she is a bad girl. Scold her severely.

***6.* What would you do if my child refused to eat the lunch you prepared for her?**
Acceptable: Say, "That's what there is for lunch today," and leave it a few minutes so she can change her mind if she wants to. Tell her, "That's okay, but there won't be any dessert."
Unacceptable: I would not let her leave the table until she ate everything on her plate. Tell her, "I'm going to put on my sad face because I worked so hard making that nice lunch just for you," and not smile until she finishes every bite.

***7.* What if she's hungry in the middle of the afternoon after having refused lunch?**
Acceptable: Reheat and offer her the same food again. Give her a nutritious snack like a sandwich and some fruit, not sweets.
Unacceptable: Give her cookies and ice cream. Tell her she may not have any food until dinner.

***8.* What if she eats only some of her lunch?**
Acceptable: Well, if she doesn't seem hungry, I won't push it. She can have a more substantial snack after her nap if she needs it.
Unacceptable: I'll promise her some candy if she's a good girl and cleans her plate.

***9.* What television shows do you like to watch?**
Acceptable: Programs shown only in the evening, children's programs you approve of.
Unacceptable: Soap operas, quiz shows, old movies, and adult daytime programs.

***10.* What would you do if my daughter refused to share a toy when a friend was over to play?**
Acceptable: Suggest that we put it away until after her friend leaves. We will put toys she is unwilling to share away before the friend comes.
Unacceptable: Tell her that she must share all her toys or her friends won't come to play with her. Give the toy to her friend and send her to her room.

***11.* What would you do if my daughter refused to take her nap?**
Acceptable: Read to her. Rock her and sing her some songs. Take her for a ride in her stroller along some quiet streets. Set the timer for 20 minutes and ask her to play quietly in her room until it rings. (Or any tactic that gives the child some quiet rest.)
Unacceptable: Order her to stay in her room alone for one hour. Tell her the bogeyman will get her if she doesn't stay in her bed.

***12.* What would you do on a rainy day?**
Acceptable: Bake bread and teach her to knead. Put on records and dance. Put on galoshes and raincoats for a rainy-day walk. Go to the library. Invite a friend to play. (Or any answer showing some flexibility and creativity and including some exercise.)
Unacceptable: Stay in and watch TV.

***13.* What kind of outdoor play do you encourage?**
Acceptable: I like to take them to the playground or the park. They love the sandbox and the climbing frames. I usually take along a big ball to play with, and a pail and shovel. If she has a tricycle we can take that, too. (Or any answer including vigorous play and willingness to tote equipment.)
Unacceptable: A ride in the stroller is nice. I wouldn't want her getting all dirty in the sandbox or climbing—it's too dangerous.

***14.* How will you manage both to do the housework and to take care of my daughter?**
Acceptable: I can plan to clean during her nap if she naps, or give her blocks or modeling clay to work with while I do some chores. I like to make games of the housework and let her help me.
Unacceptable: I'll leave her in her crib or playpen until the cleaning is finished.

WHAT TO LOOK FOR IN A DAY-CARE CENTER

Before approaching the problem of finding a day-care center for your child, first realize that it may take some time. Don't think yourself silly for rejecting a day-care center because of your gut reaction. Intuition can prove very valuable in helping you make the right decision.

Plan to visit at least two centers so you'll have some comparisons to make. If it's possible, bring your husband along: Two sets of impressions are better than one. After setting up an appointment to visit a center, make a list of criteria important to you and make notes as you tour the site. Below are some guidelines to help in your decision-making process.

SAFETY

1. Caretakers should not smoke around the children.
2. Floors should be clean.
3. Eating areas should be clean and free of insect infestation.
4. One adult should be with the children at all times.
5. Cleaning agents, medications, and any poisons should be out of reach of children.
6. Electrical outlets should be covered with plastic safety guards.
7. Toys and play items should be free of dangerous sharp edges, loose parts, or rust.

ON-SITE SPACE

1. Each child should have a place to store his or her belongings—a locker, cubbyhole, or similar area.
2. A quiet place should be set aside for naps, and each child should have his or her own crib or cot to sleep on.
3. There should be ample storage space for toys so they aren't tripped over or in the way during other activities.
4. Toilets should be easy to get to and easy to use. The bathroom area should be neat and clean.
5. The atmosphere should be bright and cheery. Are there pictures on the wall? Is the paint chipping, or are the walls in good shape?
6. There should be direct access to an enclosed outdoor play area. Are there ample toys to keep children busy while playing outside, or are there makeshift articles that serve as toys, such as rusty pipes or splintered wood meant for climbing?

7. The outdoor play area should be equipped with both a soft surface (sand, sawdust, etc.) for running and a hard area (blacktop or cement) for riding toys.
8. In case of rain, is there room to play indoors?
9. Is the space big enough to accommodate all the children?

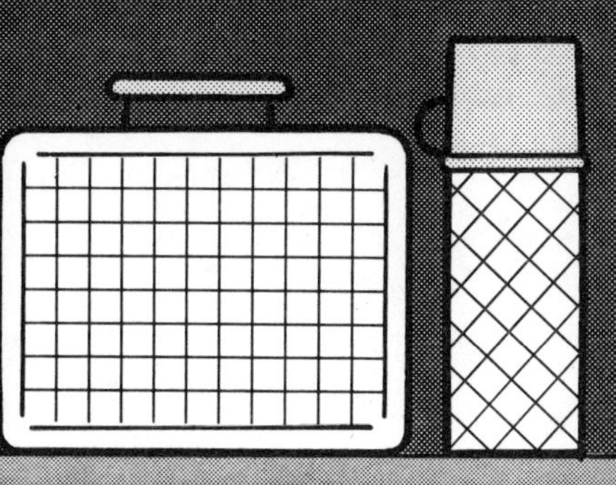

EQUIPMENT

1. There should be both books and puzzles for quiet play and riding toys and climbing structures for active play.
2. Are there enough supplies and toys to go around, or must children wait their turn to use pencils, crayons, paints, blocks, etc.?
3. Is there a choice of several activities, or are children forced to play games they don't enjoy?

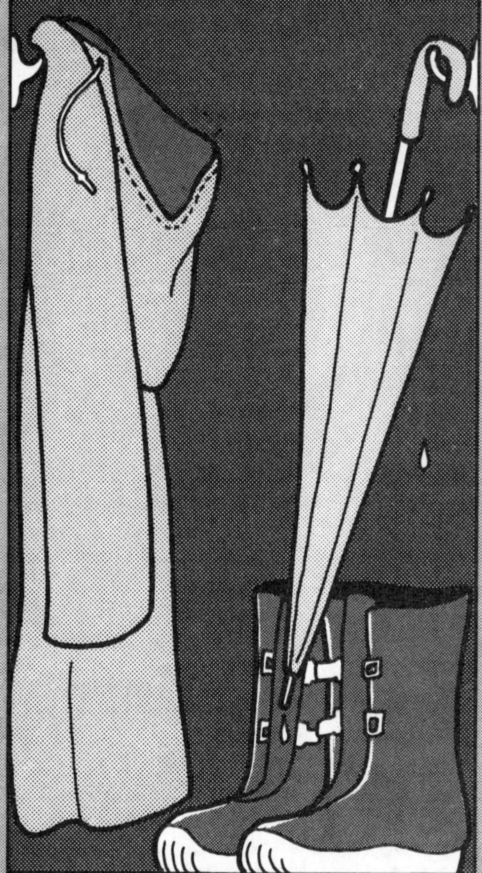

CARETAKERS

1. Are there enough supervisory adults to provide children with individual attention?
2. Are the caretakers patient, or edgy, as they go about their job?
3. Do they encourage the children or demand that the children perform?
4. Are they responsive to the children or concerned with personal matters?
5. Is there a combination of both males and females?
6. Is it the center's policy not to allow adults to physically punish the children, or is spanking permitted? If so, is there any possibility that this physical punishment could become abusive?

CHILDREN

1. Are the children happy?
2. Are they involved in activities or seemingly bored and listless?
3. Do the children fight a lot, or are disagreements resolved using rational measures?
4. Do the children play in small groups, or are there auditorium-size classes?
5. Does the center accept both boys and girls?

Special Tips If the Caretaker Is a Relative

You want to go back to work. You have a job lined up, but you cannot afford a full-time housekeeper. Your baby is too young for the day-care center near your work. You're undecided about what to do, when your sister-in-law says, "But I'd love to look after Nancy! I'm home all day anyway with Susie and Tommy. One more will be fun for all of us." A great idea—but will it work? It might. Here are some points to remember when having a relative care for your child.

- You cannot accept her services for free. It may seem awkward at first, but it will help your relationship in the long run if you pay her even a small wage. She will feel she is being treated as a professional, and you will feel less like you are taking advantage of her kindness. You can pay her in other ways, too—special gifts, reciprocal baby-sitting in the evening or on weekends, running errands or shopping for her.
- Be sure she appreciates your role as a working mother and will not use your relationship to make you feel guilty for "not taking care of your own child."
- Consider how compatible your child-raising philosophies are. A relative often feels freer to interfere with your methods than a hired baby-sitter would, since the child is, after all, a member of her family, too.
- Discuss the practical details of your arrangement right away—hours, meals, transportation. Make it clear just what services you will need before you begin.
- Your relationship will never be an employer–employee relationship, and it will take more tact and diplomacy to maintain. A sitter *expects* instructions; your relative may bristle at them.
- Your child will be cared for by someone who loves her and who loves you, she will be in a familiar home, and her caretaker will be part of her life even when you are not working: The value of these experiences may override the differences, generational or otherwise, in specific methods of child-raising.

How to Set Up a Baby-Sitting Co-op

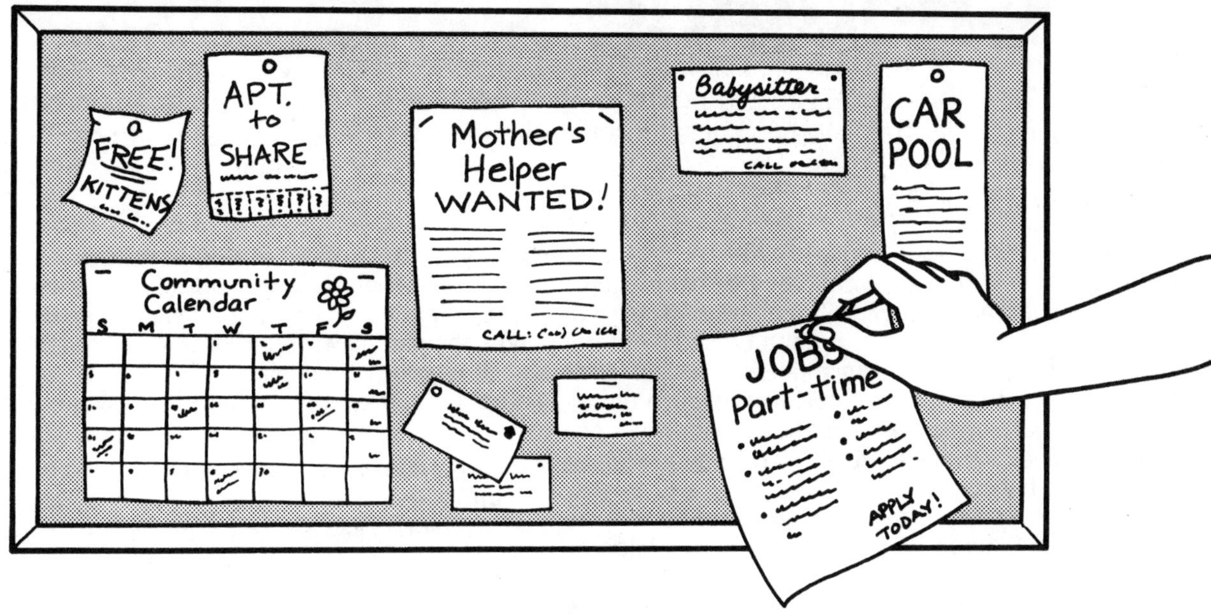

Co-oping is not just for apartment buildings—it's also for busy moms. It's a simple task to start a babysitting co-op, and the benefits are many. Among them: You'll make friends with other mothers, find new playmates for your child, obtain competent and dependable baby-sitters, have a sounding board for your problems and complaints as a mother, and develop a clearinghouse for the exchange of clothes and toys. Both you and your child will gain a lot from a baby-sitting co-op.

Here are steps to take in starting one:

- Find a home for the co-op by calling local churches, civic associations, women's groups, YWCAs, etc. Ask if they would be interested in lending you space for a set number of hours each month. Another idea is to situate the co-op in members' homes, alternating homes each week.
- Get publicity for the co-op. Advertise in local papers and on bulletin boards of supermarkets, laundromats, public libraries, shopping malls. Tell your husband to spread the word among fellow fathers. A notice might read: "Help yourself and other mothers: Form play groups, exchange information and clothing, and baby-sit for one another. A few hours a month reap days in saved time and energy." Then give your phone number and name.
- Discuss the aims you have in mind for the co-op when each mother calls. Make sure her ideas mesh with yours. If you're restricting the aims of the co-op, say to baby-sitting purposes only, be certain that other members don't expect other rewards as well. It's also a good idea to limit the size of the co-op, keeping it to no more than fifteen members.
- At the first meeting of the co-op, determine how many hours each month each mother will contribute and on which day of the week.
- Devise a schedule that fixes certain times for each mother's duties. For example, something like "Mary Carter will baby-sit from 3:00 to 6:00 every Tuesday." Have the members sign their names next to their assignments with the understanding that the commitment is final. Make sure they know that they are responsible for finding a replacement if they are unable to fulfill their obligations.

Once the co-op is running smoothly, you can make arrangements to do other parent-oriented projects, such as seminars, chauffeuring, toy exchanges, etc.

Changing Caretakers

When you find your child-care arrangements are not working out or your needs are no longer the same, or your sitter is leaving, it is time to change caretakers. The transition can be difficult for both you and your child. You will want to give him extra attention and time to talk about the changes in his life.

- **If you must fire your housekeeper:**

Do it quickly. If you have discovered that her methods of child-raising are irreconcilably different from your own, if you cannot back her up in the majority of her disciplinary decisions, if a straightforward talk does not end her chronic tardiness or her over reliance on television, if your child shows a real dislike for her, don't hesitate to look for a new sitter. Tell her you are letting her go, give her one or two weeks' salary, and ask her to leave immediately. Use your emergency backup sitters or hire temporary help from an agency while you look for a replacement.

Talk to your child about your decision. If he liked the sitter, make it clear that it was not his fault she left; if he disliked her, emphasize that it was your choice to dismiss her, not his. Be honest with him. Talk about his feelings. Assure him that you will find someone he can love and trust to take care of him while you work.

- **If your housekeeper gives notice:**

Your housekeeper is getting married, having a baby, or moving away. If the relationship has been a good one, the parting will be sad for all of you. Prepare your child ahead of time. Have her tell him if she likes. Be sure there are photos of her for his album. Arrange for visits after she leaves.

- **If your needs have changed:**

Your youngest is starting all-day kindergarten, your employer has just added an excellent on-site day-care facility available to you as a fringe benefit, you need live-in help because your new promotion means you will be traveling more—whatever the reason, you must let your wonderful housekeeper go. Give her plenty of advance notice. Help her find another job. Be generous with severance pay.

Make the transition easier for your child by focusing on the future—his new school or day-care center. If a new caretaker is moving in, have her arrive before the former housekeeper stops working, then taper off the relationship by having her work fewer days a week before she leaves.

- **Changing day-care centers:**

If you notice changes in your child's behavior that suggest he is unhappy with his day-care center, discuss the problem with him and with his teachers. Visit the center again. Talk to the staff about any problems you notice, and give them a chance to make changes. If no positive steps are taken, it is time to find a different day-care facility.

When you have found a good alternative, give the old center notice and explain to the staff why you are leaving. Tell your child as soon as new arrangements have been made, and take him to visit the new center and meet the teachers. It's a good idea to make the change when there would be a break or vacation anyway, if that is possible. Provide a treat for him to share with the other children his last day there. Keep your child in touch with his old friends—at least for a while—with weekend play dates or rendezvous at a nearby playground.

Hiring a Mother's Helper from Overseas

If you think a young man or woman from another part of the world would be an interesting caretaker for your children, there are ways to go about finding such a person. However, because of the recent crackdown by immigration officials, a number of agencies that once acted as intermediaries between prospective employers and employees have given up their overseas operations.

Now the best way to hire an overseas "au pair" is to advertise in a foreign newspaper. Decide which country you'd like your helper to hail from and learn the names and addresses of applicable foreign newspapers. A good source is the *Europa Digest,* available at your local library, which lists newspapers from all the European countries.

When writing your ad, be specific about the duties and abilities needed. Mention how long you'll want the caretaker to stay on, ask for a licensed driver if needed, and request fluent English if that is important to you.

According to the Department of Labor, the following requirements for hiring an overseas child-care worker must be met:

1. The salary must be at least $199.32 per 44-hour week.
2. Duties must relate only to the care of your child. Housework and running errands for other family members cannot be included in his or her responsibilities.
3. The person you hire must have one year of related paid experience.
4. To hire a live-in mother's helper, you must prove it is a necessity based on your job pressures.
5. You must fill out labor certification papers. Form A is for you, and Form B is for the alien. The papers are submitted to the Department of Labor, which issues a labor certificate. The papers are then submitted to the Immigration Department, which decides whether your helper can enter the United States.

A number of agencies that formerly provided overseas help have switched to handling only American domestic workers. If you're not set on hiring someone foreign, the experience could be equally interesting if your helper comes from another part of the United States.

The Overseas Custom Maid Agency of Stamford, Connecticut, (203-324-9575), one of the operations that used to deal in overseas help, now offers two categories of mother's helpers:

Summer help: The agency accepts applications, life synopses, and pictures from college-age women who wish to hire themselves out for the summer as mother's helpers. References are thoroughly checked for prospective employers. The fee is $200, and the salary is dictated by the agency at the rate of $115 to $130 per week.

Full-time help: These mother's helpers are more professional, as taking care of children is their livelihood. Both employer and employee fill out applications, and information is exchanged over the phone when a match is found. In-person interviews are arranged only if both parties are local. The weekly salary paid is $250 and up. The fee charged is usually 75 percent of the first month's salary.

12 EMERGENCY
NUMBERS
TO CLIP & SAVE

Mother at work: ____________________

Father at work: ____________________

Pediatrician: ____________________

Police Emergency: ____________________

Fire Department: ____________________

Ambulance Service: ____________________

Substitute sitter or neighbor: ____________________

Hospital: ____________________

Poison Control: ____________________

Pharmacy that delivers: ____________________

Taxi Service: ____________________

Dentist: ____________________

CLIP AND SAVE

COPING

How to Breastfeed Your Baby and Go Back to Work

Breastfeeding, experts everywhere agree, is the optimal method of nourishing your baby. Not only is it the safest, quickest, and most wholesome feeding arrangement, it also fosters close bonds between mother and child. Just because you work does not mean you must sacrifice breastfeeding. In fact, working moms who nurse have an advantage over working moms who don't, for the special warmth of the nursing relationship helps compensate for the time apart and makes it easier for the baby to weather your absences. Here are some suggestions to help you manage both working and breastfeeding.

1. Find help that will be supportive. A sympathetic husband and cooperative baby-sitter are essential. A baby-sitter who will prepare dinner, for example, can give you a chance to relax and feed the baby as soon as you return from work.

2. Pay close attention to your own nutritional needs. Try not to go back to work before you have fully recovered from giving birth and the milk supply is well established.

3. Get the baby used to drinking from bottles early on. Give him water or expressed breast milk two or three times a week well before you start to work. Use bottle nipples that resemble breast nipples.

4. Switch from demand feeding to a regular routine at least two weeks before you plan to go to work. Nurse him first thing in the morning and again just before you would leave for work. If you will be working full time, he will need at least two more feedings before you return: The baby-sitter will give him formula or a bottle of breast milk for these. Nurse again when you get home and later in the evening before you go to bed.

Or, if you work near your home or your sitter's home, you may be able to arrange two "nursing breaks" with your employer by combining lunch and coffee-break times. Either way, you and the baby need to become accustomed to a schedule.

5. Maintain your nursing schedule on weekends as well so that you and the baby won't have to keep adjusting to changes.

6. Learn to express milk either manually or with a hand pump, and don't get discouraged if it isn't easy at first. Start practicing early and freeze milk for later use.

7. After you start working, express milk during the workday when your breasts fill. If you have access to a refrigerator at work, you can freeze the milk in disposable bottles and take it home with you in an insulated bag for a daytime feeding the next day.

8. To cope with leakage: Wear nursing pads and keep a supply at the office; express milk on a regular schedule whether you save the milk or not; and keep an extra blouse, sweater, or large scarf in the office in case you need a change or a coverup.

9. La Leche League meetings can provide wonderful support and put you in touch with other working mothers of infants. Local representatives of La Leche are listed in the telephone directory. Their publications, *The Womanly Art of Breastfeeding* and "Breastfeeding and Working?" are available from La Leche International, Inc., 9616 Minneapolis Avenue, Franklin Park, Illinois 60131.

Helpful Books

The Complete Book of Breastfeeding by Marvin S. Eiger and Sally Wendkos Olds (Workman Publishing Co.)

Nursing Your Baby by Karen Pryor (Pocket Books)

When an At-Home Mom Starts Working

Mothers who stay home with small children generally find every minute of the day chock-full of chores and child care. Even when the youngest starts nursery school, precious little free time opens up. How can such a busy mom make the transition from home to the outside world of paid employment? It takes forethought, planning, and organization; it means rethinking one's priorities and working out the best ways to delegate tasks to others; it means getting the whole family to work together toward common goals instead of letting "doormat" mom do it all.

Covering All Bases

Child-care help comes first. If you will be working full time and if there is still one child at home all day or in nursery school for only three hours, a full-time housekeeper may be the best solution; if you are working part time and your child is in school half a day, exchange arrangements with other mothers may be all that you need. Look at all the possibilities: day-care centers—all day or by the hour—a helpful relative, part time baby-sitters, family day care, or, for an older child, a neighbor at home who can check up on her after school.

Assign specific jobs. Make a detailed list of all the tasks you do—both daily chores and occasional ones, like taking the kids to the pediatrician and the dentist for checkups, and shopping for their clothes—and work out who will take over the ones you will no longer have time for. Discuss the list with your husband. He may be happy to take on some of the responsibilities, especially when he sees how long the list is! Be open to a variety of arrangements, for expecting one person to replace you completely is most likely not feasible, affordable, or even desirable. You may need an older child to walk your child to school, a teenager who can take him to his karate class after school or help him with his homework, and a cleaning service to do a thorough job on the house every two weeks.

Look for help other than hired help. Older children can and should help out with household chores, caring for pets, shopping, and preparing meals. An elderly neighbor may be glad to do mending in return for shopping. Exchange services with other parents—car pools, play groups, even cleaning, shopping, and cooking—can be arranged.

Have a backup list of emergency help. If anyone in your support network gets sick, leaves town, or proves derelict in his duties, you should be prepared with someone who can step in on short notice to relieve the pressure on you.

Getting Your Life Organized

At-home moms carry vast quantities of information around in their heads: their own and their kids' schedules, countless telephone numbers, where everything in the house belongs, how to run (and often fix) an array of appliances, information on emergency procedures. All this and much more will need to be shared with the team that will be taking your place when you go to work.

Write it all down. Written messages will play a larger role than before. Organize a family message center in a much-used room or hallway near a telephone. Stock it with:

- A yearly calendar listing schedules, appointments, and holidays for every family member
- A bulletin board
- A writing board or chalkboard
- Paper, pens, and pencils
- A list of the most frequently needed, emergency, and other important phone numbers
- A well organized telephone and address book

Household information may be kept together in one file or drawer or may be stored or posted around the house wherever it is most needed: for example, wiring information and extra fuses near the fuse box, washer and dryer instructions in the laundry. Reminders not to run the dishwasher and the toaster at the same time or about any other little household idiosyncrasies should be taped on the wall where your helpers will see them.

Provide pencils and paper by every telephone—securely attached to it if possible.

Keep track of shopping needs by leaving writing materials in the kitchen near the refrigerator or pantry for an ongoing shopping list.

Write yourself messages:

- Cultivate the list habit. Take ten minutes every evening to write down what needs to get done the next day. Include any relevant phone numbers, addresses, or hours on your list. Carry it with you all day.
- Every Sunday evening, check the calendar for events coming up in the week ahead and make notes on how each day should be organized.
- Carry a small notebook in your purse to jot down information and ideas you need to remember; go through it frequently to transfer that information to the appropriate calendar, address book, or file.
- Keep an appointment book in your purse, too, and check it regularly against the family calendar to be sure important events are recorded in both.

Schedule time to talk. Written communication cannot accomplish everything. You'll want to talk to your family, and to your support network, too. The end of the workday is usually not the best time for you and your baby-sitter to exchange any but the most urgent information. Regular evening telephone chats can keep you more in touch with everything going on while you are at work.

Family meals together—at least one a day—are an important time to catch up on everyone's activities, as is daily time alone with each child and with your husband. A regular weekly family meeting at a time when no one is about to rush off somewhere will provide a good opportunity to exchange information, plan chores, work out logistics for upcoming events, and discuss problems.

Beating the Clock

Time-saving devices you may not have needed before will be well worth their purchase price now. Some of the most useful are:

- A washer and dryer
- A microwave oven
- A dishwasher
- A food processor
- A no-frost refrigerator and freezer
- A self-cleaning oven with a timer to turn it on and off

If you can't afford these right away, put them on a "wish list" of things your new salary can help pay for later.

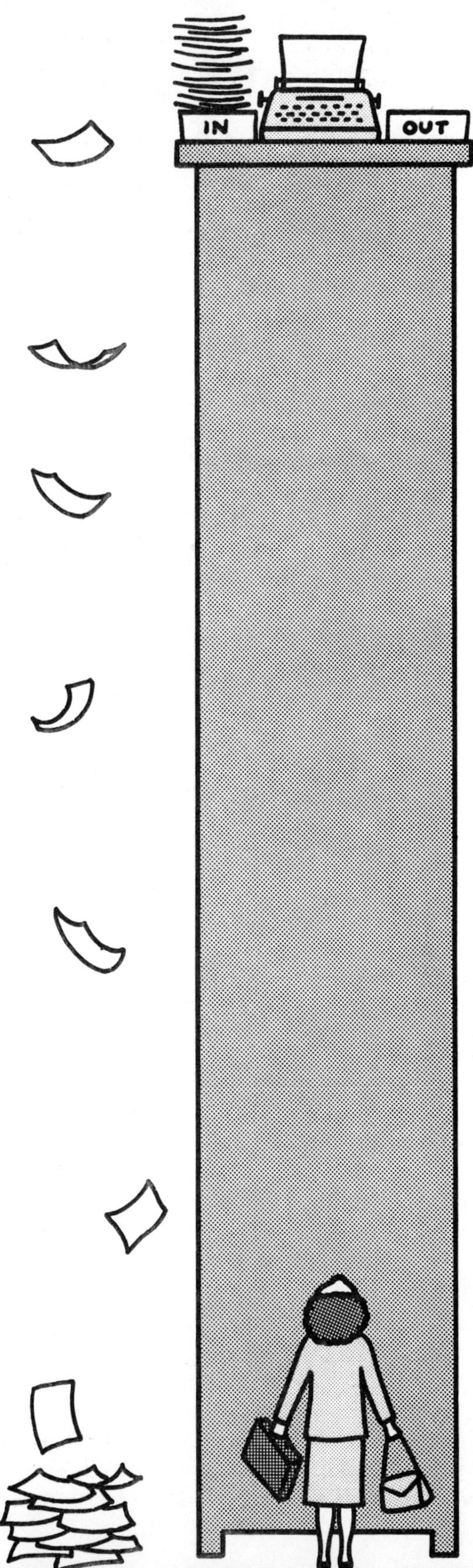

Ways to Make Your Child Feel Secure

A child's greatest fear is of being unloved and abandoned by his parents, according to Dr. Haim G. Ginott, the noted child psychologist. In the first year of life, a child forms his initial emotional attachments and is comforted by the presence of the people he has grown attached to. He uses these attachments as a stable base on which to build other attachments and to maintain his feeling of security. As long as an infant's physical and emotional needs are satisfied in a predictable and comforting way, he will develop a basic sense of security and trust, which enables him to confidently face new situations in the future.

In families where both parents work, these attachments may extend beyond the family to outside caretakers, who should be made aware of certain do's and don'ts involved in building the child's sense of security:

1. Never threaten your child by saying you will leave him or desert him if he doesn't behave. This touches on one of his most dreaded fears and will increase his feelings of anxiety.

2. Provide a routinized schedule of feeding and sleeping as soon as it's possible to do so. The knowledge that certain things will occur at a certain time and with regularity helps a young child organize his world and create a secure feeling of predictability.

3. Demonstrate your love for your child by hugging him, kissing him, and holding him as often as possible.

4. Prepare your child in advance if you're going to be away even for a short time. Not telling your child where you're going and for how long can cause intense feelings of loss and anxiety. Acting out the scenario, perhaps with dolls or some of his toys, will help him deal with the reality of your leaving and the understanding that you'll be back. You may have to repeat the sequence of events several times before your child fully comprehends it.

5. Children derive a great deal of comfort from knowing that it's okay to have ideas that are different from or even in opposition to their parents' without losing their parents' love. To build such feelings in your child, when disagreements arise, simply say, "You feel one way, I feel another way. We feel differently on the subject." This way, there is no value judgment attached to each person's feelings. Each is justified in his or her own position.

6. When parents fight, children feel anxious and insecure. Don't hide disagreements from your child, but don't flaunt fiery arguments in front of him either. If your child hears you arguing, explain that mommy and daddy disagree, but it doesn't mean they don't love each other.

7. Insisting on a certain level of competence that a child has not yet mastered will make him feel inadequate and unsure about his place in the world. Rather, if your child has trouble putting on his boots, opening a jar, or managing any difficult task, do it for him and explain that you know the task was difficult. If he performs the task successfully the next time, he'll feel good about himself, but if he doesn't, he won't feel as though he has failed.

Early-Morning Survival Tactics

One of the toughest jobs a working mother has is getting everyone, including herself, out of the house in the morning on time. There is no way to anticipate unexpected happenings like a car that won't start or a quick change of ripped panty hose, but there are many ways to beat the clock. Here are some strategies to survive the morning getaway.

❍ *1.* The morning often sets the pace for the rest of the day for working mothers. If you can start off in an upbeat mood as you go about your morning routine, it will affect your family and encourage everyone to feel the same way.

❍ *2.* Most households have several clocks, but they are not usually synchronized. Sometimes the one in the kitchen can differ as much as half an hour from the one in the bedroom. Synchronize your timepieces, and make one dependable clock the lead timekeeper. Then assign a child the responsibility of keeping it accurate by calling the local number for the right time (this needs to be done only every few days or so) and adjusting all the other clocks to the lead one.

❍ *3.* Make a list of all the things you can do before going to bed at night, and things that must be done when you get up in the morning. This list of evening chores might include laying out school clothes and your own work outfit, giving the children their lunch money, organizing school books and your briefcase, and even readying the breakfast table by setting out dry cereal and other unperishable foods.

❍ *4.* One big stumbling block to a smooth-running morning is the bathroom traffic jam. Unless your home has more than one bathroom, it's best to make up a bathroom schedule—at least for weekdays. The schedule should be rotated regularly so that no one gets stuck being the last one to use the bathroom all the time. A clock in the bathroom will help make everyone aware of their allotted time.

❍ *5.* The first time your child misses the school bus, drive him to school. But if it happens again, assuming your child is of a responsible age, insist that he walk or use public transportation to get there. If public transportation is not convenient and you worry about your child walking to school alone, drop him off on your way to work but let him know there is a penalty involved. Assigning him an extra chore around the house or depriving him of a favorite TV program once or twice will discourage habitual lateness and help him appreciate the importance of developing a sense of responsibility.

❍ *6.* Get your child into the habit of setting his own alarm clock for wake-up time. If after many reminders he still oversleeps, try changing the time on his clock to half an hour later. He'll jump out of bed at 7:30 AM thinking he's late, but he'll have an extra half hour to get ready.

❍ *7.* If your kids bring lunch to school, let them know how helpful it would be if they prepared their lunches the night before. They'll be less likely to forget them, and a job during the morning rush will be eliminated. If they buy lunch, be sure to give them the money the night before.

❍ *8.* If you own a pet that needs walking in the morning, write out a weekly schedule so that everyone in the family who can takes a turn at it. Other pet chores—changing cat litter, feeding, cleaning the bird cage—can be scheduled also.

❍ *9.* Use a rotating schedule for household chores: putting dirty breakfast dishes in the sink, making beds, picking up dirty laundry, wiping off bathroom basins. Decide which person does which chore each week and which chores you can live without having done. If bed-making is not one of your priorities but a clean kitchen is, have everyone spend a few minutes clearing the table, doing the dishes, and putting things away. Rotate chores each week.

❍ *10.* Make a habit of setting your alarm clock 10 minutes earlier than you think you might need. Then you'll be prepared for unexpected events, and if a crisis does occur, you'll have the time to handle the situation with less stress. If nothing urgent happens, you'll be able to linger over your coffee for a few extra relaxing minutes.

All working mothers grapple with the fear that they won't be available if there's an emergency. Using a page or "beeper" can go a long way in helping eliminate this anxiety. Now, even when you can't be near a phone, your children, husband, co-workers, and caretakers can still reach you.

THE BASICS

As with any technology, there are several kinds of pagers, each one offering more complicated options. Most pagers operate within a 50-to-75-mile radius, so even if you're out of town, as long as you're not too far away, they are effective. You can either buy or rent a pager. They cost several hundred dollars to purchase, or they can be leased on a monthly basis for around $25. However, for more elaborate models, you can expect to pay more. Often a security deposit of $100 is required, and if the beeper is lost the money goes toward the purchase of a new one.

HOW DO THEY WORK?

Most beepers operate on AA-size batteries, which don't need replacing very often. If you're out of the office and your child needs to reach you, she punches the number she's calling from and your beeper number into a push-button phone. (If you don't have a push-button phone, the company from which you lease or buy your pager has to install an adapter so the beeper can be called from nonpush-button phones.) If your pager is turned on, it will start to make a beeping noise that you can't miss, even if you've stepped away from the immediate area where the beeper is. The telephone number of the person trying to reach you will appear on the face of the beeper and remain there until you clear it. If you're popular (and hard to reach), you may opt for a more advanced beeper, which can display up to twenty-four numbers, twelve at a time, for multiple calls received. Some even display word messages for true emergency situations. However, if your goal is merely to provide a way for people to reach you, there's no need to get these more expensive options. (You may want to try leasing a pager before buying one to see if you like it. While pagers can be a real help to some mothers, they end up bothering others.)

PROBLEMS

Problems with beepers usually involve human error and can be avoided. Be aware of the following:

1. It's fairly easy to accidentally dislodge the on/off button to the off position, thereby cutting off your communication line to your family. However, by keeping the beeper on your desk, or placing it carefully in your purse or briefcase, you can minimize the chances of this happening. The beeper should be checked periodically to make sure it's turned on.
2. If the caller doesn't punch in the correct numbers in sequence, you will be beeped but you'll have no idea who's trying to reach you since his or her telephone number will fail to appear on the screen. Make sure you understand how to use the pager completely, and pass the information on to family, friends, and associates.
3. If your beeper isn't working properly, check the batteries. Though they last for several months because the beeper doesn't use that much juice, weak batteries can cause a host of beeper malfunctions.

Tricks to Cope with Guilt

There are 17.8 million working mothers in the United States today, and just about every single one of them suffers, at one time or another, from an attack of working mother's guilt. Occasionally you can take action to change the source of the guilt by asking yourself a few key questions: Do I need to change jobs to have fewer demands made on my time? Should I change child-care arrangements so I feel less guilty about leaving my children? Is there some way I can allocate my time differently so I have a more leisurely schedule?

Simply going over these questions is already a positive step. But if you've made all the changes you can manage or afford and you still feel guilty, you can diminish these feelings by focusing on the bright side. Try reminding yourself of the following:

* I'm providing my children with a good role model.
* I bring experience of the outside world home to my kids.
* I would be climbing the walls if I were home all day.
* My work is useful to society.
* I feel better about myself when I am working, and that makes me less critical of my children.
* My child is learning to love and trust adults other than her parents.
* If I were home it would not solve all of life's problems.
* My salary can help provide a better education for my child.
* My children are proud of what I do and like telling their friends about my job.
* My salary helps provide better food and health care.
* My salary helps provide more interesting vacations.
* My children are learning to be more independent and resourceful; I'm proud of them.
* Work is a good outlet for my talents and energies: I don't want to push my children to be what I wanted to be.
* I'm less irritable when I'm not constantly with the children.
* I like being around adults at work and having other adults to talk to.
* Work provides a good balance to my life; I get too preoccupied with the children and the housework when I'm home all day.
* My husband is learning how to be a more complete person; so am I.
* My life is more efficient and productive when I'm working; I manage my time better when I have more to do.
* My mind is sharper when I'm working, because I deal with more complex and more abstract matters than when I'm doing housework and taking care of children.
* I like working.
* Happy mom, happy children.

It helps, too, to remember that certain facts are on your side. The divorce rate is no higher in families where the wife is employed than in families where she isn't. And no studies have conclusively proved that the children of working moms are any less well adjusted or more delinquent than the children of nonworking moms. And you are not alone. Every day more and more mothers are joining the ranks of the employed. Eighteen million mothers can't be wrong.

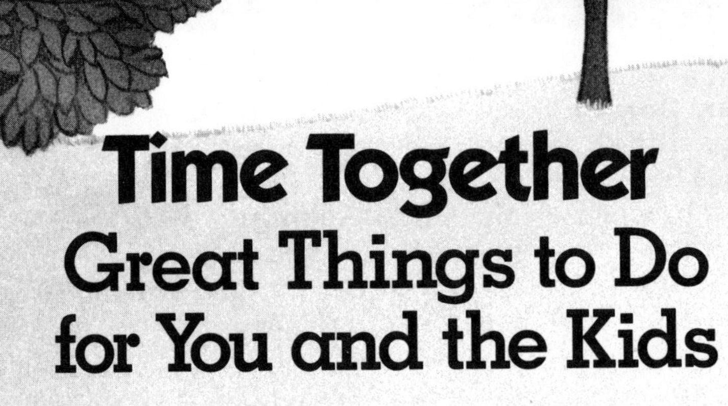

Time Together
Great Things to Do for You and the Kids

When you have time to spend with your kids, you want to make it special. But don't fall into the trap of thinking that "quality time" together necessarily involves spending money, eating ice cream or other treats, or going somewhere—although all three are fun occasionally. The best times are when you are enjoying each other's company—even if it's while washing dishes. Keep an open mind—work can be as much fun as play, homebound or neighborhood activities as much fun as visits farther afield.

If you have more than one child, plan time alone with each one, for siblings need time apart from each other as well as time with each parent. When you all spend time together, let each have a say in choosing activities.

To help plan outings and projects, keep a "Resources" file. Fill it with clippings about interesting things to see and do in your area, brochures of tourist attractions within a fifty-mile radius, a list of museums and their hours, current schedules of activities at local libraries and theaters. Include ideas for craft activities—and keep your arts and crafts supply shelf stocked.

When You Have a Full Day

* In fine weather, a full day together is best spent at the beach or exploring a large park. Take a picnic lunch, extra drinks and snacks, and plenty to play with—a Frisbee, a kite, balls, pails and shovels. Every child can help tote the food and equipment if each has a backpack.
* In cold or rainy weather, putting in a full day at a good science or natural-history museum can be very rewarding. You can take a leisurely look at dinosaurs or dioramas of wild animals. Take a pad and pencil for sketching practice. Have lunch at the museum cafeteria, or take a break and go out to eat at a nearby coffee shop.
* When you have a whole day to spend at home, try baking bread. Kids love measuring, mixing, and kneading the dough. Or organize the day around a crafts project like making puppets: Begin with a shopping trip for materials, and culminate the day with a show you can invite the neighbors over to see.

When You Have a Morning or Afternoon

* A shopping expedition can outfit the kids for the next six months and can be great fun if you are not rushed. Most kids love buying clothes, and if you pick a shop that has most of the items they

need and that carries merchandise you like and can afford, the kids can be given the freedom of choosing what they like best. Take everyone out for pizza when you're done.

* Have a cooking class while you prepare extra meals for the freezer. Give the kids as many tasks as you feel they can handle: shelling peas, husking corn, washing and peeling vegetables, stirring pots on the stove, measuring ingredients, reading out the recipe to you. Let them taste everything as you go. Keep it fun—be prepared to stop before you are finished if interest wanes. Any work you have to do around the house can be shared in a similar way—gardening, simple repairs, refinishing furniture, mending and sewing.
* Teach your child a new sport or help him increase his competence at a sport he's just starting to learn. It may mean spending the afternoon running alongside his bicycle as he tries to get his balance on his own, but he'll be grateful for your patience and encouragement.

When You Have an Hour

* Make a puzzle or game and play with it.
* Make a book and write and illustrate a story in it.
* Clean out a closet, sorting the clothes to see what has been outgrown or worn out, and make a list of shopping needs.
* Teach your child some magic tricks, then let him practice and put on a show for you.
* Share a children's magazine: Take turns reading the stories aloud, watch him figure out the puzzles, talk about the pictures.
* Build something really difficult out of Tinkertoys or Lego.
* Let your child make up a game in which he is the parent and you are the child.

When You Have Only Half an Hour

* Put on a record and dance—use a prop like a scarf to wave around or a drum to beat the rhythm.
* Listen to a record of songs together. Sing along if you have the words.
* Read a book aloud—an old favorite or something new.
* Have your child read to you (even if he's just pretending).
* Look at the family photo album or the child's baby book or your wedding pictures.
* Play a board game or a card game.
* Make music together: If your child plays an instrument, choose the easy pieces he is no longer working on, or if you play and he doesn't, have him clap out the rhythm or sing. Sing rounds together or learn a new song.
* Make paper airplanes and see whose flies farthest or stays up longest.
* Play hide-and-seek.
* Play outdoors: Toss a football, play catch, jump rope, run races.

BUSINESS-TRIP BLUES

Even if you're the happiest and most organized of all working mothers, you can be thrown into a tailspin if you have to make a business trip out of town and leave your family. And as tough as the logistics of leaving are, what's even worse is the guilt about leaving, and the nagging fear that if you were *really* a good mother, you wouldn't go. Well, most often, you *must* go—so do it with the following in mind:

DON'T APOLOGIZE

You are not committing a crime, making a mistake, or harming anyone. (If you really feel you are, don't go!) Any indecision or hesitation on your part will only make the separation more difficult, for it will make your child feel insecure: If you are worried, then hasn't he an even greater reason to be?

BE MATTER-OF-FACT

This trip is part of your job just as your daily work at the office is, and your child needs to feel that although his home life will be a little different, he will be well cared for and there will be nothing seriously wrong. Above all, you will be back.

DISCUSS YOUR PLANS IN DETAIL

Tell your child about your trip when you have the time to talk at leisure, and listen to all his questions. Let him know what the preparations are for his care, especially who will be doing the tasks you usually do yourself, whether it is fixing his breakfast, walking him to school, picking him up after school, or putting him to bed. All of these need to be done by someone he knows well, loves, and trusts. If there can be choices in any part of these plans, let him make them. These tips can be helpful:

* Talk over any problems that might arise, like what he will do if he gets lonesome or if he needs help with his homework.
* Let him know what your plans are for communicating with him—that you will call or send postcards. If you know for sure that you will be able to call him every day at a particular time, tell him that so he can look forward to it.
* Show him on a map where you are going and what the place is like. Put a map up on a wall, and mark your route with a string. Let him cut out a car or airplane to attach to the string. (It can be turned around the day you are expected back)
* A calendar marking the days you will be gone will help a small child to understand the passage of time. Give a very young child a picture of yourself or something of yours he can "take care of"—a scarf or bracelet.

* Be sure to let him know you will bring back a present for him.
* Record a different tape or VCR cassette for him to play each day while you are away.
* Hide a present somewhere around the house for each day you are gone, and tell him where to find it when you call or on the cassette.

Your husband will want to hear much the same things, only on an adult level. He, too, needs to know who will be doing all the jobs you usually do; you cannot just assume he will fill in for you. If he is not used to cooking and this is your first business trip, make the effort to cook ahead some of his favorite meals. Following your directions for reheating the food may be a good first step toward his learning to cook. (When you are going away for the first time, it's a good idea to try to avoid adding to the responsibililties of your husband and older children: Cover all bases with hired help and loyal friends. If business trips become regular, then more adjustments can be made within the family.) Your husband also needs to know when you will be where, that you will call, that he can reach you if necessary. He should know the baby-sitter well and be comfortable dealing with her. Lastly, he needs the reassurance that you love him and that above all, after X days, you will be back!

WORKING DURING PREGNANCY

Gone forever are the days of confinement. Healthy mothers-to-be are no longer expected to wait patiently at home the last several months before baby arrives, but instead can keep right on working.

Even maternity business suits are not hard to find. Still, the physical demands of pregnancy warrant some concessions, especially in the first and last trimesters. Your energy levels are apt to be lower, and your nutritional needs are definitely higher. Sudden mood changes and rapid swings of emotion are common, and your new size and shape can pose difficulties, especially when commuting and traveling. Here are some ideas for keeping your professional cool:

- Carry wholesome snacks with you in your purse to quell sudden hunger pangs.
- Avoid rush-hour trains and buses by coming in to and leaving work early.
- Take a few minutes to think things over when you find yourself ready to chew out your secretary or yell at your co-workers: It may be your condition, not their incompetence, that's making you so moody.
- Limit your social life so that you can get more rest.
- Schedule all your obstetrician appointments for the first morning or first afternoon appointment time, and arrive early so that you won't be left waiting. Ask the secretary to call you if the doctor is delayed.
- Take an exercise class for pregnant women. Being in shape will make you feel better and help you through childbirth.
- Sit down and prop your legs up whenever you can—at the office and as soon as you get home.
- Pamper yourself: New makeup and hairdo and a new outfit or two can lift you out of last-trimester doldrums.
- Invest in a few pairs of fashionable, low-heeled shoes. Fluid retention can make feet and ankles swell up, so shoes should be as comfortable as possible.
- Adjust your behind-the-desk mode of sitting to your condition. Keep your knees wide apart and cross your legs at the ankles, not the knees.
- Stay away from caffeinated beverages, especially during the first trimester. These drinks can aggravate morning sickness and make you feel more fatigued. Instead, drink very hot or very cold juices and non-caffeinated beverages, such as Sanka or Postum.
- Shop in departments other than maternity wear for your office garb. Many fashionable and flattering outfits that are also loose-fitting and comfortable can be found in such store departments as lounge wear and leisure wear.
- Keep a list of foods that are good for you during pregnancy in your desk or tacked on the wall at the office. Refer to this when the coffee wagon comes around and you have a hunger pang, and check it before an impromptu luncheon out. Particularly important are calcium-rich foods, fruits and vegetables high in vitamin C, and protein sources.
- When you're feeling particularly tired or bloated, a casual stroll around the floor or to another department in your office can help. The mild exercise will energize you and make you feel less confined. Even a trip down to the lobby of your building can help.
- Try to find another pregnant woman in your office, if it's large enough, or in a company located nearby. Sharing the experience of being an expectant working woman will be fun and also helpful.

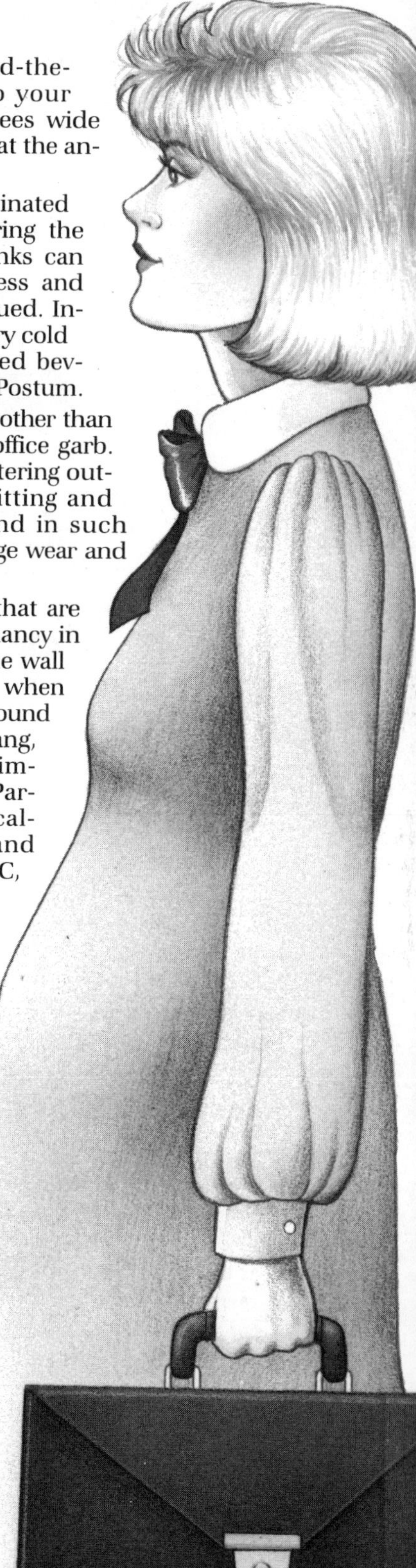

You're up before dawn, all set for a busy day. You can't believe how smoothly it's all going—time for exercise, a hot oatmeal breakfast, layering vegetables and meat neatly in a slow cooker. Your two-year-old is all sunshine, excited about going to play group. The sitter even arrives early. Then, just as you pick up your briefcase and stoop down for a good-bye hug, it all falls apart. Tears, wails, little hands clutching at your dress and legs. Or it might be an older child, disappointed you cannot be one of the mothers accompanying her class on a field trip. Sooner or later, and probably more than once, that plaintive wail "I don't want you to go to work, Mommy!" is going to come.

Handling the "I Don't Want You to Work, Mommy!" Syndrome

Usually, all you can do for a young child is gently pull away and explain matter-of-factly that you work and she goes to play group, reassure her that you love her and miss her; for the older child, a promise that you will make arrangements to go on another field trip because you see how much it means to her can be comforting.

If the complaint becomes frequent, however, or even chronic, a new strategy may be called for. First, set aside some time for thinking the problem through before taking any course of action.

1. Rethink the approach you have taken in explaining your work to your children. Have you been apologetic about it? "I'm sorry, sweetie. I really wish I didn't have to . . ." Children, especially little children, don't see adults as having to do anything. As far as they can tell, you are in control of all the choices in life. Your boss doesn't march through the door and order you to sit down and work at that computer. Nor can they comprehend the financial reasons for work. And how honest are you being if you say you wish you didn't work?
2. Go over your own hang-ups about working. Write down all the benefits—material and psychological—your work brings to you and your family. Make a separate list of any negative effects.
3. If you feel the negative effects outweigh the positive effects, reconsider your job commitments. Have you taken on more work than you should at this time? Can you create a more flexible schedule? Can you work part time? Should you change jobs?
4. Take a fresh look at what your child does all day while you are working. Is she happy with your child-care arrangements? Does she have an interesting variety of activities? Does she play often with other children? Is her life too active or overprogrammed? Find out from her what she likes and dislikes.
5. Talk over all these questions with your spouse or a close friend who can help you decide if changes need to be made. Discuss the problem with your child's teacher and her baby-sitter. Her teacher, in particular, will probably know if she is simply going through a developmental stage, how soon she is likely to outgrow it, and how best you can weather it.
6. Decide on your course of action. It may even be not to change anything at present. Tell your child as much as she is able to understand about your decision. Make it clear that your work is your decision, not hers. Be honest. Don't confuse her with apologies or long explanations. And here is the payoff for thinking all these matters through so carefully: Your assurance will reassure her and increase her sense of security at a time when she badly needs it. That alone could turn the tide.

How Kids Feel About Their Working Mothers

The news from psychologists is encouraging: Studies show that how children feel about their mother's employment has less to do with the fact of her working than it does with her attitude toward working. Kids whose mothers are happy to be working, can manage their dual roles without placing undue stress on their families, and do not feel guilty to be working are proud of their moms. Daughters, especially, are likely to name their working mom as the person they most admire and the parent they most want to emulate. That does not mean, of course, that if you love your job, your child will show daily enthusiasm for your working. His age, his comprehension of what it is you do when you are away from him, his feelings about the sitters and activities you provide for him, your own behavior, and any number of other circumstances may all influence whether or not he voices resentment on occasion toward your work. But you can guard against the possibility of such complaints becoming chronic by helping your child develop positive attitudes toward your employment. Some suggestions:

* Take your child to visit your office; let him meet your co-workers and see what sort of things you do there. Seeing his picture on your desk and some of his nursery-school artwork on the wall will help him realize you think of him even when you are away from home. Make the visit brief for a pre-schooler: His baby-sitter could bring him just before lunch, then you could go out to eat together. As he gets older, let him come for a longer period occasionally and do something for you, like run the office copy machine.

* Do talk at home about whatever aspect of your work you think your child can understand. Let him share in your pride in your achievements. Hold a family celebration when you or your spouse gets a promotion or raise.

* Don't carry the stresses of the workplace home with you. If your work is so stressful that you cannot unwind between work and home, you need to reconsider your priorities. A different job may be in order.

* Make an effort to keep any guilt feelings you may have from time to time in their proper perspective. Even small children are sensitive to their mother's attitudes; if you act guilty—even by hesitating at the door as you leave—they are likely to assume you are.

* Don't overcompensate for your absences by indulging or overprotecting your child. You will probably only undermine his self-confidence and weaken his respect for you.

* Be aware of the many factors that can temporarily stir up negative feelings about your work. Separation anxiety can surface unexpectedly in a four-year-old or a seven-year-old for a variety of reasons probably totally unrelated to whether you work outside the home or not. Look for the underlying cause.

* Remember, your own positive attitude is par mount. Feeling good about your job bolsters y self-esteem and benefits everything you dc cluding mothering.

"Make New Friends, Keep the Old . . ."

How to Maintain Friendships When You're Working

Keeping in touch with friends is as important for working moms as for anyone. The casual contacts you make at work cannot replace the true soul mates you know well and can share your life with. Friends are a valuable stabilizing influence—a sympathetic shoulder to cry on when life gets tough and an eager ear to hear your joys and triumphs when things go right. You need them, and they need you. Work, your husband, and your children may well take precedence, and their demands on your schedule may be great, but the time you find for friends, however brief, can be the most rewarding of all. The trick is to plan them into your life just as you do everything else—put them down on your lists of important calls and things to do, and find pockets of time you can fit them into even if it means doubling up on your activities. Here are some ideas:

* Lunch-hour visits are one of the easiest ways to see your friends. Make reservations so that you won't spend the entire time waiting in line, or, if the weather is fine, take sandwiches to a nearby park.

* Invite a childless friend along when you take your children to the playground. While the children play, you can catch up on each other's lives with fewer interruptions than if you were to visit in each other's homes with the children around.

* If your friend has children, two-family outings can give you time to visit, even if the children are not close friends. Pick an activity or attraction the children will enjoy while you and your friend relax and chat on the sidelines.

* Get tickets to go together to the ballet or a concert in the evening or on a weekend afternoon when your husband can take the children. This plan can let you enjoy doing things your husband doesn't much like while you have fun seeing like-minded friends. Give him a chance to see his friends the same way.

* Work out with a friend: Whether it's a regular tennis game, jogging, an aerobics class, or weight lifting, doing it together will give you both an added incentive and a chance to visit.

* Take up a hobby together one evening a week. Quilting, bookbinding, woodworking—many activities offer the opportunity to share a relaxing activity and lots of time to talk. A mutual hobby can also provide a good setting for several friends to get together to talk about common problems.

* Do your clothes shopping together. Set aside a big chunk of weekend time when you can go to a favorite store and help each other assemble the next season's wardrobe.

* Keep in touch by mail. A quick postcard can let a friend know you're thinking of her or propose a time you can get together, whether she lives in a distant suburb or right next door.

* Don't overlook the telephone. Even when you can't get together with friends, the phone can help keep you involved in each other's lives. Some of the greatest benefits of friendship, after all, are gained just in talking, and you can use your hands for mindless chores like washing dishes or folding laundry while you chat.

How to Handle Temper Tantrums as You're Going Out the Door

Temper tantrums, at the ages of two and four years, and even in teenagers, are common occurrences. It's one thing if you're home all day and a tantrum occurs. But what do you do if a tantrum flares up just as you're leaving for work? Here are ideas to consider when faced with an unexpected outburst.

Looking for Possible Causes

A temper tantrum, first of all, is merely your pre-schooler's way of trying to cope with feelings of frustration and anger.

If your child throws a tantrum as you're leaving for work, it may signify that he has negative feelings about your working. Have you discussed his feelings with him? If he doesn't have a problem with your going to work, perhaps there is one with the person who takes care of him all day. If your child throws tantrums when you drop him off at the day-care center, you should reexamine the center to make sure conditions have not deteriorated since you were there last. It also doesn't hurt to ask your child to describe his feelings about the center.

If the tantrum occurs as you and your husband are going out for the evening, it could be a response to a feeling of not getting enough attention. Review your behavior to see if you've been neglecting to hug your child or reassure him that you love him. These extra touches are important to a child, especially one who doesn't see his mother all day.

Preventing the Problem

There are several things you can do to help your child deal more effectively with his emotions so that tantrums do not reoccur.

1. Teach your child how to handle frustration and anger by setting a good example. If your child witnesses you in a frustrating situation, tell him in a calm voice how annoyed you are and that you feel like screaming but you won't. Teach him to look at negative situations and review the options he has, other than having a tantrum.

2. Reward your child for reacting calmly in adverse situations. If he is frustrated by a game and comes to you to ask for your help rather than throwing a fit, tell him how pleased you are that he behaved rationally instead of getting mad. When your child knows he'll get praise and understanding for certain behavior, he'll make more of an effort to repeat it.

3. Don't wait for the problem to become full-blown before acting. If you see signs of trouble as you are getting ready to leave, try to step in before he completely falls apart. Go over to your child, hug him, and tell him that you have to go to work but that you'll be home soon and that you'll try to call him later on. By reassuring him that you understand how he feels, and by giving him some specific events to look forward to, you will help him alleviate feelings of frustration and anger.

Solving the Problem

If a tantrum strikes despite your best efforts, *DO* try the following:

1. Ignore it, and tell your baby-sitter to do the same. This will teach your child that certain behavior is not appropriate for getting attention or getting what he wants.

2. Stand firm. Your child's noise can be a powerful tool in getting you to react, despite your resolve not to. Tell yourself as you leave that it's important for your child to learn that he can't have everything he wants when he wants it.

3. Remain calm. If your initial reaction to the noise is to yell at your child to get him to stop, ignore it. In addition to not solving the problem, you are inadvertently providing a role model that is the equivalent of your child's behavior.

4. After the tantrum, praise your child for gaining control, or have your caretaker do it if you've left. Have your sitter join the child in a game or activity that can in no way be frustrating (or you'll risk another tantrum).

Remember these DON'TS

1. DON'T try to reason or talk your child out of a tantrum. He won't be listening. He's in the middle of an exhausting battle with himself. By attempting to converse, you are acknowledging the tantrum and thus giving your child the audience he needs to keep the "show" going.

2. DON'T throw a tantrum yourself. Losing your cool will only encourage your child not to regain his.

3. DON'T belittle your child. Throwing a tantrum doesn't mean he is a bad person. But you'll make him feel as though he is if you try to prevent or stop a tantrum by telling him he should be ashamed of himself for carrying on.

4. DON'T talk about the tantrum later on. Once tantrums are over, they are best forgotten. The more attention you give to the behavior, the more you'll increase the chances of its happening again. Getting attention is one of the main reasons for a tantrum.

5. DON'T punish your child for the tantrum after it's over. He needs your reassurance that you still love him despite his behavior.

Getting Your Husband to

Compared with men thirty years ago, few husbands today openly oppose the idea of their wives working; however, that doesn't necessarily mean that they are altogether comfortable with it. Particularly when the wife's job begins to adversely affect his life-style—by altering mealtimes, by making her less available to him, by requiring him to fend for himself while she is away—the "liberated" husband is apt to squirm. But a wife's work need not add stress to a marriage; it can enhance the marriage and help both partners grow.

Getting your husband to feel good about your job will be hardest if you left your job when you got married or when your first child was born, your mother-in-law never worked and takes a dim view of "women's lib," and your husband depends on you to be his social secretary, hostess, and caterer as well as homemaker and caretaker of his children. It will be easiest if you never left work except for short maternity leaves and your husband is basically supportive. But the tools for this task remain the same: good communication, time together, respect for each other, and love. Some strategies to take:

1. Your working should be an easy topic of conversation between you, not a bone of contention. Communicate your feelings about your career, and listen to his without judging them. Appeal to his desire for you to be happy by letting him know how much your work means to you. Point out the many advantages your job brings to your family, but acknowledge the sacrifices he makes. Tell him how

What to Do When He Says, "Quit!"

When you are juggling marriage, home, children, and career, it's easy for a little chaos to seep in somewhere unnoticed. Then something dreadful—or something trivial—happens that triggers a gut response in your spouse: "If you would just quit that job!" he storms, as if the job were the perpetrator of countless crimes. What do you do?

1. Keep very quiet. He's not being rational. Think of the best ways to react to a two-year-old's temper tantrum. Sit down and wait for it to pass.

2. When the storm clouds start to clear, sort out the bits and pieces for any useful truths you can glean. Keep them—if there were any—to yourself for the time being.

3. Remind yourself that your job was not the cause of the something dreadful or the something trivial and was only indirectly the

Feel Good About Your Job

patient and understanding he is.

2. Avoid head-on confrontations about fairness and equality and women's rights: You might as well wave a red flag in front of a bull. If you want him to see your side of the workload problem, talk directly about specific tasks you need help with. Don't be offended if he suggests you hire outside help.

3. To get him to help out more, don't push. Negotiate concessions one at a time. Then use praise and encouragement to solidify your gains. Many small steps in the right direction will gradually distribute the work load more equitably.

4. Don't complain to him about problems at the office or bring stresses from work home with you. Talk to friends if you need sympathy; unwind before you come home.

5. When changes are called for, prepare him in advance and make them gradually. If your new schedule means missing dinner at home once a week, start by leaving the meal prepared for him and the children; eventually they will take over the preparation themselves.

6. Involve him in decisions about your work that will affect him: shifting from part-time to full-time work, taking on additional responsibilities, accepting a promotion that will require more business travel.

7. However busy and successful you become, don't lose track of your priorities. Make time to be together. Show your love with thoughtful acts and consideration for his needs. Even little things—a surprise gift or a favorite food, a love note, doing one of his chores for him unasked, giving him a day off from family obligations—can show him how much you care.

cause of the chaos. But don't say so. Say, thoughtfully, "Maybe you're right. Maybe I shouldn't be working. Let's talk about it later. I'm hungry; aren't you?"

4. Have dinner. (These outbursts invariably occur on empty stomachs.) Talk as cheerfully as you can about other subjects, or simply let silence reign.

5. After dinner and after the children are in bed, if the time seems right, calmly talk over the problems that led up to the outburst and think together of solutions for those problems. Perhaps the home front was disorganized, child-care arrangements were inadequate, or your husband felt overworked because a task he undertook in an effort to help out proved more burdensome than he had expected. Perhaps your own tension contributed. Renegotiate chores, plan a vacation together, think of ways to reorganize your lives to help keep chaos at bay. You might find it useful to take a day or two off from work just to implement any changes that seem imperative, whether they involve cleaning out files or closets or hiring extra help.

6. If, on the other hand, when you sit down to talk, he now says, "Oh, that! I didn't really mean it. Just blew my top, I guess," don't be overzealous in tracking down the motives for what he said and don't bend over backward seeking solutions. Above all, don't stew about it in silence. The outburst itself cleared the air for him—forgive and forget it yourself.

"I Can't Come . . ."

How to Tell Your Child You Can't Attend a School Function

It's her first part in a play; it's a school picnic; it's an assembly where she'll be playing a solo on her clarinet: Whatever the function, she's counting on mom being there, and you're counting on it, too. But suddenly you're needed at work on just that day or evening. There's no way you can squeeze out of it short of quitting your job. What do you do?

***1.* Apologize.** If possible, talk to her in person, not over the phone. Sit down with her and explain that a very important project is at stake and you can't leave work. Express your sincere regrets that you cannot be there for her performance or for the fun you had hoped to share. Let her see your quandary.

2. Be tolerant of her anger or hurt. Now is the time she is likely to vent her feelings about your working—at least the negative ones. It's only natural that she feels resentment that your "performance" is taking precedence over hers. Listen patiently. Tell her you can see her disappointment.

***3.* Suggest arranging** for another family member or friend to take your place at the event: her father, her grandmother, her favorite babysitter. Let her choose and invite the person herself.

***4.* If the function** is a performance, provide your substitute or another parent who will be there with a camera, a tape recorder, or a video camera to record the event for you so that you can watch or listen to it together later. Taking these steps to preserve her performance for posterity may even flatter your child to the point where she will forget her concern that you won't be there.

***5.* Show your interest** by finding out if you can attend the dress rehearsal or asking your child to put on a "command performance" just for you the day after the big event.

***6.* If your child knows** you're genuinely sorry you can't be there, she'll undoubtedly forgive you for it. Don't try to buy her with promises of a toy or candy. It won't lessen her disappointment; it will only make her feel that you're trying to substitute for your presence with a material object.

***7.* Plan a special time** for the two of you to be together so that she can give you a full account of what you missed.

***8.* Further restore her faith** in your love for her by making a point to be there the next time.

EDUCATION

WHAT YOU SHOULD KNOW ABOUT IQ TESTS

Before you go into a tailspin about your child's impending IQ test and worry about what you'll do if your child isn't a genius, first you should learn what an IQ test is and what it measures.

WHAT DOES IQ MEAN?

There is a widespread difference in opinion as to what the term "intelligence" means. Most people consider it a measure of the ability to learn. However, an intelligence quotient, or IQ, is a relative term. Basically, it is a score that indicates your child's ability, compared to the ability of other children her age, to reason, solve problems, understand the meaning of words, and take intelligence tests. The IQ is computed using the following formula:

$$\frac{\text{mental age of child (based on test results)}}{\text{child's actual age}} \times 100 = \text{IQ}$$

IQ PRIMER

One of the most important things to remember about an IQ is that it's not a static number, because it is always changing and developing. Heredity plays an important role in determining a child's potential, but how close she comes to achieving that potential is determined by the amount of nurturing she gets and the effect of life's experiences on her.

A child's IQ can change. It can be increased significantly in a happy child who is in a stimulating environment. Children with behavioral problems often increase their IQ scores when these problems are alleviated. There is some question as to whether an IQ test actually measures intelligence or whether it measures only the skills necessary to perform adequately at school. At any rate, the main purpose of the test is to serve as a reference point for a child's ability to learn.

WHAT IS THE TEST COMPOSED OF?

The most popular test used is the Wechsler Intelligence Scale for Children—Revised (WISC-R). It is comprised of verbal and performance tests. The verbal tests reflect a child's alertness, memory, awareness, comparison ability, concrete and abstract thinking, simple math and vocabulary, and general ability to reason. The performance tests take those basic abilities and ask children to use them to perform tasks, such as arranging pictures in the correct order, completing the missing parts of a picture, and generally using hand-eye coordination and nonimpulsive thinking.

WHAT DO THE TESTS REVEAL?

1. They eliminate any possibility that a child who completes the tests may be retarded.

2. They confirm that the child has at least an average intelligence.

3. They give an idea of the potential level of achievement that can be expected from a child.

4. A wide discrepancy (of 25 points) between the verbal and performance portions of the IQ test may be evidence of a learning disability. This can prompt the psychologist to give the child additional tests to detect where the problem lies.

BEST CHILDREN'S BOOKS

SIX MONTHS TO TWO YEARS

Animal Book by Dick Bruna (Methuen)
An ABC for You and Me by Margaret Tempest (Medici)
Baby Animals by Harry NcNaught (Random House)
The Baby's Lap Book by Kay Chorao (E.P. Dutton)
Goodnight Moon by Margaret Wise Brown (Harper & Row)
I Am a Bunny by Ole Risom (Golden Books)
Max's First Work* by Rosemary Wells (Dial)
Pat the Bunny, Pat the Cat by Dorothy Kunhardt (Golden Books)
Puppies by Jan Pfloog (Random House)
Snuffy by Dick Bruna (Methuen)

EIGHTEEN MONTHS TO THREE YEARS

Are You My Mother? by P.D. Eastman (Random House)
Ask Mr. Bear by Marjorie Flack (Macmillan)
The Carrot Seed by Ruth Kraus (Harper & Row; Scholastic)
Changes, Changes by Pat Hutchins (Macmillan)
The Golden Egg Book by Margaret Wise Brown (Golden Press)
In the Night Kitchen by Maurice Sendak (Harper & Row)
Just Me by Marie Hall Ets (Viking)
Little Bear* by Else Holmelund Minarik (Harper & Row)
The Little Fur Family by Margaret Wise Brown (Harper & Row)

Alligators All Around, Chicken Soup with Rice, One Was Johnny, and **Pierre** by Maurice Sendak (Harper & Row)
Pancakes for Breakfast by Tomie de Paola (Harcourt Brace Jovanovich)
Rosie's Walk by Pat Hutchins (Macmillan)
The Runaway Bunny by Margaret Wise Brown (Harper & Row)
The Snowy Day by Ezra Jack Keats (Viking)
Truck by Donald Crews (Greenwillow)
The Very Hungry Caterpillar by Eric Carle (Collins-World)
Where's Spot?* by Eric Hill (Putnam)
Where's My Baby? by H.A. Rey (Houghton Mifflin)

FAVORITE PICTURE BOOKS—THREE TO SIX YEARS

A Bear Called Paddington* by Michael Bond (Random House)
Bedtime for Francis* by Russell Hoban (Harper & Row)
Best First Book Ever* by Richard Scarry (Golden Press)
Blueberries for Sal by Robert McCloskey (Viking)
Caps for Sale by Esphyr Slobodkina (Addison-Wesley; Scholastic)
Corduroy* by Don Freeman (Viking)
Curious George* by H.A. Rey (Houghton Mifflin)
Doctor De Soto by William Steig (Farrar, Strauss & Giroux; Scholastic)
Harry the Dirty Dog* by Gene Zion (Harper & Row)
Harold and the Purple Crayon by Crockett Johnson (Harper & Row)
The House on East 88th Street by Bernard Waber (Houghton Mifflin)
Katy and the Big Snow by Virginia Lee Burton (Houghton Mifflin)
Little Blue and Little Yellow by Leo Lionni (Astor)
The Little Engine That Could by Watty Piper (Platt; Scholastic)
The Little House by Virginia Lee Burton (Houghton Mifflin)
Make Way for Ducklings by Robert McCloskey (Viking)
Mike Mulligan and His Steam Shovel by Virginia Lee Burton (Houghton Mifflin)
Millions of Cats by Wanda Gag (Coward McCann)
Mouse Tales by Arnold Lobel (Harper & Row)
Owl at Home by Arnold Lobel (Harper & Row)
The Story About Ping by Marjorie Flack (Viking)

*and sequels

The Story of Babar, the Little Elephant* by Jean De Brunhoff (Random House)
The Story of Ferdinand by Munro Leaf (Viking)
The Tale of Peter Rabbit by Beatrix Potter (Frederick Warne)
The Tale of the Fierce, Bad Rabbit by Beatrix Potter (Frederick Warne)
The Tale of Two Bad Mice by Beatrix Potter (Frederick Warne)
The Tall Book of Nursery Tales illus. by F. Rojankovsky (Harper & Row)
Tikki Tikki Tembo by Arlene Mosel (Holt, Rinehart and Winston)
Uncle Elephant by Arnold Lobel (Harper & Row)

BEGINNING READERS

Amelia Bedelia* by Peggy Parish (Harper & Row; Scholastic)
Arthur* by Lillian Hoban (Harper & Row)
Bennett Cerf's Book of Animal Riddles (Random House)
The Cat in the Hat by Dr. Seuss (Random House)
Cranberry Thanksgiving* by Wende and Harry Devlin (Parents)
Frog and Toad Are Friends* by Arnold Lobel (Harper & Row)
George and Martha* by James Marshall (Houghton Mifflin; Scholastic)
Green Eggs and Ham by Dr. Seuss (Random House)
One Fish, Two Fish, Red Fish, Blue Fish by Dr. Seuss (Random House)
The Stupids Step Out* by Harry Allard (Houghton Mifflin)

READ-ALOUD BOOKS

The Boxcar Children* by Gertrude Chandler Warner (Albert Whitman)
Charlie and the Chocolate Factory* by Roald Dahl (Knopf)
Charlotte's Web by E.B. White (Harper & Row)
The Chronicles of Narnia by C.S. Lewis (Macmillan)
The Country Bunny and the Little Gold Shoes by DuBose Heyward (Houghton Mifflin)
Heidi by Johanna Spyri (Various editions)
Household Stories of the Brothers Grimm trans. by Lucy Crane (Dover)
Just So Stories by Rudyard Kipling (Various editions)
Lassie Come Home by Eric Knight (Holt, Rinehart and Winston; Dell)
Little House in the Big Woods* by Laura Ingalls Wilder (Harper & Row)
Mary Poppins* by P.L. Travers (Harcourt Brace Jovanovich)

*and sequels

Mrs. Piggle Wiggle* by Betty MacDonald (Lippincott)
Nutcracker by E.T.A. Hoffman (trans. by R. Manheim) (Crown)
Pinocchio by Carlo Collodi (Macmillan); abridged version by Freya Littledale (Scholastic)
Ramona the Pest* by Beverly Cleary (Morrow; Dell)
Stuart Little by E.B. White (Harper & Row)
Trumpet of the Swan by E.B. White (Harper & Row)
The Voyages of Dr. Dolittle* by Hugh Lofting
The Wind in the Willows by Kenneth Grahame (Methuen)
Winnie-the-Pooh and **The House at Pooh Corner** by A.A. Milne (E.P. Dutton)
The Wizard of Oz* by L. Frank Baum (Dover; Ballantine)
A Wonder Book by Nathaniel Hawthorne (Airmont; Grosset)

CHILDREN'S MAGAZINES

Boys' Life, Boy Scouts of America, 1325 Walnut Hill Lane, Irving, Texas 75062
Cobblestone, 28 Main Street, Peterborough, New Hampshire 03258 (a history magazine)

*and sequels

Cricket, Box 100, LaSalle, Illinois 61301 (a literary magazine)
Ebony, Jr.! Johnson Publishing Company, Inc., 820 South Michigan Avenue, Chicago, Illinois 60605
Highlights for Children, 2300 West Fifth, P.O. Box 269, Columbus, Ohio 43216
National Geographic World, National Geographic Society, 17th and M Street NW, Washington, D.C. 20036
Ranger Rick and **Your Big Back Yard,** National Wildlife Federation, 1412 16th Street NW, Washington, D.C. 20036
Sesame Street, Electric Company, and **3-2-1 Contact,** One Lincoln Plaza, New York, New York 10023
Stone Soup, P.O. Box 83, Santa Cruz, California 95063 (stories written by children)

POETRY COLLECTIONS FOR CHILDREN

A Child's Garden of Verses by R.L. Stevenson (various editions)
A Light in the Attic and **Where the Sidewalk Ends** by Shel Silverstein (Harper & Row)
I Went to the Animal Fair ed. by William Cole (World)

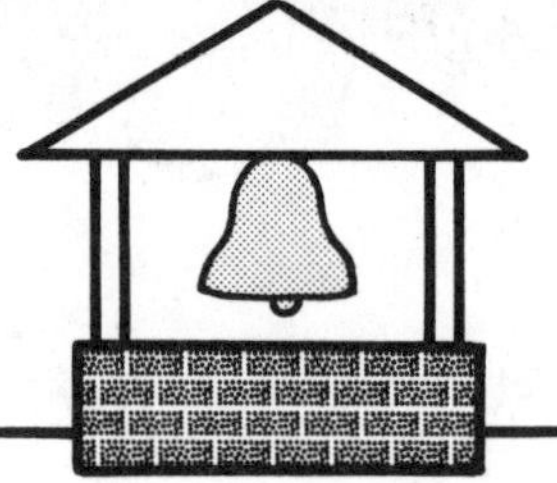

GETTING THROUGH THOSE FIRST-DAY-OF-SCHOOL JITTERS

Even though kids today get plenty of pre-school schooling—whether in day care, nursery school, or kindergarten—the first day of "real" school can make them apprehensive. Nor are these jitters necessarily limited to the first day in the first grade. Successive Septembers can bring renewed fears as children move on to new classrooms, new classmates, new teachers, and increased responsibilities. Each "first day" is different, but parents can take similar approaches in dealing with all of them.

1. Let Your Child Know What Lies Ahead

- Your child should be acquainted with the setting and the staff. Whether it is a day-care center, a nursery school, or an elementary school, have her visit the classroom and meet her teachers.
- Explain what to expect at school, what days and hours she will be there, what arrangements have been made for after-school care, and how she will get there and back.

2. Having Friends Helps

- Make sure your child knows at least a few of her future classmates. If necessary, arrange introductions and visits before school begins.
- Get together with other parents and their children for a picnic or an informal party. Encourage developing friendships with play dates, or form a play group.
- If your child has been away all summer, renew old friendships with children who will be in her class.

3. Calm Worries About Getting There and Back

- If she will be riding a school bus for the first time, find out if she will have friends riding with her or arrange to go with her the first few days until she gets to know other children on the bus.
- If she will be walking to school alone for the first time, arrange for an older child to go with her until she is comfortable with the idea. Walk the route with her before school starts.

4. Talk

- Talk positively about the new school or grade, and listen to her reactions.
- If she expresses any fears, listen sympathetically and reassure her that she can handle the new situation.
- Suggest strategies for dealing with the problems she thinks she might face.

5. Build Up Her Ego

- Boosting her self-confidence is the best way to prepare her to cope with new experiences. Give some thought to ways you can help increase her self-esteem—for the "first day" and every day.
- Don't undermine all your efforts by betraying any jitters of your own!

Fielding Questions About Sex

Kids go through three basic stages in their curiosity about and comprehension of sex: The first is typical of pre-schoolers, the second of school-age children in the so-called "latency" period, the third of children at puberty. Just as we would not answer a two-year-old's query about what makes a car go with a long, detailed description of the internal combustion engine, we need to gear our responses to their questions about sex to the appropriate age level.

Level 1: Pre-School Kids

With a small child, put yourself at ease. Your main job will be to identify anatomical parts with their correct names, to let him satisfy his curiosity by occasionally seeing other children and babies and his parents undressed, to teach him that there is a difference between public and private behavior—that he may masturbate in the privacy of his room but not in front of other people—to respect his privacy and teach him to respect yours, and to suggest other activities if playing doctor becomes a fixation.

He will ask about body parts and their functions, where babies come from, why he has a penis and you don't, why you have breasts and he doesn't, what tampons are, and about anything else that comes into his realm of experience.

Simple, honest, straightforward answers are best. Be matter-of-fact and to the point. Don't overload him with information he didn't ask for. That babies come from their mothers' wombs—a special place inside their bodies—is probably enough to satisfy his curiosity for the moment.

Avoid misleading terminology and metaphors: They can cause confusion and even anxiety. Babies do not come from their mothers' *stomachs,* for example; nor do fathers *plant seeds* inside mothers-to-be.

Level 2: "Latency"

School-age children can ask more trenchant questions and often require fuller answers. As they learn to read, they will ask real toughies like "What does s-e-x mean?"

Your single most useful response, many experts suggest, will be, "What do you think?"—not because you are being evasive but because you need to find out what he knows already and what it is he really wants to know. Then you can tailor your answers accordingly.

Answer all questions: "That's something we'll talk about when you are older" is not an answer.

Make your answers accurate and informative. But don't overdo it. Many school-age children are satisfied with brief answers and really don't want to hear more, perhaps because it all sounds a little peculiar and farfetched. As with small children, watch for their limits.

Don't restrict your answers to information: Communicate your attitudes and values, too. Children need to know not only the facts about reproduction, but how to cope with sexual feelings and what is responsible sexual behavior.

Find opportunities to talk about sex in ways not directly related to your child's behavior. He will learn about rape or abortion or birth control or gay rights by reading the newspaper or hearing newscasts. Help him understand what these terms mean.

Level 3: Puberty

At the onset of puberty, if your kid has found you an "askable" mom, questions about sex are likely to increase—even from a child who couldn't have cared less about the subject a year or two before. What then seemed remote is suddenly happening to him or his friends; it has immediate relevance to his life.

Brush up your knowledge of these developments. Puberty is not one event, but a gradual process of growth and change that lasts four to five years for boys and three to four years for girls. A clear, detailed description of the physical changes that will take place and the approximate schedule of their appearance will lessen anxiety.

Talking about your own memories of puberty and your feelings about it at the time will further assist in reassuring your child.

Dispel myths about homosexuality, fantasies, and masturbation.

Promote frank, open discussion of important sexual issues. Children should be made aware of specific methods of birth control, the risks of sexually transmitted diseases, and the exploitative possibilities of sexual relationships. Whether your child asks directly about these matters or not, he needs to learn about them to behave responsibly when he becomes sexually active.

Helpful Books

For Pre-Schoolers:

A Baby Starts to Grow by Paul Showers (Crowell)

The True Story of How Babies Are Made by Per Holm Knudsen (Children's Press)

For School-Age Children:

The Wonderful Story of How You Were Born by Sidonie Matsner Gruenberg (Doubleday)

How Was I Born? by Lennart Nilsson (Delacorte Press)

For Pubescent Children:

What's Happening to My Body? by Lynda Madaras (Newmarket Press)

The What's Happening to My Body? Book for Boys by Lynda Madaras (Newmarket Press)

For Families:

The Family Book About Sexuality by Mary Calderone (Harper & Row)

Sex: The Facts, the Acts & Your Feelings by Michael Carrera (Crown)

For Parents:

Talking with Your Child About Sex by Mary Calderone and James W. Ramey (Random House)

Learning Games for Toddlers

Toddlers are avid learners. Their pride and joy at being able to navigate on two feet spill over into every area as they gain command of language, begin to feed and dress themselves, and learn to manipulate crayons and pencils, blocks and toys. Your happiest times together will be when you are teaching her new skills, whether by playing with her toys, by reading and singing to her, or by making games out of daily routines. Here are some simple games that will enrich her learning experiences. No fancy equipment is required. Some are activities she will pursue while you do other work nearby; others will involve you more in the fun.

* Put all your pots and pans with lids on the floor. Take all the lids and put them in an empty grocery carton. Then let your child match up pots and lids.

* Buy an assortment of different-colored plastic blocks. Show your child how to sort the blocks according to color, and tell her the name of each color. Talk about the colors to help her make comparisons: "This block is red, like your toy telephone."

* "Washing dishes" teaches nothing about washing dishes but a lot about fluid dynamics. Stand your child on a step stool or her high chair so that she can reach the sink. Fill a large mixing bowl or dishpan with water, and give her a plastic pitcher and cup, spoons, bowls, a colander, and a funnel to play with. Urge her to keep the water in the sink, but be prepared for spills. A waterproof smock on her, bare feet, and bath mats on the floor will help somewhat.

* Matching socks, folding washcloths, and sorting clean laundry into personal piles for each member of the family are real tasks a toddler is proud to help out with, and they will develop her matching and sorting skills.

* Get down on all fours and pretend to be animals together. Imitate the sounds and movements of dogs, cats, ducks, chickens, rabbits, frogs—whatever appeals to her.

* Play hide-and-seek indoors or out. Pretend you can't find her and look in funny places, naming them as you go. Give her voice clues or peek out if she has trouble finding you.

* Another version of hide-and-seek: Hide a toy in a different room and give your child directions for finding it. Start with very simple directions: "Go to the dining room and find the red ball under the table." Make your directions longer and more complicated as she gets more proficient.

* Make an "obstacle course": something to climb on, something to crawl under, something to go around or step over. Show her the route to take, describing it as you go and emphasizing words that indicate the sequence, actions, and spatial relations: "*First* we *climb up* on this chair; now we *slide down* the pillows and *crawl under* the table; *then run around* the other chair back to where we started."

* Put three or four objects your child is familiar with in a laundry bag or pillow case. Choose things of different sizes and textures, for example, a washcloth, a rubber ball, a small brush, a pencil, a toy car. Show her and name each item as you put it into the bag. Then have her reach in and pick an object without looking and guess what it is by feeling it. Ask her to describe how it feels.

* Let your child help you find products in the supermarket. If you are using coupons, let her hold the coupons and tell you where the product pictured on each is. Or you can stop in front of the produce section and ask, "Where are the bananas?"

* Make up your own learning games for toddlers. The best ones let them use their whole bodies and all their senses. Let them handle objects. Give everything a name. Ask questions about similarities and differences. Give them a chance to solve problems. Once your child has learned a game, reverse roles. Teach your child's favorite games to her baby-sitter. Above all, have fun.

Helpful Books

Playtime Learning Games for Young Children by Alice S. Honig (Syracuse University Press)
Teach Your Baby by Genevieve Painter (Simon & Schuster)
Learning Games for the First Three Years and **Learning Games for Threes and Fours: A Guide to Adult-Child Play** by Joseph Sparling and Isabelle Lewis (Walker Publishing Co.)

Back-to-School Checklist

The first day of school is one of the most important of the year for your child. He'll race home with a list of school supplies a yard long! And, of course, he'll insist he must have everything—or else. You can ease up on the back-to-school panic kids—and parents—go through by preparing as much as you can before opening day.

Before the first day of school . . .

Sometime in August, plan to take a day off and spend it with your child, shopping for school needs. Prepare a list of the supplies you can buy in advance. The advantage of doing it this way is that you'll be able to shop in a calm, relaxed manner, and you won't be caught up in the mad rush of shopping that goes on during that first week after school opens.

Clothing will probably be at the top of the list, since he's grown since last fall, and the fads have changed, too. Most stores are already well-stocked with fall clothing by mid-August each year, so if you shop early, you'll have the best selections. Before you shop, check what's needed: underwear; socks and tights for cooler weather; basic school clothes—jeans, corduroy pants, jumpers, skirts, dresses, turtleneck tops; shoes—sneakers, dress shoes, boots for stormy weather; and outer wear—sweaters, a light jacket, rain gear, and snow pants and jacket. Of course, you may have already stocked up on some of these items at end-of-winter sales last spring and checked the local thrift shops and rummage sales over the summer, for buying a whole new wardrobe every fall can cost a mint. If last year's snow gear is not completely worn out and still fits, consider using it to start the season and buying new things in January when the prices come down.

In addition to shopping for clothing, there are a few other items that need your attention.

- Bike tune-up. If your child uses his bicycle to ride to and from school, now is the time to have it checked thoroughly.
- Wristwatch. Since it's important for your child to start being responsible for his own schedule, a wristwatch makes a wonderful back-to-school gift.
- Lunch box. Even if he doesn't bring his lunch to school every day, it's a good idea to keep a lunch box and thermos handy for class trips or those days when he can't face cafeteria food.
- Library card. Neither the school library nor you have all the books your child may need for research or reading. So now is the time to see that he has his library card—either a new one or an updated card. Go with him the first time, so that you both know where the library is located and the hours it is open.
- Inoculations. Check with the school and your doctor to see what shots or boosters your child may need. It's wise to take care of this before school begins, since some inoculations can cause mild reactions.
- Eye checkup. If your child wears glasses, or if it's been a while since he's had a checkup, make an appointment so that the necessary adjustments can be made before the first day of school.

After the first day . . .

You can't predict exactly what school supplies your child will need, but the basic list will probably include the following:

1. Notebooks
2. Looseleaf binder, paper, subject separators
3. Pens and pencils
4. Pen and pencil case
5. Erasers
6. Ruler, compass, protractor
7. Construction paper
8. Small stapler and scissors
9. Crayons, markers, or colored pencils
10. Paste or glue
11. Small assignment notebook
12. Reinforcements

Helping Your Child Learn To Read

Learning to read does not begin in school—it begins at birth. Studies show that children who are talked to and read to grow up to be readers. Talk to your baby. Sing or recite nursery rhymes. Help her copy the sounds you make. Read early and read often. Children as young as six months can get great pleasure from looking at picture books. Choose sturdily constructed board books with bright colors, interesting graphics, and realistic illustrations of familiar objects. Read with gusto. Provide appropriate sound effects and movements. Here are some specifics to keep in mind to make reading a happy sharing time for both of you.

---

1. As your child begins to talk, listen. Let her "read" stories to you. Help her to understand the stories you read by asking questions about objects and experiences mentioned. Let the story initiate a dialogue about events in the child's own life. After reading a story, talk over what happened in it.

2. Don't be discouraged by your child's requests to hear the same book over and over. She learns much through repetition. When *you* are tired of it, try going through the book just talking about the pictures instead of reading text, then quickly suggest a new activity.

3. Take your child to the library and let her choose books for herself while you choose books you want to share with her. Let your librarian suggest the best books for her age and interests. Look for books you liked as a child, for your enthusiasm will communicate itself in your reading. Introduce your child to art by selecting books with beautiful illustrations. Include non-fiction as well as fiction, verse as well as prose.

4. When your child *does* begin to read, listen patiently and praise and encourage her efforts. Don't stop reading aloud to her. Her curiosity and ability to comprehend outstrip her beginning ability to read; she will be frustrated and discouraged if she is limited to only simple books. By reading aloud you can broaden her knowledge of a field she is interested in and increase her vocabulary; at the same time you will be aiding her progress toward reading more difficult books.

As your child grows older, encourage her to read to you. Let reading be a source of both information and pleasure, a useful skill and shared joy.

Helpful Books

Teach Your Child to Read in 20 Minutes a Day by Barbara J. Fox (Warner Books)
The Read Aloud Handbook by Jim Trelease (Penguin)
Good Books to Grow On by Andrea E. Cascardi (Warner Books)

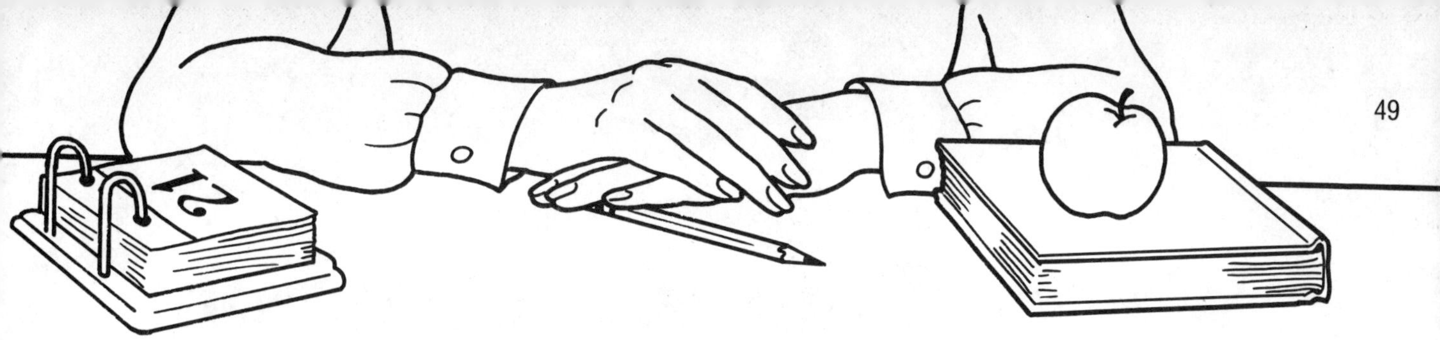

How to See Kids' Teachers

Some responsibilities of a working mother require a certain amount of maneuvering to accomplish. The parent/teacher conference is one of the easier tasks to rearrange to fit your schedule, if necessary. Most teachers are aware of the needs of working parents (they frequently have the same problems themselves), and they will be willing to bend to fit your needs. Here are some ideas on the best ways to proceed.

* Inform your child's teacher at the beginning of the school year of your interest in your child's schooling and your desire to be as involved as you can be. The flip side of the coin, however, is your full-time job that necessarily places demands on your time.
* Ask to be kept abreast of all school events well in advance so that you can best plan for them.
* Exchange phone numbers with the teacher and ask to be kept informed on a regular basis of your child's progress and problems in school. You needn't feel as if you are imposing.

The parent/teacher conference is usually heralded with a note that accompanies your child home from school. The note explains the purpose of the conference. Various available dates and times are listed for you to choose from. If you can't attend any of the available time slots, don't fret. There are always ways to improvise.

Most teachers, aware of the schedules of working parents, will leave extra time open for evening and early morning conferences. You can call the teacher and request one.

Since there are often two conferences scheduled during the school year, another option is for you and your husband to share the task, since it is unlikely that both of you will be unable to attend both conferences. It is ideal for you and your husband to keep abreast of your child's progress in school without neglecting your responsibilities at the office.

If it happens that neither of you can attend a conference, there is always the option of sending your child's grandmother, aunt, uncle, or even a trusted babysitter. Anyone sent in your place should be involved with your child on a continuing basis so he or she can respond to the teacher's observations, providing relevant feedback and background information.

Though not as widely used, phone conferences are a way of communicating with your child's teacher when in-person meetings are impossible. This should be arranged beforehand to take place at a time that's convenient for both of you. If you take the call at work, try to schedule it for a time, such as your lunch hour, when you're reasonably sure you won't be disturbed. If you take the call at home, perhaps your husband can participate by listening in on an extension.

Depending on your situation, there may be other solutions that fit the needs of both you and your child's teacher. Communicating by letter is another option. Teachers enjoy parents who are interested and involved with their children. If you display that interest, your child's teacher will be more than willing to assist you in any way possible. The parent/teacher conference is a good way to keep involved with your child's education.

Ways to Deal with Common School Problems

When kids start school, moms breathe a sigh of relief. No more worries about full-time child care. However, school problems can crop up. Here are some common ones:

Coping With A Difficult Teacher

Helping your child get along with a difficult teacher is tough, for it's hard not to get angry at the teacher yourself. But simply taking your child's side does not teach him how to cope; what's more, it may worsen their relationship and destroy your chances of mediating.

1. Listen. Let your child express his anger verbally, or, if he wants to, have him write down his grievances. Venting his anger may dissipate it. It can also help him see his own share in creating the problem—he talked out of turn, he forgot his homework, whatever. And it helps you find out what specific problems are. Be sympathetic without judging either him or the teacher.
2. Suggest strategies. Draw on experiences you've had with temperamental, strict, or unfair teachers and bosses.
3. Make an appointment to see the teacher. Find out if she is aware of your child's unhappiness with school. Ask her for suggestions to help you deal with it. You want her to feel you are working with her to help your child.
4. If your child and his teacher are really at loggerheads, see the principal and tactfully arrange to transfer your child to another class.

Classroom Misbehavior

As distressing as it is to get a report from your child's school that he is misbehaving in class, don't just blow up at him or kick yourself. Be as objective as you can be—you want to help your child.

1. Talk it over with your child. Ask him what's been happening, and listen to his side of the story. He may be having difficulties with the teacher or with another child.
2. Call the teacher right away and confer with her on the best ways to deal with the problem. Sometimes a change in seating arrangements or schedule helps.

Friction With Classmates

Kids can be mean, nasty, vindictive, bigoted, and cruel—just like grown-ups. When your kid is the victim of teasing, ostracism, or bullying by other children, your protective hackles rise. What can you do?

1. Enlist the teacher's aid. She should know what is going on and how your child is being hurt.
2. Bolster your child's self-esteem. Give him pride in his heritage and racial background. Give him confidence in his physical abilities by letting him choose a sport and helping him gain mastery in it.
3. Share his agony. Acknowledge that people can be cruel and life isn't always fair; we cannot always get redress. But help him realize that we risk becoming unjust ourselves if we let frustration turn to bitterness.
4. See the school principal if real disciplinary problems with bullies develop in the classroom or schoolyard. Your child's safety—and probably that of other children—is at stake.

Poor Schoolwork

If you have been in close touch with your child's teacher and his schoolwork, report cards will carry no surprises. But they may still be disappointing. You know he is not dumb. How can you get everyone else to see that? How can you help him do better?

1. Talk to the teacher about your child's lack of progress. Find out what she believes the source of the problem to be. If she suspects he has learning disabilities, have him tested both by your pediatrician and by a testing service recommended by the school. If he is disabled, learn all you can about his disability and work with it.
2. If a particular subject is giving your child difficulty, extra one-to-one assistance from a tutor may be the answer. Ask the school for a list of names to choose from. A good tutor can increase a child's motivation as well as help him over a tough spot.
3. Think over the best ways of arousing his desire to learn and improving his study habits:
   - *Build on his current interests:* Magazines and books on his favorite subjects will get him to read more.
   - *Provide a new work area for him:* Convert a closet into an "office" for him, or make a screen around his desk to help him focus on his work.
   - *Don't nag* but do discuss with him the importance of education in modern life. Encourage regular study, praise all his efforts, and reward diligence.

Phobias

Children who acquire early morning headaches or stomachaches that miraculously disappear once the school bus has departed require special attention. The source of their anxiety may be any of the problems already discussed; it may be fear of not doing well on an exam or of having to compete in a sports event. Kids feign illness because they don't want to reveal what the real phobia is; it's up to you to unearth the reason.

See the school counselor or psychologist if you feel you need more help. It might be easier for your child to open up to someone less directly involved with his life.

Helpful Books

***What Did You Learn in School Today? A Comprehensive Guide to Getting the Best Possible Education for Your Child* by Bruce Baron, Christine Baron, and Bonnie MacDonald (Warner Books)**

How to Raise a Brighter Child

Scores of books are available in libraries and bookshops that promise to show you how to teach a two-year-old to read, how to raise your child's IQ, how to program your child for academic success. Their methods may work, at least in accomplishing the short-term goals their authors have in mind, but at what long-term cost in creativity and happiness we may never know. Each child is unique. Each is born with her own special talents. Discovering and nurturing your child's innate abilities are some of the joys of parenthood—and ones you won't have to miss, despite your busy schedule.

1. Provide opportunities for your child to increase her competence at doing things for herself. A step stool to reach the faucets, clothes in which she can dress herself, low open shelves or easy drawers she can arrange her things in—all give a young child confidence in her abilities that will carry over to other realms of learning.

2. Encourage self-expression by keeping supplies of crayons, paper, scissors, glue, and clay or Playdough where she can reach them easily and use them safely. Let a younger child dictate her stories for you to staple into a homemade book she can illustrate. Have her sing made-up songs into a tape recorder.

3. Widen your child's horizons. New foods; trips to age-appropriate museums, puppet shows, films, and theaters; travel to new neighborhoods or distant countries; visits to the local fire and police station—all broaden her knowledge of the world.

4. Bring the world home with books, radio, television, records, photographs, reproductions of works of art, newspapers, and magazines. You will want to explore and discuss some of these materials together; others you may simply wish to make available for her to look at or not as she pleases.

5. Build up a reference library you can both use at home: Include an atlas, an encyclopedia, a good children's dictionary, and a good collegiate dictionary. Reference guides to music, art, film, and any other special subjects you care about can be useful, too.

6. Remember that your input, your enthusiasm, and your loving concern are the best motivators for learning. The time you spend playing games, reading books aloud, and telling her things you know is much more valuable than hours spent watching "educational" television.

7. Learn together. If she wants to start music lessons, take up an instrument yourself. Don't let competition mar your pleasure in sharing a new activity together; she will probably learn faster than you do anyway and will be delighted to let you play second fiddle.

8. See that your child has a chance to develop extracurricular interests, whether in sports or the arts or both. Seek out child-oriented teachers who know how to make learning fun and who won't try to push children beyond the capacities of their stage of development. Encourage your child to focus on the one or two activities she really likes and stick with them.

9. Coordinate learning experiences. When you take a trip to the aquarium, find other ways of exploring marine life as well. Go to the beach or to a fish market. Read and talk about stories about fish, both fiction and non-fiction. Supplement the passive experience of looking at and reading about fish with more active participation—draw fish, buy a fish and make fish prints, or make a papier-mâché whale.

10. Know when enough is enough. Don't try to continue a learning game after your toddler's interest wanes. Don't push educational toys or books your child isn't interested in.

10 Do's and Don'ts for Hassle-Free Homework Times

Teachers assign homework to give children a chance to think out problems on their own, to extend learning beyond the classroom, and to help children develop independent work habits. You can contribute to this effort by keeping these goals in mind. Your job is to make it easier for your child to take the responsibility of doing homework on himself.

1. *DO* make homework a high priority. Set limits on after-school activities. Homework, chores, and practicing an instrument should be the regular events around which others may be scheduled as time permits.
2. *DO* set a regular time for doing homework. Let your child decide what works best for him, whether just after school, after dinner, or between an after-school activity or playtime and dinner.
3. *DON'T* make exceptions easily. Invitations to birthday parties and other outings, and special programs on TV come up all too frequently. Set limits, and arrange for some other activity to give way so that the homework still gets done.
4. *DO* provide a quiet, well-lighted study area where your child can be away from siblings and distractions, although not necessarily alone. Some children work best at the kitchen table while mom fixes dinner or cleans up afterward.
5. *DO* see that your child understands the assignment, but don't answer questions he is supposed to figure out himself.
6. *DO* let him call a classmate for help if neither of you can comprehend what needs to be done. If other children in the class are equally mystified—this does happen sometimes — call the teacher yourself and diplomatically explain your confusion.
7. *DO* provide sympathy and encouragement if the homework seems excessively long or difficult. Listen to complaints and acknowledge your child's feelings of anger and frustration, but don't attack the teacher yourself.
8. *DO* go over his homework when he is finished—if he wants you to. Let him know if you find errors, and see if he can find them before telling him where they are.
9. *DON'T* edit his homework.
10. *DO* see that he puts the finished homework in his book bag right away, and have one place where the bag is always kept.

HOW TO CHOOSE AN ENCYCLOPEDIA FOR YOUR CHILD

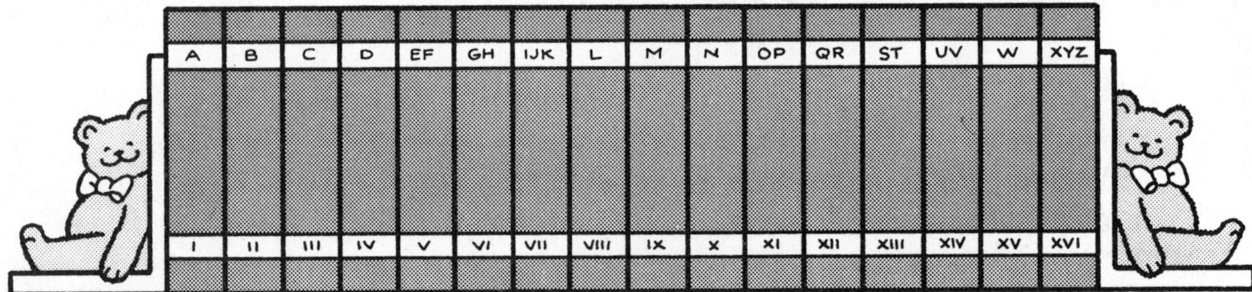

There are special problems associated with encyclopedias published for children. One problem is the vocabulary level. You have to make sure it's not too difficult and not beyond the reach of your child. Another consideration is whether your child will outgrow the set before you've finished paying for it. It's better to get a more advanced version than too simple a version.

The American Library Association suggests following *these* criteria when trying to assess the quality of a set of encyclopedias.

1. Authority: The authority of an encyclopedia with a good reputation is usually taken for granted. You can assume it will cover familiar topics, such as ancient Greece and philosophy, well. However, the fast pace at which technology is advancing means that there are a number of emerging subjects in which there are new developments every day. A good encyclopedia will update the information with each printing and handle each subject thoroughly. To help make a decision about whether the encyclopedia you choose is an accepted authority, look at the list of credentials for both the editorial staff and contributors, and note their experience and education.

2. Arrangement: Encyclopedia topics can be arranged either thematically or alphabetically by word or by letter. A word-by-word arrangement is easiest for a child to follow. Also note the method used to help readers locate related information on a particular subject. The child-turned-student will appreciate a detailed index to help draw together information that may pertain to the same subject but may be scattered throughout the set of encyclopedias.

3. Subject Coverage: To help determine how well an encyclopedia covers its subject matter, consider the following: What type and range of topics are included? How much space is allotted to each subject? Does the point of view of the editors show through? Are both living and dead persons covered? Any good contemporary encyclopedia should devote approximately half of the total text to geography and the pure and applied sciences. The rest should be devoted to liberal arts. Children's encyclopedias should also devote attention to such topics as pets, health, and handicrafts.

4. Accuracy: Never assume that information published in an encyclopedia is correct. Generally, editors strive to keep as accurate as possible articles about American politics, space exploration, major scientific breakthroughs, and geography. Inspect topics you're familiar with to see if articles about them are accurate.

5. Subjectivity: This is especially important for children, whose views on certain subjects may well be influenced by the information (or viewpoint) presented in an encyclopedia. Note any sexual or racial bias or stereotypical placement of women or men in solely traditional roles.

6. Quality: One crucial factor in determining the quality of an encyclopedia is the length of the articles. An encyclopedia that attempts to cover a world of information in two-hundred-word segments may be serviceable, but it is unlikely to provide enough background for an eight-year-old who is trying to understand a complex subject. The length of articles should vary depending on the importance and complexity of the subject. Biographies should provide lengthy summaries of important persons' lives, focusing on concepts and contributions rather than on dates and degrees earned.

7. Style: Like good writing, the information included in an encyclopedia should be delivered in a lively, orderly, coherent, simple, direct way. Even though the subject matter is factual, the reader should not fall asleep while attempting to read it. The language should be appropriate but on a reading level that a child won't outgrow too quickly. (Most reading matter aimed at the general public is geared to an eighth-grade reading level anyway.) Technical and advanced terms should be defined when they first appear. Most important, an encyclopedia article should be a pleasure to read.

8. Bibliographies: Many encyclopedias include bibliographies of suggested reading for further study at the end of articles. The works listed should be current, relevant, and generally available.

9. Illustrations: Drawings, maps, portraits, photographs, and other graphics included along with articles are stimulating and help the reader identify with the subject matter. In trying to assess the quality of these illustrations, you should determine whether they are clear, pertinent, informative, and pleasing to the eye. Captions should be complete enough to avoid confusion on the part of the reader. Portraits of living people should be recent.

10. Physical Format: The binding, typography, and design of the encyclopedia are also important considerations. Notice whether the books are durably and attractively bound. Is the binding strong enough to stand up to years of use and abuse? Are letters and numbers on volume spines easily visible? Test a volume to see whether it lies flat when opened. The center of double-page maps should not disappear into the binding. The paper should be opaque so the information on one side doesn't show through on the other.

ENTERTAINING THE KIDS

12 EASY BIRTHDAY PARTIES

The countdown is on. Your three-year-old knows her birthday comes soon, and she seems to think of it constantly. Everyone in the neighborhood is on her party list. How are you going to meet this challenge? Share in her eager anticipation of this wonderful event by planning simple parties that everyone will enjoy. Birthday parties, after all, are a celebration of life, a time for you to remember one of your happiest moments; they should be fun for moms, too.

1. Involve your child in all the planning and preparation. She can help make or write invitations, pick out favors, prepare food. She might also have lots of ideas for activities her friends will enjoy.

2. Rent a space. Schools and nursery schools have large rooms with child-size furniture that are quick and easy to clean up afterward. Rental fees are usually very low.

3. Clowns, magicians, storytellers, or guitar players can hold small children spellbound for amazing lengths of time. They need not cost a mint: talented teenagers, college students, or struggling actors are often available. Ask other parents; call a local college or acting studio.

4. Old-fashioned party games are so often overlooked today that your child's friends will be delighted by such easy, time-honored standbys as Blindman's Buff, London Bridge, and Drop the Handkerchief.

5. Simple craft activities are fun: Staple ribbons to paper plates and decorate with crepe-paper streamers and tissue-paper flowers to make party hats; make banners to carry in a parade; decorate cupcakes with frosting, nuts, and candies.

6. Hunting games are easy. Have a scavenger hunt (two teams try to find all of the items on a list) or a treasure hunt with clues leading to a stash of prizes, or for younger children simply a hunt for something you have hidden in a room or garden—peanuts or poker chips (these could be turned in for small prizes) or little favors.

7. Many children's museums and restaurants (such as McDonald's) will organize a party for you, providing entertainment or food or both.

8. A sports activity your child loves can be the main attraction: bowling, ice skating, roller skating, softball, swimming. Ice and roller rinks usually have special group rates and provide seating space where you can serve refreshments you bring or they provide. College or hotel pools may also be available for rental.

9. Loosely structured outdoor parties are great fun and very easy if you can count on the weather (or have a viable alternative) and have some parents help with the transportation. Take along a picnic to a park or playground. Or go to the beach even if it isn't warm enough for swimming—you can all build sand castles.

10. Go to a movie and out for a pizza afterward. Reserve ahead and arrange for cake and ice cream.

11. Organize a hike. Let the guests help carry the food in backpacks.

12. For older children, a slumber party for a few close friends is a good idea. Let them plan their menu and do their own cooking; you provide a super breakfast.

HELPFUL BOOKS

Birthday Parties for Children: How to Give Them, How to Survive Them by Jean Marzollo (Harper & Row)

PLANTS KIDS CAN GROW

Children are fascinated by the magic of growing. Watching seeds sprout and measuring the stems as they inch higher remind the child of his own amazing origins and gradually changing self; he, too, is a part of nature.

It's a good idea to start with a seed he can see develop: a lima bean or an avocado pit. Sprouting root vegetables is another easy way for your child to grow plants. Seeds from the foods he eats—oranges, apples, grapefruit—may be tested in a pot kept handy on the kitchen table or windowsill and transferred to individual pots as the seedlings develop.

The following plants will provide the quickest satisfaction for your young gardener:

LIMA BEANS

Take a clear plastic cup and line it with damp paper towels. Then fill the inside with damp wadded-up paper towels. Carefully slip lima beans between the cup and the damp towels about halfway down the cup. Put it away in a dimly lit place. Within a day or two, the beans will begin sprouting small roots and stems. In three or four days, real leaves will appear and the plant will need sunlight to keep growing. In a week or ten days, your child can move the seedlings carefully to small pots. This technique also works with dried legumes that have been presoaked a day to two.

AVOCADO PLANT

An avocado plant is tricky, because some pits can take up to three months to sprout and some will not grow at all. It's best to save up several before trying; you and your child will feel less cheated if at least one works.

Let the pit dry. Peel off the papery brown coating. Stick three or more toothpicks around the middle of the pit and suspend it in a small jar or glass so that the flat side is down. Fill the jar with water just to the bottom of the pit and put it in a dark place to germinate. Add water as needed to keep the base of the pit wet. In a month or more, the pit will split in half and a small shoot will emerge. Move the jar to a sunny window, and let the roots grow to about 5 inches before planting the avocado in a pot.

Use a 6-inch pot and a good potting soil mixed with perlite. The top of the pit should just show above the soil. Keep the soil moist, and give the plant lots of sunshine. As it grows, show your child how to pinch off the top leaves every few inches to get a bushier tree.

ROOT VEGETABLES

Carrots, beets, and turnips will grow leafy tops. Cut off about half an inch at the top of the vegetable and plant it in a shallow container filled with a quarter inch of sand or perlite. Water frequently. The leafy stems will last a few weeks in a sunny location.

A sweet potato grows a lovely vine. It helps if the sweet potato has been recently harvested and not treated for long storage. Suspend the potato with toothpicks in a jar of water with the stem end up,

and keep it in a dimly lit place until the root sprouts appear. Move to a sunny window. Break off all but three or four of the strongest stems, and replant the potato in potting soil when the stems are 5 or 6 inches tall. Make a trellis, and attach the vines with string or twist-ties as they grow.

EXPERIMENTING WITH SEEDS

Keep a small planter in a sunny window in the kitchen or your child's room. Have it ready with a layer of small stones for drainage at the bottom and sterile potting soil on top. Let your child plant whatever seeds he finds in his food. Plant small seeds near the top; push larger seeds farther down. Make small signs on sticks to remember what is where. Some will grow, many will not. Transplant any seedlings to small pots.

For greater success with seeds from fruits that grow in cold climates—apples, grapes, peaches—give them a "pretend winter" in your refrigerator: Fill a plastic container half full of moist peat moss, put the seeds on top, cover, and store in the refrigerator for six weeks. Check regularly to be sure the moss is damp. Then plant them in your planter or simply move the container to a warm place and cover it with a plastic bag until the seeds sprout.

A SPONGE TERRARIUM

A quick, easy way to grow chives or dill for salads or catnip for your cat is to make a simple terrarium. You will need some small seeds, a sponge, a saucer, and a clear plastic dome made from a two-liter soda container. Break the dark outer collar off the bottom of the soda container, saw off the top, then use scissors to cut the plastic into a dome 6 or 8 inches high. Wet the sponge, place it in the saucer, spread the seeds on the sponge, and cover with the plastic dome. Give your little garden a bright spot to grow.

FORCING BULBS INDOORS

Crocus, hyacinth, daffodil, and tulip bulbs are not difficult to force indoors for winter blooms. Start early—it can take four months for hardy bulbs to flower. Buy several bulbs of each variety you choose, 4- or 5-inch flowerpots with drainage holes, and a good potting soil. Provide a layer of small stones at the bottom of the pots for drainage. Position the bulbs—flat side down—in the pots so that the soil will just cover the tips. Several bulbs of the same variety may be put in each pot, depending on the size of the bulbs—six or seven crocus bulbs, four or five tulip bulbs, three hyacinth or daffodil. Leave at least a quarter inch of space between the bulbs. Water thoroughly after planting.

Now the bulbs need to be wintered: Put the pots in a cold basement or an unheated room, or wrap them loosely in plastic bags in the refrigerator. Be sure the soil stays moist. In six weeks or more, growth will begin to appear. As this happens, move the pots to a cool room with indirect light. In two or three weeks, when the buds are formed, move the pots to a sunny spot until the flowers open. To extend the life of the blooms, do not keep them in direct sunlight or in very warm rooms.

HELPFUL BOOKS

Grocery Store Botany by Joan Edna Rahm (Atheneum)

Kids Gardening: A First Indoor Gardening Book for Children by Aileen Paul (Doubleday)

Plant Fun: 10 Easy Plants to Grow Indoors by Anita Holmes Soucie (Four Winds Press)

The Don't-Throw-It-Grow-It Book of Houseplants by Millicent Selsam and Deborah Peterson (Random House)

ORGANIZING AN AFTER-SCHOOL ACTIVITY PROGRAM

Your child is finally in school for six hours a day—but you work eight. How do you provide supervision and worthwhile activities for him for the two or three hours remaining before you get home? Instead of regular baby-sitting care, you now need the help of other parents, responsible teenagers, or retired people who are available for briefer stints at the end of the day. You can take advantage of many institutional sources of after-school care. Try a variety of approaches, with different sorts of activities each afternoon. He can have gymnastics on Monday, a play date on Tuesday, story-acting at the library on Wednesday, music lessons on Thursday, and quiet play at home on Friday. Here's how:

After-School Programs

Many schools offer a broad spectrum of recreational and educational activities for an hour and a half or two hours after school lets out. If your child's school offers none, check other schools in your area. Often he may attend an after-school activity at a school other than his own. You will probably need to find a reliable older student to escort him from one school to the other.

Y's, community centers, settlement houses, churches and synagogues, and municipal recreation centers also offer after-school courses in sports, crafts, and music. These are often advertised in local newspapers. Some of these programs have made arrangements with schools to bus the children from school to their facility. Or another parent may be able to take your child along with his if you offer to pick up both children on your way home.

Exchange Visits with Other Children

An at-home dad might be delighted to take your child every Tuesday afternoon, say, if you will take his child a weekend morning or afternoon for the same number of hours. Or perhaps he would be grateful for some evening baby-sitting in exchange. This gives your child a break from group lessons.

The Library

Libraries offer story-telling hours, films, and other programs on a regular basis. A responsible teenager could walk your child there and perhaps help him with his homework after the program.

Unstructured Time at Home

If you have cleaning help once a week, hire someone who will pick up your child at school and clean while he plays quietly alone. Your son will have company, and he can help out with some of the chores. But most important, he will have time alone to think, to draw, to listen to records, and to relax.

Older children who are ready to be at home alone will still want outside activities to relieve any tedium and anxiety. The same ideas will work for them. In addition, they can now take on more responsibilities themselves. They can provide escort service for younger children or do other jobs such as walking a neighbor's dog or delivering newspapers. They can also broaden their experience by doing volunteer work at a hospital, a nursing home, a police station, a museum, or a school. They can take charge of more work at home. Instead of being part of the problem, they are now becoming part of the solution.

Best Board Games

Board games have an endless fascination for children of all ages. They can also provide a much-needed respite for a harried working mother. Keep a good supply on hand and encourage your children to play—either with each other or with their friends. As a special treat, you can sit down and play a round or two with them.

Ages Three–Six

Good games for very young children require simple skills such as counting and color differentiation, but winning is based entirely on chance. This puts your five-year-old on an equal footing with her older brother, helping her to gain in self-confidence and to learn good sportsmanship. Favorites are:

1. *Chutes and Ladders* (Milton Bradley)
2. *Goldlilocks and the Three Bears* (Selchow & Righter)
3. *Candy Land* (Milton Bradley)
4. *Winnie the Pooh Game* (Parker Brothers)
5. Bingo
6. Parcheesi

Ages Six and Up

Games requiring some skill and strategy to win are best for older children. These will help them develop their abilities to make decisions, to plan strategies, and to solve problems. Parents can help their children learn these games, occasionally giving them a chance to win to bolster their confidence. Top games in this category are:

1. Checkers
2. Backgammon (a *Backgammon for Juniors* is available from Selchow & Righter)
3. *Scrabble* (Selchow & Righter; a junior version is also available)
4. *Monopoly* (Parker Brothers)
5. *Othello* (Gabriel)
6. Chess* (An excellent beginner's book is *Chess for Children Step by Step: A New Easy Way to Learn the Game* by William Lombardy and Bette Marshall [Little, Brown and Company].)

*Many schools now start children as young as five and six years old playing chess. The idea is to teach them to think strategically. Studies have shown that young chess players can master the game far more quickly than older children or adults. The skills and thought patterns learned in chess can serve a child well his entire life.

Toys for Different Ages

Toys can develop a child's physical abilities, teach him a variety of skills, stretch his imagination, and help him come to terms with the realities of the adult world. What's more, they're fun. Everyone loves toys. But choosing toys for your kids and their friends, not to mention nephews, nieces, and friends' kids, can be confusing and time-consuming.

What to Look For

1. You want toys that are safe, durable, and age-appropriate. The best are adaptable to different kinds of play and stimulate the imagination. They should be the right size for the child to handle and easy for the child to learn to use. They should have long-lasting appeal.

2. Most of all, you want toys that match the interests of the particular child. Be guided by the type of toys he or she has shown a preference for in the past: Does she like to build things or play house? Does he like crafts or sports? Adding to a set of toys a child already has and loves—such as hardwood blocks or Lego, clothing, or equipment for a favorite doll, bridges and tunnels for an electric train—is always a safe bet.

3. Be sure there's some variety of toys to fit different moods—active toys and quiet-time toys, toys that develop mental skills and toys that develop physical skills, toys that stimulate fantasy play and toys that stimulate curiosity.

What to Choose

Here is a list of popular toys to help you in making your selections. Age recommendations are only approximate. Many toys span several years of use—stuffed animals, dolls, music boxes, balls, tub toys, and sand toys, to name a few; others grow and change as the child grows and goes through the various developmental stages.

Birth to twelve months:
Mobiles * Teething rings * Rattles * Music boxes * Crib-gym exercisers * Washable stuffed animals * Soft balls (with no exposed sponge rubber) * Washable dolls * Activity boards that attach to the crib or playpen

One to two years:
Stuffed animals * Push and pull toys * Shape sorters * Stacking rings * Sand toys * Cars and trucks * Tub toys * Plastic beads that snap together * Pop-up toys * Nesting boxes or cups or dolls * Pounding bench and hammer * Balls of all sizes (but larger than 1.5 inches in diameter) * Simple puzzles with knobs on the pieces * Rocking horse or boat * Pull-apart toys with three or four pieces * Low climbing structure with slide * Play tunnel * Ride-on toys

Two to three years:
Dolls and doll clothes * Toy stroller * Shopping cart * Pots and pans * Tea set * Toy appliances * Toy telephone *Play house or tent * Cash register and play money * Simple dress-up clothes * Farm, garage, village, and other play sets with small cars, people, and animals * Bristle blocks * Duplo (large-scale Lego) * Large cardboard blocks * Simple puzzles (four to ten pieces) * Play-Doh * Inflatable punching toy * Large wooden beads for stringing * Spinning top that works by pumping a knob * Tricycle and other pedal ride-on toys * Small trampoline (jumping board)

Three to six years:
Dress-up clothes and costumes * Doctor kit * Simple dollhouse with furniture and family * Colorform sets * Paper dolls * Puppets * Trains and auto-racing sets * Walkie-talkies * Modeling clay * Tinkertoys * Lego * Constructo-Straws * Wooden unit blocks * Slinky * Sewing cards * Pegboards and pegs * Coloring books * Kaleidoscope * Puzzles (twelve to twenty pieces) * View Master * Magnets * Doorway gym bar * Wagon * Large tricycle or bicycle with training wheels * Beginner skates

Six to nine years:
Puppet theater * Makeup and disguise kits * Dollhouse and furniture * Fashion dolls * Jigsaw puzzles * Jacks * Marbles * Activity books * Loom * Model building sets * Craft kits * Board games * Printing set * Science sets * Kites * Gyroscope * Bicycle * Pogo stick * Stilts * Roller and ice skates * Bat and ball * Hula hoop * Badminton set * Croquet set * Jump rope

Nine to twelve years:
Marionettes * Magic tricks * Advanced model building sets and craft sets * Science sets * Ant farm * Computer games * Computer video games * Ping pong * Archery set * Sports equipment * Electric trains

TOY SAFETY GUILDELINES

1. Toys for small children should have:
   * No sharp edges, sharp wires, exposed nails or pins
   * Nontoxic paint
   * Contents of stuffing clearly labeled
   * No loose or poorly glued small parts
   * No parts that could be chewed off easily
   * No parts that could pinch small fingers or catch hair
2. They should be:
   * Unbreakable
   * Large enough not to be swallowed (any toy smaller than 1.5 inches in diameter is too small).
3. Electrical toys and riding toys for older children should be carefully chosen and maintained. Children should be taught to use them safely.

TV OR NOT TV?

Television can be a very positive influence in your home—if you use a little forethought. It can teach, it can inform, it can entertain. And you can decide how to get the most good out of it.

Long before your child knows which button to push to turn it on, think of how the medium can affect your lives. Reflect on your own television habits: Do you control it or does it control you? If you use television intelligently, your children will learn to, also.

Be sure that anyone taking care of your children while you are away is in complete agreement with your television viewing policies—your husband and other family members included.

- Use TV sparingly with small children. Choose the programs you think are best for their ages, and keep control of both what they watch and how much. A suitable half-hour program at the end of the day when he is tired and while you are preparing dinner can be wonderful for pre-schoolers. It's even better if you can watch so that you can talk about what is happening.

- An expensive but valuable investment in television control is a video recorder. Then you can choose not only the program but the time to air it. And you can borrow tapes from public or rental libraries—excellent animations of popular children's stories and classic films for children are easily available. These can be weekend treats for the whole family or for the children when the adults want some time to themselves. You can collect good programs that are aired after your children go to bed—sports events, cultural performances, nature documentaries — and save them for a rainy weekend or a holiday when you have to work.

- Keep viewing time down. One half-hour program on weekdays is plenty for children in grammar school. Longer programs—one hour or ninety minutes—are best reserved for Saturday or Sunday. Have an overall weekly limit—somewhere between four and seven hours.

- Provide a rich enough after-school schedule to obviate any wish for mindless TV viewing—sports, library visits, music lessons, play dates, homework time, chores to be done. See that unstructured time is spent more creatively, in imaginative play with friends or siblings, in pursuing a hobby, in children's radio programs as a substitute for TV time.

- Keep abreast of what is being broadcast. Read the listings, read reviews, ask other parents; if necessary tape a program and watch it after your child is asleep.

- Don't be afraid to veto any program you feel is objectionable. Tell your child why you will not allow him to watch that program.

- Choose programs together. Encourage programs that you feel are worthwhile, and plan to watch them together. Let television time be family time, and talk about the programs you watch together.

- When you watch commercial television, explain to your child the purpose of the advertisements he sees and teach him to understand the gimmicks commercials use to sell products. Don't undermine your efforts to make him an intelligent consumer by buying him a toy or box of cereal he's seen advertised just because you're tired of hearing him ask for it.

- Avoid the temptation to buy a second TV set "for the kids." You will be better able to monitor and supervise their viewing if you have one set in a room the whole family uses. Even overhearing a program you are not yourself watching will enable you to talk about the program with your children. For conflicting programs, a video recorder is a better investment, for then everyone can watch both worthwhile programs together.

Sandcastling

Beach jaunts can be more fun when the whole family joins in and builds a sandcastle. Although it takes plenty of time and patience, it's relatively easy and provides an outlet for any untapped artistic abilities your child may have. Work with him at building his castle until he can manage on his own.

Materials: *Pail and shovel (of the beach toy variety), plastic, Styrofoam, or paper cups, toothpicks with paper attached to look like a flag.*
NOTE: *For best results, build your castle near enough to the shore to make the gathering of damp sand easy, but far enough from the shore that when the tide comes in, your castle isn't washed away.*

1. Fill the pail with damp sand gathered from the edge of the shore. Be sure to fill the pail completely and pack the sand down hard. Turn the pail over and tap the bottom to loosen the sand. Carefully lift the pail off. You may have to practice a few times before you get the knack. Repeat this procedure four times, placing each sand pile in a corner to form a square. This is the boundary of the castle.

2. Using your hands, construct a wall to connect each sand pile. Smooth the castle walls with your shovel. If you are blessed with steady hands, try to cover the walls with a water and sand mixture that will help stabilize them.

3. Pack one of the smaller cups with damp sand. Carefully overturn it on top of a sand pile in one of the corners. Repeat this at each corner until each pile is covered with a small "tower."

4. Depending on how detailed you want your castle to be, you can build a moat. Dig a trench around the castle deep enough to hold water. You may find the sand keeps absorbing the water, but just keep filling the moat until the sand is waterlogged.

5. Make your castle fancier by adding little touches like sculptured walls. Be sure to wet the sand first. Use your shovel to scallop the edges.

6. Stick a toothpick flag into one of the towers to claim the castle for your very own, then stand back and admire your creation, and if you've brought a camera to the beach, be sure to snap a picture so your child can have a memento of his work and you can have a reminder of a happy day.

NOTE: *The more elaborate your castle, the greater the chance of its being damaged along the way. With young children, who are easily frustrated, it's a good idea to encourage simplicity.*

RAINY-DAY CRAFTS

Stormy weekends need not adversely affect the climate indoors. Kids love making things, and a rainy day offers the perfect opportunity for them to indulge their whimsies and leave you with a little free time for yourself.

BE PREPARED

1. Keep a shelf stocked with craft materials—most are available at the supermarket or dime store. Poster paints (red, yellow, blue, black, and white; powdered or liquid), water colors, assorted brushes, glue, tape, paper (a role of plain white shelf paper, blocks of colored construction paper and white paper, colored tissue papers), fabric crayons, a hole puncher, rubber bands, paper clips, brad fasteners, modeling clay, colored pipe cleaners, and squares of brightly colored felt are all useful items.

2. Start a "stuff box": Wash out used milk and juice cartons, margarine tubs and lids, foil pie plates, plastic bottles, egg cartons, and plastic trays, and store them in a cardboard box. Add other useful discards: empty spools, paper-towel and toilet-paper rolls, small boxes, and scraps of wrapping paper.

3. Save old magazines, catalogues, and greeting cards that have pictures that appeal to children. Keep them in a special place or mark the discards with a small X in the corner to let the children know you're finished with them. Keep a small stack of newspapers on hand.

4. Make a scrap bag for scraps of fabric and yarn. Save buttons.

ORGANIZE A PROJECT

1. BLOCKS:

Open out the flaps of milk cartons, stuff them with crumpled newspaper, cut and fold the flaps down to lie flat, and tape in place. Decorate the blocks with colored construction paper or cover them with white paper and paint. Doors and windows may be painted on to make houses, buses, or trucks. Vary the size of your blocks by cutting the cartons down or using other boxes. Build a city.

2. DOLL FURNITURE:

* Turn a half-gallon milk carton over and cut out a parson's table using the bottom of the carton for the tabletop and four edges for legs. Using quart-size cartons, cut out benches the same way.
* A round tabletop can be cut from cardboard or from the side of a milk carton and glued to a spool.
* To make a sofa, cut off the top and cut a carton lengthwise down the middle. Slide the two pieces together. Add a back and arms by fastening on pieces cut from other cartons with brad fasteners. Decorate the furniture by pasting on cloth or construction paper.

3. MUSICAL INSTRUMENTS:

* *A Drum:* An oatmeal box or a coffee can with a plastic lid makes an excellent drum. Your child can play it with his hands or use spoons or chopsticks as drumsticks. Tape or tie two

or three boxes of different sizes together to make bongo drums.

* *A Kazoo:* Poke a couple of holes in a toilet-paper roll with a pencil. Cover one end of the roll with a piece of wax paper held in place with a rubber band. Hum into the other end.
* *A Tambourine:* Punch holes around the rims of two aluminum pie plates. Fill with half a dozen bottle caps or buttons and sew the plates together with a piece of yarn. A small piece of tape wrapped around one end of the yarn makes the lacing easier.
* *A Banjo:* Cut a large hole in the middle of the lid of a shoe box or other sturdy box. Wrap four rubber bands around the box and across the hole. Vary the size of the rubber bands to get different notes.

Decorate your instruments (paint them, glue on pictures), and have a parade.

4. ROBOTS:

Glue or fasten boxes together to form a body and head; tape on cardboard-tube arms and legs. Paint or cover with colored tissue paper. Make button eyes and pipe-cleaner antennae.

5. JEWELRY:

Paint empty spools and thread them on colored yarn. Make simple link chains out of the twist-ties that come with plastic bags and form them into necklaces, bracelets, rings, and earrings (held in place by curving a tie to fit over the back of the ear).

6. DECORATIONS:

* *A Flower Arrangement:* Use the green pipe cleaners for stems and leaves, shape the other colors into tulips and daisies, and attach them to the stems. Buttons can be flower centers or more flowers. Arrange the flowers in a ball of modeling clay and place in a margarine tub "vase" or on a plastic lid.
* *A Bug Mobile:* Shape colored pipe cleaners into spiders, bees, and butterflies. Hang them with thread from the ends of pipe cleaners, arranging them into a mobile.

Your supplies will suggest countless other activities. Have the kids embellish their underwear or T-shirts with fabric crayons (you will do the ironing), play skittles with plastic bottles and a ball, cut pictures from magazines and glue them into construction-paper books. Very small children love just exploring the shapes and sizes of things in the stuff box; a three- or four-year-old will play store; a six- or seven-year-old will create his own craft projects.

HELPFUL BOOKS

Toys: Fun in the Making, published by the U.S. Department of Health and Human Services, U.S. Gov't. Printing Office, Washington, D.C. 20402

What to Do When "There's Nothing to Do" by the Boston Children's Medical Center and Elizabeth M. Gregg (Dell)

Toys to Make at Home

What mother hasn't heard the plaintive cry, "I'm bored! There's nothing to do!" from her children? Now, the next time the kids get restless, suggest they try making toys. It's good fun for you and your children, both during the creation and long after. Best of all, you don't need to spend much money on special supplies, because you probably have many of them on hand. Here are some easily made toys to try.

SHOE BANK

Materials: High-top sneaker in good condition; colorful shoelaces; sport sock; empty tubular potato chip or cracker can with plastic top; white glue.
Instructions: Wash the sneaker in the machine and allow it to dry thoroughly. Insert the foot of the sock into the sneaker and stuff it with crumpled newspaper. Lace up the sneaker. Cut a slot for coins in the plastic cover of the potato chip can. Slide the can into the sock and pull up the sock to the top of the can. Glue the top of the sock to the edge of the can to hide the can.

CLOTH BOOK

Materials: Heavy cloth (canvas is best); crayons; blotting paper.
Instructions: Cut four or five pieces of solid-colored cloth into 12- x 16-inch pieces (or smaller if you prefer a smaller book). Lay them evenly on top of each other and sew a seam down one side to bind them together. Your child can decorate each page with crayons. When he's finished, press each page with a warm iron as follows: Put one sheet of blotting paper on top and one underneath each page, then hold the iron down firmly for a few seconds. The crayon decoration will melt into the cloth and become permanent. If your child likes, he can then glue extra decorations like sparkles, stars, bits of lace, or fabric on the cover or inside on the pages of the book.

CLOTHESPIN DOLL

Materials: Old-style clothespins (the kind cut from one piece of wood, with no springs); bits of cloth and yarn; crepe or construction paper; straws; pipe cleaners; tooth picks; crayons; pens.
Instructions: Have your child wrap bits of cloth around the clothespins for dresses or wind fabric around each prong for pants. Use bits of yarn or paper for hair. Make hats from crepe or construction paper. For arms, use straws, pipe cleaners, or toothpicks. Use a crayon or ballpoint pen to draw faces. Make several dolls and act out scenes with them. Construct a stage with cardboard or a box and put on a play.

BOWLING ALLEY

Materials: Half-gallon milk or juice cartons; soup can.
Instructions: Collect ten half-gallon milk or juice cartons. Rinse very well. Set them up in a V shape, the way pins are set up in a bowling alley. Use an unopened soup can as a bowling ball. Let the kids roll the can across the kitchen floor (or the sidewalk) to knock over the "pins." Make the game competitive by keeping a score card.

CIRCUS TOSS

Materials: Old bed sheet; colored markers; sponge or soft ball; thumbtacks.
Instructions: Cut a large hole in the bed sheet. Let your child decorate the sheet with the markers. Use the hole as a clown's mouth, an elephant's ear, or a hippo's eye. Drape the decorated sheet across a doorway and secure it with thumbtacks. The fun begins when the kids try to throw a dry sponge or ball through the hole. Offer prizes or points to make it more challenging.

PLAY DOUGH

Recipe:
1 cup salt
1½ cups flour
½ cup water
2 tablespoons vegetable oil
Food coloring

Mix ingredients in a bowl until they form a smooth ball of dough. Distribute a chunk of dough to each child. Let them use cookie cutters, plastic glasses, popsicle sticks, and other items you have around the house to make various playthings. After the objects dry, they will be permanent toys. Keep leftover dough in a plastic bag or an airtight jar and store in the refrigerator. Play dough will keep moist for five days.

FAMILY MATTERS

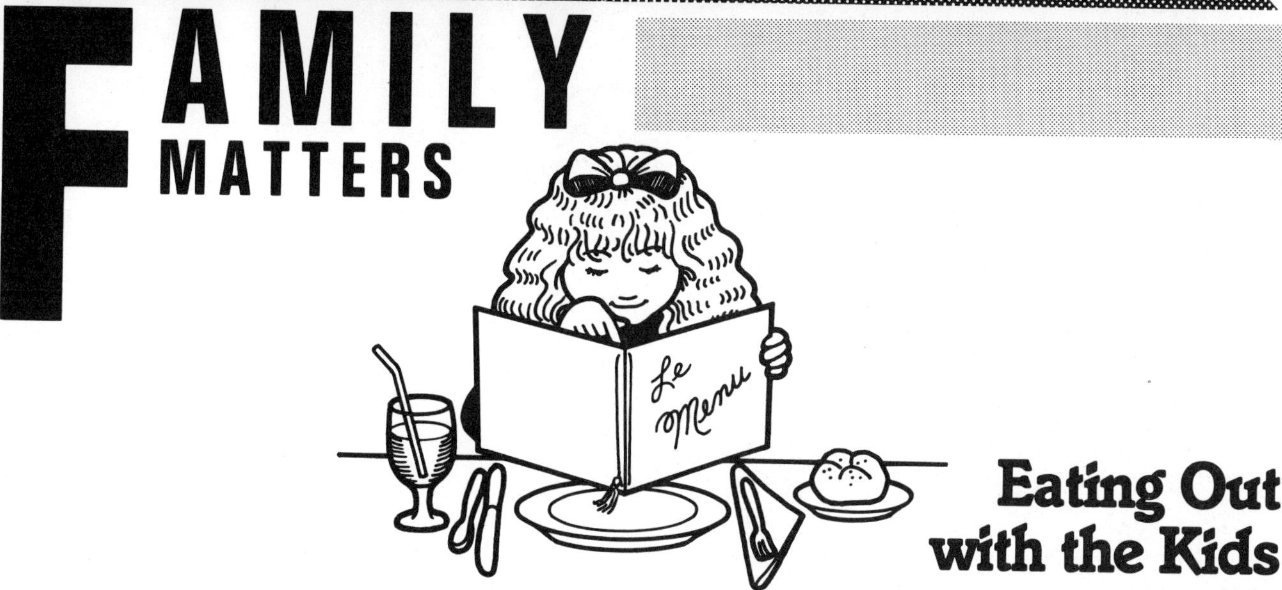

Eating Out with the Kids

If you occasionally dream of having a really nice meal out *en famille*, fast-food restaurants need not be your only choice. Just remember to be prepared—you don't want your dream to turn into a nightmare of screaming kids, flying food, and fuming parents.

1. Choose Your Restaurant Carefully

• A bright, bustling ambience appeals to kids, and the din masks any noise they may make.

• Look for a reasonably broad menu—or one with at least one item each child really likes.

• Entertainment is a plus. A jazz emsemble or an oompah band are fun to watch and are noisier than kids. The Japanese chef who chops and grills your vegetables and meat right at your table, the pizza maker who spins the dough in the air, the waiter who tosses the salad, flambés the bananas, or warms the crepes at tableside all provide amusement for at least part of a meal. A view provides entertainment, too.

• An outdoor setting—a garden restaurant or a sidewalk café—is usually more relaxed even when it doesn't include play space. An outdoor café alongside a park where your children can run and play is, of course, ideal.

2. Go Early

• Kids are less tired and cranky, restaurants are less crowded if you go out a little earlier than the usual mealtime.

3. Call Ahead for Reservations

• Ask about the availability of a high chair or a booster seat if you will need one. Let them know you are bringing children. Ask whether they have a children's menu, and if not, whether they mind if your very young children split an order.

4. Dress the Kids Up

• Have them wear their nicest clothes even though they'll doubtless be dripping food all over them; most kids behave better when they know they look their best, perhaps because they overhear the admiring comments of other diners and sense their parents' pride in them.

5. Be Prepared in Case There Is a Wait

• Tuck pads and pencils, small books, and small toys into your purse. Have some simple finger games (for younger children) or puzzles and tricks (for older children) up your sleeve.

6. Prepare Small Children

• Prepare small children by forewarning them: "When we go to a restaurant we need to sit and wait for a while for our food."

• Ask the waiter to warn you if the preparation time for any dish is particularly long or to tell you which dishes are the quickest. It may not occur to him that you don't want a long wait.

7. Take Everyone to the Restroom

• After placing your order, take everyone to the restroom. Kids love the tour, and it fills up some of the time.

8. Have Dessert Served Early

• If the kids start getting restless after they've finished eating their main course and you're still at it, ask for their dessert to be served. Then you can finish your meal at a leisurely pace while they eat it.

9. Take Only One Child to an Elegant Restaurant

• You can accustom kids to more elegant, quieter restaurants by taking one child at a time as a special treat. With undivided parental attention and no partners for mischief, a kid can really shine.

"There's a New Baby on the Way!"

You've just gotten the news yourself: You're expecting again. You share it right away with your husband and then your parents. Your father dashes a little cold water over your enthusiasm by commenting dryly, "That will sure put Joey's nose out of joint!" Not to worry. It's good to realize that your firstborn may not be overjoyed, and there are ways you can prepare him that will help cushion the blow.

■ Tell your child you are pregnant as soon as you tell your friends. It may seem a long time off, but it is better he hears from you than from someone else about this important event.

■ Explain how life begins, how the baby is developing inside you, and how it will be born. Let him feel the baby move and listen to the heartbeat.

■ Involve him in preparations for the new baby, such as setting up the crib or repainting the high chair. If he must give up his crib for the new baby, make the move well ahead of time—several months, if possible—and reward his graduation to a big-boy bed with new sheets and a quilt he can help choose.

■ If toilet training is imminent but not yet begun, consider postponing it until some time after the new baby is born. That way you can both avoid the annoyance regression would cause.

■ Take out his baby book and pictures to show him what he looked like as a newborn and how much love and attention he got.

■ Tell him exactly what will happen when the baby comes, where you will be going to deliver the baby, who will help look after him, how long you will be away, and whether he will be allowed to visit. Write it out as a story with simple drawings for him to follow.

■ Be sure the person staying with him while you are in the hospital is someone he knows well, loves, and trusts. This is not a good time to accept an offer of help from a relative he's never met or to hire a new housekeeper. If someone new will be moving in to care for the new baby, have her start work well before the baby comes.

■ Call him from the hospital so that he can hear your voice even though you may not hear much of his. Leave little presents for him, and tell him over the phone where he can find them. Send home instant snapshots of the new baby alone, with each parent, and with both parents to give him a chance to see how tiny the baby is and to adjust to seeing you together.

■ When you return from the hospital, let your spouse carry the baby so that you can greet your firstborn warmly.

■ Give your firstborn lots of attention during this period of adjustment. Find time to play with him alone. Go on outings together without the baby.

■ Show him how to hold the baby, how to make the baby's fingers and toes curl around his own, how to play gently with him. Let him help by fetching diapers or formula. Read to him while you nurse the baby. Let him hold the bottle when you bottle feed.

■ Let him express his annoyance or anger verbally—he needs to do this to gain control over it. Talk about his feelings. Let him know it's okay to say what he feels and that you still love him.

A Well-Mannered Child...

Manners are the outward sign of our consideration and respect for our fellow human beings and are best taught just as we teach our children other values: by example. Your own manners are important, especially those that affect your child directly. How you treat him is going to have a great influence on how he treats others.

Teach Courtesy with Play-Acting

Show your child how to introduce people, how to shake hands and exchange greetings, by setting up pretend games in which introductions are necessary. Have fun making up your own preposterous situations in which a polite phrase will save the day. Answering the telephone can be practiced with a toy telephone.

Table Manners

Table manners can be taught early, beginning with pretend tea parties with real little sandwiches and herbal tea. Family dinners are the practice field for learning how to use utensils and how to behave at table. To keep the scene from becoming a battlefield, the focus should not be on correcting bad manners, but on conversation and conviviality. A bit of formality helps, too. A tablecloth, a seasonal centerpiece—maybe your child's own creation—and candlelight can evoke the right atmosphere for gracious dining. This may not be possible every night, but it should be manageable once a week, and on holidays and special occasions.

Conversation

One of the banes of motherhood is the interrupting child. Teach your child good conversation habits by giving him your full attention, maintaining eye contact, and letting him have equal time in your conversations with each other. When your friends come to visit, include him in the conversation for a few minutes before suggesting another activity for him to do.

To teach a child not to interrupt, don't respond to his appeals for attention when you are talking or listening to someone else. A finger to his lips will remind him he should wait until you are finished. Turn to him only when a pause in the conversation occurs, and let him speak his piece.

Telephone conversations are harder for young children to understand, especially when you aren't doing the talking. For very small children, a drawer full of toys strategically placed under the telephone table and opened only when needed is the best resource.

Swearing and Four-Letter Words

Along with everything else they learn in nursery school, kids pick up a good many words you might not be delighted to have your innocent little babe know. When he comes home with one, don't overreact and add the thrill of getting a rise out of mom to the simple joy of a new word. Since most are slang terms for various bodily functions, you can call them bathroom words and tell your child he may say them all he likes so long as he is alone in the bathroom. Don't be surprised if you find him practicing them there in front of the mirror. He is not, however, to use them elsewhere, and may be escorted to the bathroom if he forgets.

Swearing is also easily picked up, for we all need words to vent anger or frustration, and kids imitate what they hear. If you disapprove of swearing, you probably never do it yourself and can explain to your child that you find certain ways of speaking offensive and that many adults agree with you. If you do sometimes swear, you will want to teach your child when you believe it is appropriate and when not: It's okay with me, but not in front of your grandmother. You might suggest substitute words—"Oh, Fudge!" or "Watermelon!"—and practice them yourself.

Carry-Over

You cannot monitor your child's behavior twenty-four hours a day, but your best weapon against the natural temptation to backslide or rebel is your trust that the child will behave well. Saying, "Now you behave yourself!" as you drop him off at a birthday party implies you have little faith that he will. If you really feel he needs reminders, ask him to tell you what he will do at the party, or go over specific points before you leave home. Then send him off with a hug or a smile. A self-confident child will try to live up to his positive self-image and be less vulnerable to peer pressure to misbehave.

Helpful Books

What Do You Say, Dear? by Sesyle Joslin (Scholastic)

How Much Allowance?

Having an allowance can help a child learn how to handle money, how to shop wisely and how to plan her spending. It's a valuable tool in teaching responsible fiscal habits.

When to Start an Allowance. Preschoolers can be given small amounts of money on a regular basis when they are old enough to count it and to keep it in a safe place. A four- or five-year-old will feel very grown up getting a few pennies or a nickel a week to spend as she likes, probably on candy, gum, or trinkets from a gumball machine. She can begin to learn that once it is spent it is gone and that by saving several coins she can buy a little more.

Children in elementary school are usually ready for a more serious kind of allowance, one that can be budgeted for specific expenses and that will give the child a sense of independence and responsibility. A strongbox with a key and manila envelopes to hold funds earmarked for particular purchases will help her in learning to organize her money and to save up for more expensive items. She will also need a wallet for carrying to school with her only the amounts of money she spends daily.

How Much? To determine how much allowance to give a child, you need first to figure out what her expenses are. Keep track of all the money you give her for a couple of typical weeks. Include what she spends on lunch, school supplies, snacks she buys after school, and any other regular expenses. These are her fixed expenses; you are spending the money anyway, so why not teach her to take care of it herself?

Additional "discretionary funds" are a good idea so that she can start to set money aside regularly to buy books or toys for herself or gifts for the family. You may also want to include some "pocket money" for gum and candy.

Talking to other parents may give you an idea of what your child's friends are getting, but you shouldn't feel you have to give her the going rate. Discuss your decision with her and tell her how you arrived at the amount you think is reasonable. If she asks for more, listen to her side and see if together you can reach a happy medium. It's better to start low and increase the allowance as your child's needs grow and as she proves her ability to handle money responsibly.

Review her allowance needs and modify her budget as the situation requires. If circumstances change and she needs carfare for an after-school activity or money for a new, worthwhile hobby you want to encourage, an increase is in order. As she as gets older and as she learns to handle money well, she can be entrusted with bigger responsibilities, such as buying her own clothes.

Your Input. Make it clear to your child how much of her allowance is intended to cover her fixed expenses, but leave the decision of how to spend her discretionary funds and pocket money entirely up to her. You can encourage saving for special items she wants, you can talk to her about how to get the best value for her money, you can even express your objections to her plans to purchase a worthless gimmick, but leave the decision to her. If she does waste her money on junk, she will learn through her disappointment to resist better the temptations of market hype. And she will need your sympathy and your faith that she will choose more wisely in the future.

Give her the allowance on a regular schedule—once a week on a specific day. Or, if the amount is high, twice a week may be easier for her to handle. Be consistent. Just as you count on your paycheck, so she expects her allowance.

Don't tag allowance to behavior. Cash bonuses for good behavior or fines for punishment can get quick results, but used regularly, they teach the child to measure human worth in monetary terms.

"We're Moving!"
12 Ways to Help Your Child Adjust

Moving is as American as apple pie, an ever-present option in our mobile lives. Whether you are relocating because your or your spouse's work requires it, or because you've found a better community in which to raise your kids, or because you need a larger house for a growing family, you usually see the change as a positive step. Your kids, however, may have a harder time coping with the change than you do. The loss of friends and familiar surroundings and routines, and the fear of the unknown loom a little larger in their lives; nor is it easy for them to see the advantages the move will bring. It's important to prepare them for the change and ease them through it. Here are some pointers:

1. Tell your children right away, as soon as you and your husband have decided to move. Tell them why you are moving and as much as you can about what the new environment will be like. Answer their questions honestly, and be understanding if their immediate reaction is to be angry or hurt.

2. Let them talk openly about their fears, and confess your own if you have some. Putting up a false brave front yourself can only increase their anxiety. Admit that it will take time to learn to like the new place and make new friends, but reassure them and yourself that *it will happen.*

3. Help them see the move as an exciting adventure, a new experience the whole family will have together—like the Pilgrims landing at Plymouth Rock or any other historical analogy that appeals to their imaginations.

4. Include the children in plans for the move, especially house- or apartment-hunting if that is possible. Listen to their ideas about what the new place should be like.

5. Let your children visit the new neighborhood often before you move. Show them their new house and new schools, and the nearest playground, swimming pool, or pizza parlor. If it is too far away for them to visit before the move, bring them pictures of the new house and neighborhood, and brochures from their new schools, library, or community center.

6. Take time to say good-bye to close friends and favorite places in your old neighborhood.

7. Have the children help with the move itself: unfolding and taping cartons, packing their treasures, writing labels for boxes, helping load and unload the van—whatever contribution they can make.

8. Involve the children in decorating and arranging furniture in their new rooms, letting them choose the colors and fabrics. Some children will love the opportunity to strike out in a totally different direction; others will want to make the new room resemble the old one as closely as possible. Very young children and infants, in particular, will probably have an easier time of it if the arrangement is familiar.

9. Keep old friendships alive for a while after the move. Letters, long-distance calls, and visits back and forth will ease the transition.

10. Set a good example by making new friendships yourself. Join community organizations; be outgoing and friendly to neighbors.

11. Take time off from work for the first week after the move, and spend it with your children getting settled, learning your way around, making new acquaintances, and starting them in school or other activities. Start normal routines as soon as possible.

12. Be tolerant of regressive behavior. A return to thumb-sucking, bed-wetting, or any other behavior you thought they'd given up months before is only symptomatic of the normal stress they are feeling. Time and TLC should bring a renewed sense of security in the new environment.

HELPFUL BOOKS

Mr. Rogers Talks About . . . by Fred Rogers (Platt and Munk)
Moving Day by Tobi Tobias (Knopf)
I'm Moving by Martha Hickman (Abingdon)
Moving Molly by Shirley Hughes (Prentice-Hall)
I'm Not Going by Nancy Mack (Raintree)
Maggie and the Good-bye Gift by Sue and Jerry Milord, (Lothrop, Lee & Shepard)
A Tiger Called Thomas and **Janey** by Charlotte Zolotow (Lothrop, Lee & Shepard)
Good-bye, House by Ann Banks and Nancy Evans (Crown)

Pets may seem like one worry a working mother should be spared. But pets have a special role in family life, for they teach kids a lot about nurturing and responsibility and bring pleasure and companionship to children and adults alike. If your child hankers for a pet—or if you want one yourself—don't rule the possibility out right off the bat. Here is a sampling of some of the most popular pets and what you can expect if you bring one home.

DOGS

High on the list of every kid's most wanted pets is a dog. Few other animals can match the dog for affection, loyalty, and companionship. Few other pets, however, are as much work.

The first year is the hardest. A puppy needs frequent, regularly spaced meals. He will need to be housebroken, which requires consistent, patient training and outdoor walks. And he needs to be taught to obey simple commands to make his behavior acceptable.

If you really want a puppy, your best bet is to acquire him at the beginning of a vacation you plan to spend at home and take a week or two getting him on a feeding and training schedule, then hire someone to take over his care when you return to work and the children go back to school.

Older dogs will still need regular walks, exercise, and companionship; regular feeding and grooming; and medical care, including annual shots against rabies and other canine diseases. Fleas and ticks can be a problem even in the city. Life will be easier if a female dog is spayed and a male castrated.

Among the breeds you might want to consider are: basset hound, bearded collie, Bernese mountain dog, boxer, bulldog, cocker spaniel, collie, golden retriever, German shepherd, and poodle (both miniature and standard). All are even-tempered, tractable dogs with good track records with children; they vary a lot in size, personality, and aesthetic appeal.

CATS

Cats are much easier to take care of than dogs. They are more independent to begin with and don't mind being at home alone all day, and they don't need to be walked, trained, or groomed. Housebreaking is usually simple. Allergies to cat fur are common, however; be sure no one in the family is allergic before acquiring a cat.

Kittens will need frequent feedings, and cleaning the litter box is a daily chore—not to be done by you if you are pregnant. Your cat will need shots and occasional medical care. Neutering is advisable for both sexes.

CAGED PETS

Rabbits, guinea pigs, hamsters, gerbils, mice, and even rats are popular apartment and schoolroom pets. Your child may not develop the close ties he would with a dog or a cat, but rabbits and guinea pigs especially are cuddly and affectionate, and kids enjoy watching the smaller animals perform on the ramps, ladders, and wheels in their cages. All can become quite tame with gentle handling.

Rabbits and guinea pigs, being larger, require large, solidly built pens. The cage will need daily cleanup to remove droppings, usually only in one corner, and a thorough weekly cleaning. These animals are usually fed twice a day.

Good, secure cages are also important for the smaller animals. They should be large enough to provide room for exercise and should have equipment to play on. A cage for a mouse or a rat must be made of metal. The floor covering will need changing twice a week, and the entire cage should be washed once a month. These smaller animals are not the best pets for very young children, who could easily hurt them by mishandling, nor can they survive too much cuddling. They consume little more than a tablespoon of food daily.

FISH

Fish are fascinating and educational to watch and require little care. They don't mind an empty house all day and won't suffer if you're away over a weekend. Goldfish can live in a small bowl. The water will need changing every two or three days.

Or you can get a tank with a pump to provide oxygen and forget about changing the water, only adding more occasionally to replace what evaporates. A tank can also house mollies, swordtails, or guppies.

Tropical fish need warmer, more acidic water: A heater, chemicals, a pH kit to test the water, and a pump are essential. Still, once the tank has been set up, your principal tasks will be feeding twice a day and checking the water regularly. One drawback is the susceptibility of fish to diseases that can fell a whole tankful in short order.

BIRDS

Like fish, birds are also beautiful to look at. Male canaries are, in addition, splendid singers, and parakeets and cockatiels can be trained to mimic words and do simple tricks. A very young child may hold a bird too tightly or accidentally let it escape, but a child over five can easily handle the care and feeding on his own. Rarer, exotic breeds are best avoided: They're fragile and hard to keep. Expect some mess under the cage—seed pods and feathers will add to vacuuming chores—and even more mess if you let the birds fly around outside their cage.

Pets stores usually carry helpful paperbound books on fish and bird care.

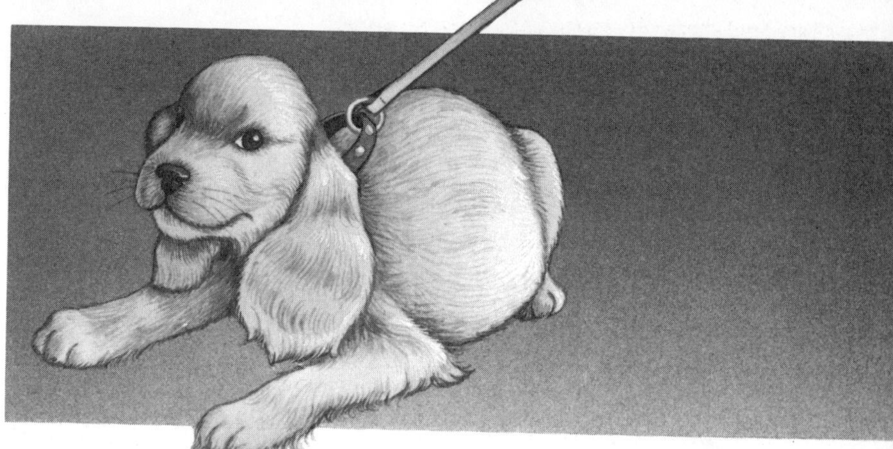

Train Your Dog in One Week!

Believe it or not, according to most dog experts, it's possible to housebreak your puppy in just one week! Although some dog owners let the process drag on for months, it's not good for the dog and it's certainly terrible for you. The key to successful training, according to the experts, is the proper mix of praise and strictness. Here are some things to keep in mind:

1. Establish regular eating habits for your puppy before attempting to housebreak him. In this way, he'll be better able to control himself according to the timetable you set up.

2. Discipline your puppy to stay in a particular area of the house. This is essential to success during the training period, since dogs will usually not relieve themselves in the same space in which they live. You can use the bathroom or a sectioned-off area in the kitchen.

3. Follow a strict outdoor walking schedule. He should be walked a minimum of twice a day, always at the same time. Young dogs usually need to be walked three times a day.

4. Give plenty of praise. Praise is a crucial element every time your dog does something correct. Put enthusiasm into your voice and stroke him affectionately. This kind of positive reinforcement will encourage him to continue the behavior just praised.

5. Use corrective training. Mistakes are to be expected during the seven-day learning period. The most effective way of curbing undesirable behavior is to catch your dog in the act. Immediately yell, "No!" very firmly. Then carry or push the dog out the door. Hopefully, he'll pick up where he left off. Then praise him.

If you're able to catch only the evidence, fetch the dog and pull him over to the scene by the collar. Point to the mess, stick his nose near it, and scold him using a loud, firm voice. However, never strike him.

6. Always get rid of telltale odors. Even if *you* can't smell the remains of yesterday's accident, your dog's sensitive nose can, and it will be a signal to him that it's okay to repeat the act.

Getting Started

The night before beginning the training program, take your dog outdoors. Be sure he relieves himself completely. Confine him to a closed-off area for the night.

As soon as your alarm goes off in the morning (you may want to allow yourself some extra time), take your dog outside. When he relieves himself, praise him warmly. If he doesn't do anything, take him inside, put him in his area, feed him, and give him water. Repeat the outdoor procedure in 15 to 20 minutes.

Before you leave for work, confine the dog to his temporary space.

When you come home from work, take him outside immediately. Praise him if he cooperates. Return him to his pen and let him eat and drink some water but, don't leave the bowl with him. Take him outdoors one more time before you go to bed.

If all goes well, in seven days, your pet will be an even greater joy to have around the house.

"Stop It!"

How to Cope with Kids' Quarreling

Few things are more nerve-racking and discouraging to parents than squabbling children, for there is no way to stop kids' quarreling entirely. It is normal and probably even healthy, as kids learn how to solve problems by verbalizing their differences. What's more, kids evidently enjoy it. Parents can only hope to minimize the acrimony by not feeding sibling jealousies and by calling a halt to battles that threaten to go the way of that famous encounter between the gingham dog and the calico cat. Here are some suggestions:

1. Foster caring attitudes among siblings. See that each remembers the others' birthdays and makes or chooses cards and gifts for them. Encourage an older child to read to a younger one or prepare her for her new school by telling her what it is like. Take siblings to see their sister perform at a recital or in sports events. Remind them that they are very special to one another because they are siblings.

2. Give each child one-to-one time every day, even if it's only 15 minutes. It may be sitting down for a chat together, going over his homework, listening to her read or play the piano, or sharing an activity you both enjoy. Be sure your attention is undivided and uninterrupted, and let your child choose how you spend that time together. Make time to take each child on an outing alone with you at least once a month—have a meal together at a restaurant, visit a museum, or engage in a sport you both like.

3. Treat each child as an individual. Don't try to be "fair" by giving each child the same things or treating them exactly alike. Respect and encourage their individual preferences in clothing and activities.

4. Be aware of the times your kids are most likely to start fights, and forestall them by providing separate activities for each child. Often children quarrel simply because they are tired or hungry or both. Pre-dinnertime snacks and parental attention help.

5. When arguments occur, don't get involved. Stay out of a dispute even when you think you know how it started. If one child comes to you for a decision, tell her she must settle the issue (if there is one) with her sister. Then let them work it out for themselves. Keep aloof or leave the room.

6. If the dispute gets out of hand—if it is excessively noisy or becomes physical—call a time-out and send each child to a separate room to cool down.

7. If an object is being fought over, remove it. Tell them they must both do without it for a specified period.

8. If you are driving in the car when quarreling erupts, pull over and stop. Explain calmly that you will not continue on your way until the arguing stops. Wait until it does before starting the car again.

9. Discuss continued hostilities at a family council. Issues of fairness can best be dealt with here. Listen to all sides and work out compromises together.

Discipline Do's & Don'ts

All parents need to provide firm, consistent discipline for their children. Working moms especially, tempted as we are to make every moment with the kids pleasant, have to remember that discipline is a means of showing kids we care about them. Standards of discipline should not suffer because mom is going back to work, nor should guilt over the hours spent away interfere with clear thinking about who's in charge. Discipline makes a child's world manageable and secure—to relax it at a time when he is adjusting to your increased absence or learning to manage on his own can only aggravate feelings of insecurity. Through your discipline, your child will learn self-discipline and grow up to be the kind of responsible adult you want him to be.

Rules, Rules, Rules

Rules are the best way to deal with issues that will come up again and again. It is easier to say, "That is the rule" than "No." Rules help both of you to remember precedents and obviate the need for repeated requests and decisions.

At first you will set the rules, tailoring them to the child's stage of development. As your child gets older, his input will increase. Family councils can decide when rules need to change. Be guided by your child's wishes, peer practice, and your own standards and expectations. Some compromise will make them more effective. Avoid rules that you cannot enforce.

Making Rules Work

Moms in management have the advantage here, for they have experience and regular practice in getting people to do things. Managing children takes many of the same techniques that work in an office.

1. Respect is paramount. Children deserve to be treated as the human beings they are. They should never be subjected to belittling criticism or verbal abuse.

2. Don't nag. A reminder may be helpful, especially when a rule is new, but don't overdo it. You want the child to make keeping the rules his responsibility, not yours. Show that you have confidence in him.

3. Make desirable behavior attractive. Make unpleasant tasks fun by playing games or singing. Cheer up morning slow pokes with some snappy music. Provide incentives where appropriate: "If you are ready for bed by eight-twenty, we will have ten minutes to read a story together."

4. Improve your child's self-image by telling him he has positive qualities. "You are very gentle with your little brother." "You are generous with your toys." "You are very brave when you fall down." "You worked hard on that difficult piece today." Always focus on good points.

5. Break work down into small steps. Begin with one request. Instead of saying, "Clean your room!" ask, "Would you please put your dirty clothes in the hamper?" Then ask him to put his toys away. Then to make up the bed. Make the first request easy to get him started; once he is involved, you can gradually escalate your demands.

When Rules Are Broken

You can't fire your kid. When the rules are not followed, you will have to find constructive ways of dealing with the situation. You want to teach him to appreciate the need for his cooperation. There are several tacks you can take:

1. Time out. Having the child stay in a chair or his room until he can better control his behavior may be necessary to cool him down. This measure works best if he chooses when he is ready to rejoin the group or go back to what he was doing. Some parents isolate the child for a specified time and set a timer so that the child knows when the punishment is over.

2. Withdraw. Sometimes, especially if the child is trying to manipulate you with temper tantrums or whining, the best thing for you to do is leave the room. It may increase his anger, but don't give in. Don't return until the uncontrolled behavior has stopped.

3. Give your child a chance to learn the consequences of his actions. If his basketball uniform didn't get washed because he forgot to put it in the hamper, don't feel sorry for him and do an extra load to get it done. Let him play in his practice uniform or in his dirty one, or show him how to work the washing machine and dryer.

4. Build consequences into your rules, and carry them out when the rules get broken. If your three-year-old is not behaving well at the playground, let him know that if he misbehaves he will be taken home.

5. Dock allowance or privileges. The elimination of television or telephone time or after-school activities can be used to give your child time to carry out his obligations. Present these as consequences of his actions. "If your homework is not done, you may not watch your television program." "If you have not finished your practicing before school, you may not go swimming after school." Allowance can be used to pay for something your child has carelessly broken or to replace money he has lost. His loss should be somehow related to or arise from his misbehavior; it should not be punitive, but corrective.

6. Discuss the problem with him or at a family council. Listen to his point of view and suggestions. Often compromises can be made and new rules set that he will feel he has a stake in keeping.

How to Argue Constructively in Front of the Kids

Arguing constructively in front of the children is one of the more challenging responsibilities of being parents. When conflict erupts, everything you have been telling them about "using words," not shouting, not bullying, not running off and slamming doors, but settling differences through rational discussion—all this is now on the line: It's your chance to provide a valuable "live" demonstration that they will watch not as curious bystanders, but as intensely involved family members. Small children in particular are frightened that parents' anger will be turned on them; older children may worry about divorce. All have a vested interest in family harmony.

Arguments start as a breakdown of family communication and organization. They aren't scheduled or planned, and they tend to occur at the worst possible times. Turning this breakdown into a positive experience for everyone requires great tact and forebearance at a time when these qualities are hardest to summon.

Mom gets an important phone call just as she is preparing dinner. The beans burn, the children are creating a commotion, dad is trying to hear the news on television. The accusations begin the moment mom hangs up. "Hey, look—you burned the beans!" "*I* burned the beans? Why weren't you watching them? You knew I was on the phone!" "Why didn't you tell him to phone back later? You're always talking on the phone!" "I am not! This was important, and I could hardly hear a word with the kids screaming and you watching TV. Why don't you read to them or something?" "We're all just waiting for dinner. Why isn't dinner ever ready on time?"

This argument is rapidly descending to destructive levels: We'll soon have a mother-in-law denigrated or crockery flying. But arguments can be constructive. Here are some helpful rules:

RULE A: AVOID ACCUSATIONS OF ANY KIND. Even accusations that seem one hundred percent correct to you ("You burned the beans!") can invite angry responses. Be especially chary of words like "always" and "never": They are rarely accurate and almost invariably inflammatory.

RULE B: BE OPEN AND HONEST ABOUT YOUR FEELINGS. Send "I messages." Say, "I am angry! I do not like all this noise and commotion! My nerves are all frazzled, and I'm hungry, too!"

RULE C: CONSIDER THE OTHER PERSON'S POINT OF VIEW. Remember that the same event can look quite different to different people and can evoke quite different reactions. Consider, too, all the circumstances that abetted the anger—being hungry, being tired, feeling pressured at the end of the day. It will give you a fuller picture of what led to the argument in the first place. In this case both parents had reasons to be annoyed. If they can put themselves in each other's shoes, it will be easier for each to admit his or her own mistakes. "You're right; you were counting on me to get dinner cooked tonight, and I was off on the phone." "I'm sorry; I could have stepped in to help you."

RULE D: DEFLECT INVITATIONS TO QUARREL. Don't rise to the bait; it takes two to fight. Be patient and kind. Your apology might be met with an angry "Damn tootin'! I do my share of the cooking around here. All I wanted was to get my turn to relax before dinner." Keep calm: "Yes, you do. I really do appreciate all your help."

RULE E: ELIMINATE EXTRANEOUS ISSUES. It's easy for arguments to get hung up on minor points. Don't waste time and energy on them. The burned beans can be quickly replaced with a frozen vegetable. Everyone's hunger can be appeased by sitting down to eat. Then try to talk out the problem, even if it's over dinner.

RULE F: FOCUS ON THE PROBLEM AT HAND. Find out what the issues are, if any. Are you really upset about the cooking arrangements? Do you think your husband spends too little time interacting with the children? This step is hard because discussion of problems and feelings can easily deteriorate into more angry exchanges. You will need to accept all the feelings that get expressed and try to understand them. Be tactful and courteous. It might be best to postpone the discussion until both of you have had time to think things over, maybe even write down what you perceive to be the problem.

RULE G: AGREE ON A GAME PLAN. Work out the changes in organization and communication that will help solve the problems that brought on the argument. Chores may need to be reassigned, schedules shifted, new strategies found, and new rules made. The couple in our example might decide to move up the dinner hour or have high-protein hors d'oeuvres set out ahead of time. They might set a house rule of no interruptions at the dinner hour: to take the phone off the hook and turn off the TV.

RULE H: HUG AND MAKE UP. Restoring harmony after the conflict is essential. Even if fuller discussion and agreement on a game plan are delayed until a more convenient time, a positive agreement has been reached, and all can be confident that a solution will be found. Reassure the children of your love for them and of your love for each other.

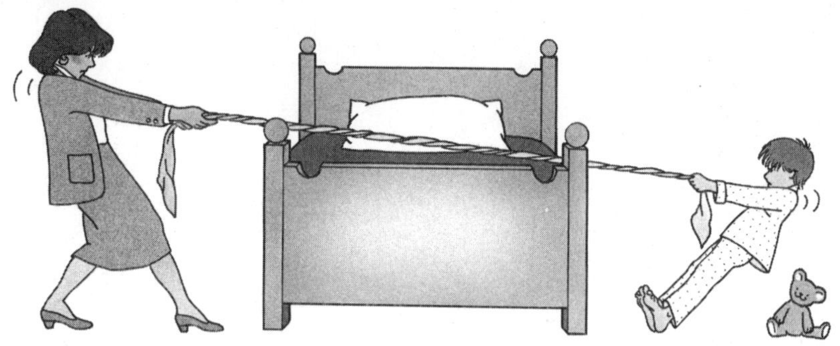

HOW TO STOP THOSE BEDTIME BATTLES

One of the most stressful times for every working mother is the bedtime hour. Suddenly, even the most docile, obedient child can turn into a difficult, screaming, and stubborn little person, with her own ideas about when she should go to sleep.

Children dislike going to bed for many reasons, so your first step when bedtime battles begin is to figure out the causes. Very young children may be afraid of the dark. Children just beginning to assert their independence from their parents also fear it, and these ambivalent feelings may surface at bedtime. Some children need more attention and know they can get it by being difficult at bedtime. For others it is a time to gain more control over their parents, or a child simply may be too excited to sleep or may not be very tired.

SET A REASONABLE HOUR FOR BEDTIME

Children have different sleep needs: If you know a child functions well on eleven hours of sleep a night, it is useless to try to keep her in bed for twelve. Either let her stay up later or provide an early morning quiet activity, a snack, and an alarm clock set for the hour she may come greet everyone with a cheery good morning.

The hour you set will change with changing needs. Summer bedtime hours may be later; when the child starts school, she may need more sleep and the hour will have to be earlier. If you are being realistic and discuss her sleep needs with her, she will be more likely to understand and cooperate; no one likes to drag through the day on insufficient sleep.

WORK OUT A PLEASANT, REASSURING BEDTIME ROUTINE

A bath, a snack if she is hungry (milk toast is a good soporific), toothbrushing, a story or a song. Allow choices within the framework you set up, but set limits. She may choose which three songs you will sing to her, or which two animals she will take to bed with her.

DEAL REALISTICALLY WITH FEARS

Assure her there are no monsters, but close the closet door if it makes her feel better. Provide a night light if she wants it, and put one in the hallway and in the bathroom also to encourage independence should she need to get a glass of water or to use the toilet. A flashlight may be a great success: The kind you have to pinch to light will last longer than one that might be inadvertently left on all night.

Music can help calm a restless child, and it is soothing to a tired parent as well. Put on a quiet, relaxing record that both of you can enjoy.

Whatever routine you work out will succeed best if you can give the child your undivided attention. Take the phone off the hook, and put a note on the doorbell. Your time together need not be very long, but it should not be drawn out by interruptions.

Once she is tucked in, leave. Try not to answer calls or cries you know are unfounded. Check on her if you really think something is wrong, but don't encourage the crying by giving in to demands for more stories or food. Your best bets are firmness and a matter-of-fact approach. Don't let yourself feel guilty for wanting some time for yourself.

HELPFUL BOOKS

Dr. Balter's Baby & Child Sense *by Dr. Lawrence Balter (Simon & Schuster)*
Solve Your Child's Sleep Problems *by Dr. Richard Ferber (Simon & Schuster)*

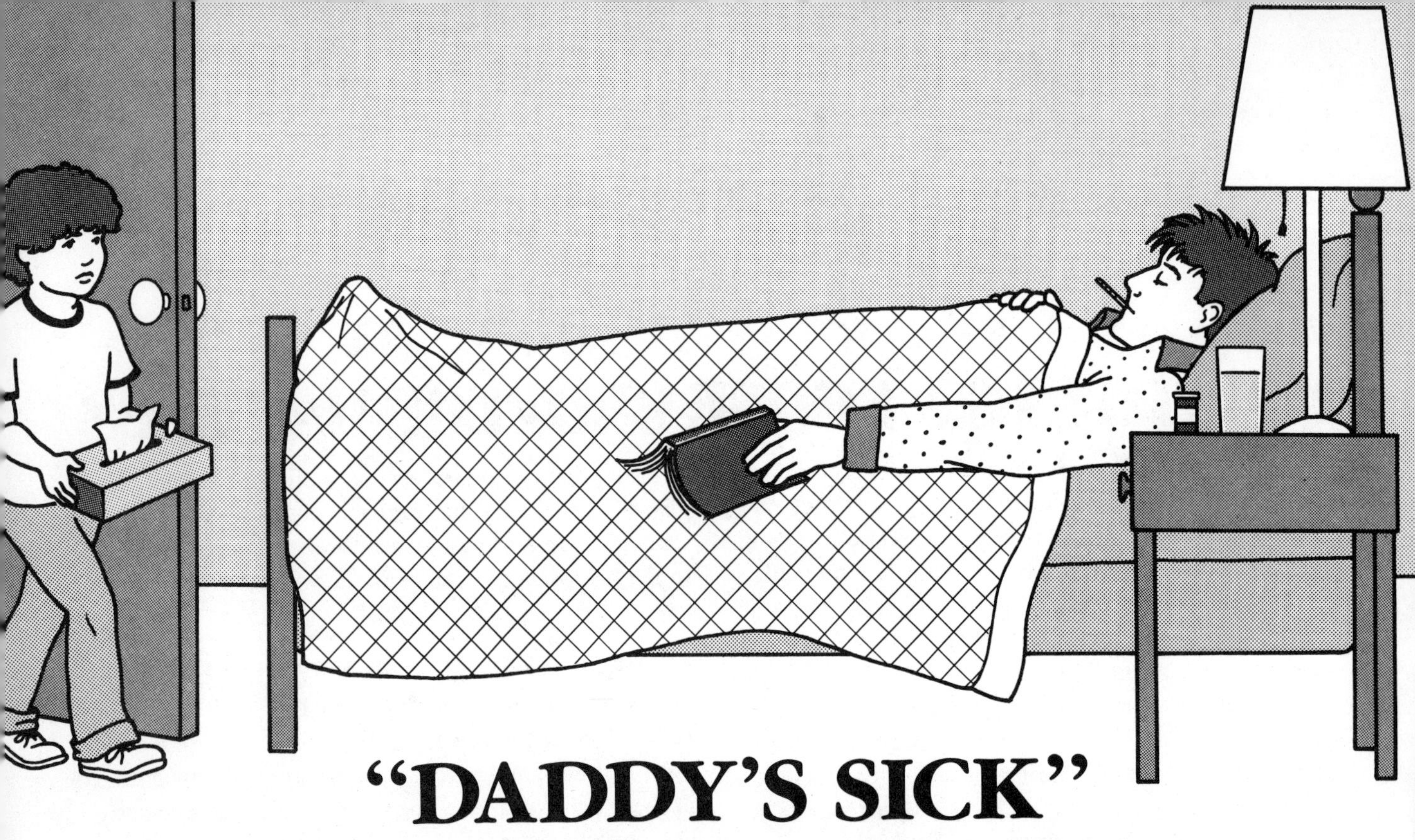

"DADDY'S SICK"

How to Reassure a Child When a Parent Is Ill...

When a husband is ill or hospitalized, a working mother is often hard put to manage the household alone, care for her sick or injured spouse, and take care of the kids. The psychological impact on children is also a great concern, and it's important to reassure them that their father's illness is not their fault and that he still loves them and will return. Their disrupted home life needs to be made as stable as possible.

* Talk as frankly and openly as you can about the illness or injury. Translate it into terms your children can comprehend.
* Reassure them that even though you may seem upset and may even cry, you can still take care of them.
* Get help. This is the time to call on friends and relatives who can give both you and your children support. Ask for help in running the household and caring for your spouse so that you can be more available for the kids.
* If a father is hospitalized, arrange for the children to visit. Many hospitals that do not ordinarily permit children to visit may be prevailed upon to make an exception. Prepare the children for any equipment in the room they might find frightening. If visits cannot be arranged, have them telephone frequently.
* Keep your children's lives on as even a keel as possible. They should not have to give up any of their usual activities even though it may be difficult for you to provide transportation and pickups. They should not be made to feel guilty for continuing their lives.
* Encourage children to help in whatever ways they can to care for and cheer their sick father, whether it is by making small gifts or cards or by taking in a sick tray.
* If a husband is terminally ill, honesty is important. Ask your doctor or the hospital about support groups for children and spouses of terminally ill patients, or write to the national organization for the illness involved, such as the American Cancer Society. Knowing and talking to others who are undergoing or have undergone the same painful experience can be the greatest help of all.

Helping Kids Handle Divorce

Divorce is painful for everyone involved—even the partner who most desires it. It's easy for a mother facing a divorce to become so caught up in her own emotions that she underestimates the impact divorce will have on her children. But it is possible to make even this difficult time less traumatic by remembering their needs, too.

Breaking the News

The hardest part will be telling your children, but it should be done right away, before anyone outside the family is told. Your children should hear the news from you, with your husband there with you if possible, at a time you can all talk over together the changes that will take place.

At your first talk—and at the many that will follow—four important points need to be made:

1. That you and their father have decided to get divorced—or separated, if that is the case. Don't pretend it will be a temporary arrangement, however, if you do not intend it to be. This is not a time for "white lies": They will only make your children distrustful of you and increase their bewilderment and anxiety.

2. That you and their father have made this decision because you are no longer happy living together or because you have problems that are best solved by living apart. Don't go into specific details. If your husband has left, he may seem to be entirely at fault, but try to be accurate and give a balanced picture without denigrating him or bending over backward to glorify him.

3. That the children are in no way to blame. Kids are quick to take guilt upon themselves and will need constant reassurance that they are not the cause of parental conflicts.

4. That you both still love them. It's easy for kids to fear that because love between married adults can come to an end, their parents might stop loving them. They will need frequent reminders of your love. If, however, your spouse has left, it is not entirely up to you to assure them of his love.

Easing the Transition

Your children will have many questions about how the divorce will affect their lives. To help calm fears about the future, stress those things that will remain the same. The fewer additional changes they will have to face, the more secure they will feel. If they can continue to live in the same home and go to the same schools, at least for the first year, the adjustment will be easier.

Your children are also apt to feel embarrassed about telling their friends about the divorce. Help them feel less isolated by pointing out friends or relatives who are divorced. Ask them how their friends with divorced parents feel.

Maintaining Discipline

One form of security you can provide during this difficult period is to continue to set limits as you always have. It won't be easy. Your kids are apt to act out their anger in inappropriate ways, test your love through disobedience, and regress to infantile behavior. They will need patience, encouragement, and reassurance.

Enlist school support by having a conference with each of your children's teachers as soon as the decision to get divorced has been made.

Don't overindulge the children with presents. Security cannot be measured in toys or any other possessions. They need your love and understanding much more.

Don't load on extra responsibilities. Your children are still children. They cannot be expected to take over the role of their absent father.

Don't compare your child's bad behavior to that of your former husband. It is destructive to his self-image and possibly quite frightening.

Don't assume that all of your children's misbehavior is attributable to the divorce. It won't be. Your children will continue to go through the normal phases of development and will have difficult and easy periods.

Reestablish Normalcy

As soon as possible, let your lives settle into normal routines. Custody arrangements will establish when the children will visit or live with their father. Help your children adjust to their new two-home lives. If you are not the custodial parent, build them each some private space where you live so that they have a place to leave things between visits. Let them help decorate it.

Remember that holidays are usually the toughest times. Retain all the traditions you reasonably can, and let the children contribute their ideas for any changes. If you and your former husband are on good enough terms, a holiday meal together need not be out of the question. Just try not to unwittingly encourage children's fantasies that you will remarry.

Helpful Books

For pre-school children:

What Would You Do? A Child's Book About Divorce **by Barbara S. Cain and Elissa P. Benedek (Youth Publications/The Saturday Evening Post)**

Divorce Is a Grown-Up Problem **by Janet Sinberg (Avon)**

For older children:

How Does It Feel When Your Parents Get Divorced? **by Terry Berger (Julian Messner)**

For parents:

The Parents Book About Divorce **by Richard A. Gardner (Doubleday)**

What Every Child Would Like His Parents to Know About Divorce **by Lee A. Salk (Harper & Row)**

Toll-Free Numbers

Toll-free and hotline numbers can be a boon to busy moms. You can obtain information on a variety of subjects—or even register complaints—without spending valuable time at the library or writing letters. Many companies use toll-free numbers to give consumers information about their products. State and federal government agencies offer services dealing with everything from complaints about movers to free travel information. Whatever you need, there's a good chance a friendly voice is waiting at the end of a toll-free telephone line to help you out. You can also call the toll-free information number—800-555-1212—to find out if the service, agency, or company you wish to speak to has a toll-free number. Here is a sampling, with exceptions where noted:

1. Child Abuse Hotline
   Florida: **800-342-0152**
   New York: **800-342-3720**
2. Consumers Product Safety Commission (to register complaints about a specific product)
   U.S. (except Maryland): **800-638-2666**
   Maryland: **800-492-2937**
3. Division of Tourism (for information about travel in the United States)
   U.S. (except South Dakota): **800-843-1930**
4. Housing Discrimination Hotline (to register complaints if you feel you've been discriminated against when applying for housing)
   U.S. (except Washington, D.C.): **800-424-8590**
5. Interstate Commerce Commission (to register complaints about movers)
   U.S. (except Washington, D.C.): **800-424-9312**
   Florida: **800-432-4537**
6. Ladies Center, Inc. (birth-control information)
   U.S. (except Florida): **800-327-9880**
   Florida: **800-432-0460**
7. National Highway Traffic and Safety Administration (to register complaints about your car)
   Connecticut, Delaware, Maryland, North Carolina, New Jersey, New York, Pennsylvania, Southern Ohio, Virginia, West Virginia: **800-424-9393**
8. National Committee for Citizens in Education (for complaints about public schools)
   U.S. (except Maryland): **800-638-9675**
9. National Runaway Switchboard (for runaways to call to send messages home)
   U.S. (except Illinois): **800-621-4000**
   Illinois: **800-972-6004**
10. Operation Peace of Mind (runaway hotline)
    U.S. (except Texas): **800-231-6946**
    Texas: **800-392-3352**
11. Nexus (clearinghouse on post-secondary education)
    U.S. (except Washington, D.C.): **800-424-9775**
12. Poison Control Centers (for information on what to do in case of poisoning)
    Colorado: **800-332-3073**
    Georgia: **800-282-5846**
    Nebraska: **800-642-9999**
    Utah: **800-662-4225**
    elsewhere, consult your phone book
13. World Book
    800-621-8202
    Illinois, Alaska, Hawaii: Call collect, **312-341-2677**
14. Polaroid
    800-225-1384
15. Zayre Discount Department Stores
    U.S. (except Massachusetts): **800-225-2242**
    Massachusetts: **800-982-2266**
16. Beech-Nut Infant Nutrition Hotline
    U.S. (except Pennsylvania): **800-523-6633**
    Pennsylvania: **800-492-2384**
17. Johnson & Johnson
    U.S. (except New Jersey): **800-526-2433**
    New Jersey: **800-352-4777**
18. Little Tykes Toys
    800-321-0183
19. Federal Deposit Insurance Corporation (for complaints about banks)
    U.S. (except Washington, D.C.): **800-424-5488**

WHEN YOU HAVE TO DISCIPLINE ANOTHER PARENT'S CHILD . . .

A child visiting your home needs to heed the same general household rules your child does. It is easy enough to let her know in a matter-of-fact way what these rules are if she begins to infringe upon them—in fact your daughter will probably tell her first. "We don't bring toys to the table; your bunny can watch you eat from over here." "We don't watch television at this time." "You may not slide down the banister; it's too dangerous." "We take off our shoes when we sit on the sofa." Enforcing even minor rules lets a child's friend know that a certain standard of behavior is expected and reminds your own child, too. It may also help discourage them from real mischief-making.

Serious misbehavior should be treated very much as you would your own child's misbehavior, especially if safety is involved. You will need to consider, though, how much more frightening and embarrassing it is to be reprimanded by someone else's parent.

* Moderate your voice. One can be stern without shouting.
* Don't hit.
* Make your objections to her behavior perfectly clear. Make sure she understands what she did wrong and why you think it was wrong—parents have different standards and expectations, and this child is not used to yours.
* Don't punish; if both children are involved, have them sit in separate places for a few minutes while you think of what needs to be done next. If they are old enough, discuss how they can make amends for what they have done. Perhaps there is a mess they can volunteer to clean up.
* Clear the air as soon as possible. Working together to clean up is a start. Change the scene. Start a new activity.
* Reassure your child of your love for her. A smile, a hug, a squeeze of the hand, praise for something helpful she did.
* Let the parent know later what happened and what you did to discipline her child, but never do this in front of the child. She has already been disciplined; she does not need to have her misbehavior rehearsed again. The mother may wish to discuss the matter with her daughter later—that is up to her.

Helping a Child Cope with Bereavement

Bereaved children feel much the same feelings as bereaved adults: anger, fear, guilt, a sense of loss, loneliness, sometimes even hopelessness, depression, and despair. But they may deal with these feelings in different ways than adults do. Don't be surprised if behavioral problems develop. An increase in aggressive behavior may be your child's way of acting out her anger. Or she may regress in her toilet training. Most disconcerting for the bereaved adult is that she may show no sign of bereavement at all, in fact may seem quite cheerful about her loss. "Grandmother died!" she announces with a bright smile to the cashier in the supermarket. An older child may not even talk about it, but may instead treat the time off from school to go to the funeral as a great lark and put on her roller skates to race around the block even as relatives are arriving with food and sympathy.

The main thing to remember is that children do feel grief and like adults they need to find appropriate ways of expressing it. How can you help?

T. L. C.

- Don't excuse bad behavior, but try to understand it. Deal firmly with the behavior itself, but give the child more time and attention.
- Be gentle and uncritical about regressive behavior, yet try to help the child understand the reasons for it. "Are you sucking your thumb because you feel sad? Come, sit in my lap—you haven't done that for a long time either."

Talk

- Tell the child your own feelings in terms she can understand. Talk about all the feelings, not just sadness, but anger and guilt, too—these are the more difficult ones to express and the ones your child may be finding it hardest to cope with.
- Encourage your child to talk about her grief, her thoughts about the person who has died, and her feelings.
- Physical closeness is important, too. Hug or hold her as you talk.
- Answer her questions about death as honestly as you can. She will see through any attempt on your part to make up stories about the afterlife if you don't yourself believe in it; if you do, share your religious beliefs with her.
- Remember that small children cannot comprehend the finality of death. Be patient; you may need to repeat many times that her grandmother will not be coming back.

The Funeral

- Take your child to the funeral if she has been very close to the deceased, if you think she can manage reasonably well to sit through it, and if you think she will not be unduly distressed by the emotions likely to be shown there.
- Tell your child ahead of time in detail just what the funeral will be like and that grown-ups will be crying.
- An open coffin may be especially frightening to a child. If she shows any hesitation, don't insist on her viewing the body. Sit with her while this is done, and have a close friend or relative sit with her while you make your farewells.
- If she does not attend the funeral, arrange for her to stay with a well-loved sitter or friend who can answer her questions. Don't let her feel left out.

Family Closeness

- Let the bereavement bring your family closer together. Family relationships change when a family member dies, and closer ties and new intimacies can develop among the survivors if the bereaved reach out to each other for consolation. Give your children a chance to help console you. They cannot give the kind of support adult friends and family members can, but they can give hope for the future.
- Keep memories alive. Don't be afraid to talk about the deceased. Bring him up in conversation. Dig out old photographs to look at. Pictures and anecdotes help us to remember lost friends and relatives and to pass along to our children the special qualities we loved in them.

When a Pet Dies

Bereavement caused by the death of a beloved pet can be as serious to a child as the loss of a loved person. Treat it that way. Help the child in the same way you would if she had lost a close relative or friend: Talk about death, talk about the pet, talk about feelings of grief, guilt, and anger. Encourage her to talk. Hold her close. Have a funeral for the pet, and let her hold the body and bury it. Give her time to mourn. It is a valuable experience for her that will help her learn to deal with other losses.

25 Fabulous Fifteen-Minute Desserts

Nothing makes a meal more memorable than a wonderful dessert. So even when preparation time is short and the meal itself is simple, it's worth a little effort to make something special, whether it is for family or for guests. Try one of these quick but easy-to-make treats:

1. Pears poached in red wine with cinnamon and cloves
2. Tapioca pudding
3. Apple crepes with powdered sugar
4. Stewed rhubarb with sour cream
5. Plum-jam sandwiches fried like French toast
6. Sliced oranges dribbled with honey and chopped walnuts
7. Yogurt supreme: plain yogurt with honey, granola, fresh or dried fruits, and nuts
8. Ricotta cheese whisked with confectioner's sugar and flavorings: For example, add ¼ teaspoon almond extract and garnish with slivered almonds.
9. Banana fritters
10. Cranberry relish: cranberries, sugar, and a whole, unpeeled orange mixed in the blender—served with plain yogurt
11. Chocolate pudding mixed with nuts and topped with whipped cream
12. Broiler s'mores: melted marshmallows on graham crackers, dipped in chocolate sauce
13. Jiffy *pots de creme:* Put 6 ounces chocolate bits, 1 egg, 2 tablespoons sugar, and 1 teaspoon vanilla or rum in the blender. Add ¾ cup boiling milk and blend for 1 minute. Pour into 4 or 5 small cups or glasses and chill.
14. Strawberry jam omelette
15. Farina pudding with maple syrup
16. Grapes with sour cream: Spread a single layer of seedless grapes in a shallow baking dish or pie tin, cover with sour cream, and sprinkle with brown sugar. Run under the broiler until the sugar dissolves.
17. Cottage cheese, crushed blueberries, brown sugar, and cinnamon: Mix well and chill.
18. Bread "fried" in sizzling maple syrup, served with cream or ice cream
19. Strawberry Jell-O: When the Jell-O is almost set, fold in fresh strawberries and whipped cream.
20. Ice cream sandwiches made with graham crackers or chocolate wafer cookies
21. Baked apples with raisins and brown sugar
22. Instant sherbet: Mix frozen orange-juice concentrate with milk, sweetened yogurt, or ice cream. Chill.
23. Rice cream made by mixing leftover boiled rice and whipped cream: Add chopped up fruit and marshmallows.
24. Vanilla ice cream stirred up with mashed bananas and topped with crumbled graham crackers
25. Peaches, or any fresh fruit—pineapple, strawberries, etc—in champagne. Serve perfectly ripe fruit in a tall stemmed glass, and pour a splash of champagne—or any sparkling white wine—over it.

Quick Breakfasts for Busy Mornings

With everyone scrambling for school and office in the morning, it is often a hassle to prepare and eat a real breakfast. How much simpler to gulp down some juice and eat a slice of toast on the run.

But breakfast food need not be elaborate or time-consuming. Think of easier and quicker alternatives to the standard bacon and egg breakfast, and simplify ways of cooking traditional breakfast foods. Here are some ideas to get you started.

*Provide bacon and eggs in one easy package by making a breakfast quiche. Basically an egg custard in a pie crust, quiche is a delicious and simple dish that can be made and baked ahead of time and popped into the oven for reheating in the morning.

The basic quiche recipe consists of eggs, Swiss cheese, cream, onions, bacon or bits of ham, and spices. For variation, add vegetables like broccoli, mushrooms, or zucchini; pieces of cooked chicken or turkey; cheeses like cheddar, Parmesan, or ricotta; and shellfish such as shrimp, lobster, or crabmeat.

Quiche Lorraine

1	9-inch unbaked frozen pie shell*	3/4	teaspoon salt
1	tablespoon butter	1/8	teaspoon black pepper
4	eggs		pinch cayenne pepper
2	cups heavy cream	1/4	pound natural Swiss cheese, grated (about 1 cup)
		12	slices bacon, fried until crisp and crumbled into bits

Preheat oven to 425 degrees. Rub butter over the surface of the pie shell. Mix eggs, heavy cream, salt, peppers and beat until well-blended. Sprinkle grated cheese and bacon bits on bottom of pie shell. Pour in egg and cream mixture. Bake for 15 minutes at 425 degrees, then reduce the oven temperature to 300 degrees and bake for 40 minutes longer, or until a knife inserted into the center of the quiche comes out clean. Makes 6 to 8 servings.

*Transform leftovers from the night before into tomorrow morning's breakfast fare. A beaten egg and grated onion added to mashed potatoes can make delicious potato cakes. Top with applesauce before serving.

*Cooked roast beef can be diced or shredded and blended into a cream gravy for chipped beef.

*Tomato sauce or beef stew can be dribbled over waffles or toast for a hearty breakfast meal.

*Fried or poached eggs are delicious over cooked spinach and English muffins.

*Creamed vegetables, prepared the night before with dinner leftovers, can be eaten in the morning spooned into toasted pita bread.

**Frozen pie shells make the quiche preparation even simpler. Mix the ingredients in a bowl the night before, then pour into a frozen pie shell in the morning and put in the oven while showering and dressing.*

Jazz Up the Ordinary

If you usually have something quick, easy, and very ordinary in the morning, why not add something different to make it more interesting—and more delicious?

*Add fruited yogurt instead of plain milk to cold cereal.

*A bagel can be made more nutritious and tasty by spreading it with peanut butter and adding sliced banana.

*Spread toast with ricotta cheese instead of butter, top with a few grains of nutmeg, and put under the broiler for a minute or two until warm.

*For a mini-breakfast pizza, top half an English muffin with bottled or canned tomato sauce and a slice of Swiss or mozzarella cheese, then put under the broiler until the cheese is bubbly.

*Spread a bran muffin with cream cheese mixed with chopped dates and walnuts.
*Cover a slice of date nut bread with cottage cheese and orange sections.
*Sprinkle frozen yogurt with chopped nuts, grated coconut, and granola for a morning treat kids will love.

Why Not Salads and Sandwiches?

Salads are a natural for lunch, even dinner, but have you ever thought how handy they can be for breakfast? They're healthy and easy, and taste just as good in the morning as they do later in the day.

Here are some ideas to try:

*Make a breakfast fruit salad by combining bananas, apples, grapes, grapefruit and orange sections, and strips of melon. For variation, add canned peach halves, canned apricots, cherries, strawberries, blueberries, and pineapple chunks. The salad can be made the night before, refrigerated, and then served in the morning. For extra protein, add a scoop of cottage cheese to each serving.
*For a robust chef's salad, combine strips of ham, turkey, and cheese, with hard-boiled egg halves, and place on a bed of lettuce. This, too, can be made the night before and tossed with a light oil and lemon dressing in the morning before serving.
*Tuna fish salad, chicken salad, even egg salad make good breakfasts. In the morning, they can be eaten on slices of toast, or plain accompanied by a whole orange and a cup of coffee or tea.
*Pieces of leftover meat can be made into a morning salad. For example, strips of cold roast beef can be mixed with rings of green pepper, Swiss cheese slices, tomato wedges, broccoli flowerets, and cucumber slices, then dressed with a mixture of sour cream and horseradish.

Leftover vegetables can also be tossed into a morning salad, combined with salad greens. Beets, carrots, green beans, corn niblets, lima beans, slices of white potato or peas all provide enough complex carbohydrates to give your family an energy boost for the entire day.

Sandwiches, too, don't have to be limited to the lunch box. Even a peanut butter and jelly sandwich is better for breakfast than nothing at all—after all, it's protein and carbohydrates. For something more adventuresome, however, consider the following:
*For an open-faced grilled cheese sandwich, add two slices of American or cheddar cheese to a piece of bread, top with a tomato slice and, if you have time, a strip of cooked bacon. Put under the broiler until the cheese is melted.
*Meat loaf, if there's any left from the night before, tastes wonderful in the morning. Try it served on whole wheat toast spread lightly with mustard, or on a sesame seed bun with some tomato sauce.
*Corned beef hash, a traditional morning favorite, can be enhanced in sandwich form. Top a slice of rye bread with canned corned beef hash, a few dollops of ketchup, then sprinkle with grated cheddar cheese. Heat under the broiler until the cheese is melted.
*Creamed chicken and turkey, even chipped beef, can make great hot sandwiches for breakfast. Make them either open-faced or topped with bread, depending on your preference.

Time-Saving Tips

Do as much leg work as possible the night before to cut down on preparation in the morning. For example:

*Set the table with utensils, plates, and napkins the night before.
*For a simple scrambled egg and toast breakfast, beat the eggs the night before and refrigerate; count out slices of toast, and have butter, jelly, and jam ready so that the eggs just need to be scrambled and the bread toasted in the morning.
*Make batter for French toast the evening before. Have bread slices ready to be dipped, and the pan on the stove, ready for heating.
*Use convenience foods and pre-packaged foods as much as possible. Canned and bottled juices, even single-serving juices help save time, as do things like frozen waffles, muffins, and coffee cakes; mixes for pancakes, biscuits, muffins, and popovers.
*Use quick-cooking cereals or dry cereals occasionally, but enliven them with raisins, nuts, and dried fruits.

Tips for Cooking Ahead

The period before dinner is one of the most difficult in the daily routine, vying only with the early morning rush for the "Most Hectic Hour Award." Everyone needs to unwind after a busy day; everyone wants attention. And you need to get the evening meal ready. Wouldn't it be wonderful just to pop a ready-made dish into the oven and relax with the children while it heats? With planning, it can be done. Figure out your best cooking hours—weekends, late evenings, or very early in the morning. Cook ahead and stockpile meals in your freezer. Here are some tips:

* Buy larger cooking pans so that you can make double or treble batches of your favorite soups, stews, and casseroles.

* Shop with leftovers in mind.

* Buy a slow-cooker: Prepare the ingredients the night before and refrigerate; load them into the pot as you make breakfast.

* Buy a food processor to help cut up all the extra vegetables when you make large quantities; it can also whip up bread dough and piecrust in a jiffy (that leftover pot roast can become beef potpie).

* Keep a loose-leaf notebook, and glue in recipes and ideas for leftovers clipped from magazines and newspapers.

* Prepare your own mixes for making pancakes and muffins by measuring and storing the dry ingredients together.

* Mix salad dressing by the bottle and keep it ready in the refrigerator.

* Stock up on plastic containers, plastic bags, foil, and labels. Keep a list of freezer contents handy and up-to-date.

* To freeze stews and casseroles: Choose a wide, shallow pot you can use to reheat the meal, and line it with foil, leaving extra foil hanging over the edge. Put the cooked food into the lined pot, cover, and freeze. Remove the pot when the food has frozen, wrap the food closely with the foil, and label. When reheating, peel off the foil; the frozen chunk will fit right into the pot.

* Or freeze one-dish meals in self-sealing plastic bags. Reheat by boiling the bag in water.

* Invest in a microwave for super-quick defrosting and shorter cooking times for all foods.

* Make extra pancakes and waffles at a leisurely weekend breakfast. Stack with wax paper between them, and wrap in foil to freeze. Reheat them in the toaster or spread out on a cookie sheet in a hot oven.

* Most baked goods freeze well: cookies, cakes with or without buttercream frosting, bread, muffins, unfilled cream puffs, meringues, pies. Slice breads and cakes before freezing for quick thawing. Use wax paper between portions.

* Keep ground meat frozen in hamburger-size patties. Later, if you want to use the meat for a different purpose, the patties will thaw faster than a large ball of meat.

* When freezing stews and casseroles, undercook slightly and provide plenty of gravy. Thickening and final seasoning can be done as the meal is reheated.

Helpful Books

The I Hate to Cook Book by Peg Bracken (Fawcett)

Pressure Cooking Day by Day by K. F. Broughton (International)

The Freezer Cookbook, 2nd edition, by Charlotte Erickson (Chilton)

The Best of Electric Crockery Cooking by Jacqueline Hériteau (Grosset & Dunlap)

Will It Freeze? An A to Z Guide to Foods that Freeze by Joan Hood (Scribner's)

Microwave Cooking: Meals in Minutes by Thelma Pressman (Irena Chalmers)

Homemade Mixes for Instant Meals the Natural Way by Nina and Michael Shandler (Rawson, Wade)

Working Parent Food Book by Adeline Garner Shell and Kay Reynolds (Sovereign)

WEEKLY MENU PLANNING

There are some days when the chore of deciding what to serve your family for dinner can seem overwhelming. Those are the nights to resort to take-out food or a quick trip to the local deli. However, with a little advance planning—and if you make a conscious effort *not* to be in the running for a Julia Child cooking award—you can provide tasty and innovative meals for your gang. You'll cut down on shopping time and also find it comforting to know exactly what you'll be making each night of the week. Save the weekends for experimenting or recreating those gourmet meals you see pictured in the food magazines.

Here are some tips to get you off and running:

- Make up a seven-day menu plan and repeat it every week. The rotating schedule might include chicken, pasta, beef, fish, veal, and pork. Though your staple remains the same, the preparation can be altered. The beef dish might be hamburgers one week, steak the next, roast beef or chili another.

- Pick one night a week to order take-out food, and vary the selection. Chinese, Mexican, or other family favorites can be a special Friday-night dinner, followed by a family outing to a movie or a trip to the local dessert or ice cream place.

- Plan to experiment with foreign cuisines once or twice a month. Though your children may balk at first, being introduced to such exotic foods as Indian, Thai, Vietnamese, Korean, or other far-off delights will help broaden their horizons—a positive influence for any child.

- Choose one day a week—perhaps Saturday or Sunday—to sit down and plan your menus. Ask for input from your husband and children. Involving them in planning dinners is the first step in getting them to help with the meal preparation.

- Invest in a few cookbooks that promise delicious meals in an hour or less, and keep your eyes open for time-saving recipes printed in your local newspaper or the women's magazines.

- Don't discount frozen foods. You shouldn't feel ashamed to offer your family frozen dinners occasionally. If you're concerned about nutritional value, prepare a salad or other vegetable on the side.

- Don't be afraid to make quick but unconventional dinners for your family, such as scrambled eggs or various types of omelettes.

- At least twice a month plan on a large roast or turkey that is guaranteed to provide enough leftovers for another meal. Sunday's turkey dinner can turn into a Wednesday-night Chinese feast of turkey lo mein, or turkey à la king, for instance.

Healthy Snacks to Have on Hand When You're Not There

Snacking itself is not a bad habit, only eating the sugar-filled junk that is usually handed out to hungry kids is. So, instead of looking to TV commercials for snack ideas, find snack foods that will supplement the healthy fare kids are all too apt to turn down at mealtimes. One important step is simply not to buy soda pop, foods that boast sugar first on the list of ingredients, and other high-calorie, high-fat, high-sodium snack foods, however "vitamin-enriched" or "vitamin-fortified" or "natural" they claim to be.

Keep your kitchen supplied with fresh fruits and vegetables, dairy products, whole-grain breads, and cereals. Easily available year around—and less expensive than heavily advertised junk foods—are apples, bananas, cheese, yogurt, unsalted dry-roasted peanuts, granola, peanut butter, dried fruit (raisins, prunes, apricots, dates), carrots, celery, whole-grain breads, unsweetened dry cereals, wheat germ, popcorn (unsalted and unbuttered is best), frozen fruit juices, herb teas, and milk. These ought to be staples, on hand at all times, ready for instant munching or for combining with other ingredients into wholesome snacks. Here are some ideas (starred items can be made ahead and left for the starving masses after school; all can be made by an older child):

Peanut Butter Lollipop

Peel a raw carrot, trim the ends, and stick it into the peanut butter jar for an instant "lollipop."

Yogurt Pops*

Mix 1 cup plain or lemon yogurt with ¼ cup frozen lemonade concentrate. Freeze in popsicle molds or in small paper cups with popsicle sticks.

Banana Delights*

Slice bananas into half-inch rounds, spread with peanut butter, and sprinkle with wheat germ. Put the slices on a cookie sheet and freeze. When they are frozen, store them in a plastic bag and let the kids eat them directly from the freezer.

Gorp*

Everyone's recipe varies, but the idea's the same: a mixture of nuts, seeds, dried fruits, and cereals that makes a tasty, nutritious snack. Your recipe might include peanuts, sunflower seeds, raw cashew nuts, almonds, currants, chopped dates, wheat germ, carob chips, and granola. Keep a stash mixed and stored in a canister or plastic bag. In the unlikely event it lasts more than a couple of days, store in the refrigerator.

Peanut Butter Balls*

Combine ½ cup peanut butter, ½ cup powdered milk, ¼ cup wheat germ, and ¼ cup honey. Form into balls and roll in wheat germ. Store in the refrigerator.

Applesauce*

There's nothing in the world like homemade applesauce, and it's a snap to make. Peel and core at least half a dozen Macintosh apples. Cut them into quarters and put them in a saucepan with 1 cup water. Cover and cook over a low heat, stirring occasionally until the apples are very soft and begin to form a sauce. Mash them with a potato masher, add brown sugar, cinnamon, and nutmeg to taste, and store in a covered bowl in the refrigerator when cooled.

Homemade Granola

Much better than the store-bought variety, this granola mix can be adjusted to fit your family's particular taste preferences. You might like less coconut and more oats or want to eliminate the sunflower seeds. However you adjust it, it makes a delicious and healthy snack that kids love.

3 cups oats	½ cup honey
1 cup sunflower seeds	½ cup vegetable oil
1 cup flaked or shredded coconut	1 tablespoon vanilla
1 cup coarsely chopped cashews or blanched almonds	¾ teaspoon ground allspice
½ cup packed brown sugar	½ teaspoon salt

Preheat the oven to 325 degrees. Mix the oats, sunflower seeds, coconut, and cashews in a large bowl. Mix the remaining ingredients; toss with the oat mixture until evenly coated. Spread in two ungreased 15 ½ x 10 ½ x 1-inch jelly roll pans. Bake uncovered, stirring frequently, until golden brown, about 30 minutes; cool. Store in a tightly covered container no longer than two months.

Peanut Butter Bars

If you make a batch of granola, there are other things to do with it besides eating it by the handful or in bowls with milk. This easy recipe is just one example.

- ½ cup light corn syrup
- ⅔ cup creamy peanut butter
- 3 cups granola

Heat the corn syrup to boiling in a 2-quart pot. Boil 1 minute; remove from heat. Stir in the peanut butter until smooth. Stir in the granola. Pat the mixture onto a greased 9 x 9 x 2-inch baking pan with a buttered spatula. Let stand one hour. Cut into bars and store in the refrigerator.

What to Do When Your Kid Won't Drink Milk or Eat Vegies

Tests have shown that, given a chance to help themselves to a wide variety of foods, in the long run, toddlers choose nutritious foods over junk. Older kids seem to have less reliable instincts. Whether the rebellion begins at two or three or when the child is older, the day eventually arrives when your cheerful cherub pushes away the milk and vegies with a resounding "Yuk!" (There is no recorded instance of the same treatment ever being given to ice cream or chocolate chip cookies.)

DRINKING MILK

Milk is an excellent food, but there are times when kids adamantly refuse to drink a drop. Before you resort to chocolate milk, try some of these suggestions:

1. Make a rule that milk is *the only* beverage served with lunch and dinner.

2. If necessary, make the servings smaller—temporarily. Use baby cups or small juice glasses. As the rule gets accepted, slip in larger cups and glasses.

3. Buy a new drinking cup with a lid and straw, or buy some crazy straws, any little trick that will make drinking milk fun.

4. Sneak milk in wherever you can—oatmeal, meatloaf, scalloped potatoes. Add dry powdered milk to baked goods. Make milk shakes in the blender with milk, a banana, and an ice cube. Try warm milk and honey or Ovaltine. And serve plenty of cottage cheese and yogurt.

(If your child *loves* to drink milk, be sure it is not at the expense of other essential nutrients: Three 8-ounce glasses of milk a day should be the maximum allowed.)

EATING VEGIES

Vegetables are important sources of vitamins and minerals. Fortunately there are many of them to choose from, and many fruits offer similar nutritional value. Just remember to include at least one vegie high in vitamin A (carrots, spinach, squash, sweet potatoes) and one high in vitamin C (broccoli, green peppers, potatoes, tomatoes) every day. To encourage vegetable eating:

1. Cook a variety of vegetables. Don't fall into the trap of always cooking peas because that's all they'll eat.

2. Make a three-bite rule to keep them tasting. Eventually they'll like something.

3. Always have raw vegetable snacks on hand, particularly just before dinner when they're sure to be hungry.

4. Be sneaky. Vegetables can be chopped up and slipped into shepherd's pie, meatballs, even hamburgers. Or add pureed vegetables to soups and gravies. Many a kid who'd never touch eggplant if he knew what it was loves eggplant parmesan. Kids who "hate spinach" but love salads may never guess what that dark green "lettuce" is.

5. Try novelty. Kids seem to love any food if they can have it in a state it was not intended to be eaten in. They'll refuse vegies in any normal form and then devour a plate of frozen succotash.

6. Make mealtime educational and fun.

- Don't overwhelm your kid with huge portions.
- Don't require a totally clean plate at every meal.
- Don't push seconds because you don't want to bother storing leftovers.
- Ignore the "Yuks" or simply say, "I know it's not your favorite, but please try some of it anyway."
- Don't let arguments about food take over.
- Make mealtimes together pleasant family experiences. Talk about the day's events. Play word games. Plan future outings or parties. Tell them about what they were like as babies or about your own childhood. Then act surprised and say, "Now where did all that food go?"

HELPFUL BOOKS

Healthy Babies, Happy Kids by Stanley A. Cohen (Delilah Books)
How to Help Your Child Eat Right by Antoinette Hatfield and Peggy Stanton (Acropolis Books)
The Taming of the C.A.N.D.Y. Monster by Vicki Lansky (Meadowbrook Press)
No-Nonsense Nutrition for Kids by Annette Natow and Jo-Ann Heslin (McGraw-Hill)
The Well Child Book by Mike Samuels and Nancy Samuels (Summit Books)
What's to Eat? And Other Questions [illegible] Ask About Food, U.S. Gov't. Printing Office, Washington, D.C. [illegible] [illegible]r ages nine to twelve)
Kids Are What They Eat by Betty [illegible] Si Kamen (Arco)

Doctoring Canned or Frozen Foods

Frozen and canned foods are a mainstay of the American diet, and they figure prominently in the working woman's kitchen. Food manufacturers have made great strides in improving the taste of their products, but there are still some tricks you can use to make these quick and easy meal aids even better.

---

1. Purée leftover vegetables and add them to canned soup for a richer, more flavorful soup.

2. Frozen fish sticks will taste much better if you squeeze on lots of fresh lemon juice and provide homemade tartar sauce for dipping.

3. Mix spaghetti sauce from a jar with dried oregano, a couple of tablespoons of olive oil, and sautéed garlic for a real home-cooked flavor.

4. Add extra mozzarella cheese, pepperoni, or sautéed mushrooms to frozen pizza before heating.

5. Frozen Mexican food entrées can be spiced up with cumin, chili powder, and pickled hot peppers. Grated cheddar cheese sprinkled on top before heating also adds an authentic touch.

6. Make homemade hollandaise sauce for frozen broccoli spears to spruce up a drab winter meal.

7. Canned or frozen beans can be livened up with minced onion and slivered almonds that have been sautéed in a bit of butter. Then add the cooked beans and sauté for a minute or two before serving. A grind of fresh pepper will make the beans even more tasty.

8. Frozen waffles or pancake mix can taste almost like your own if you add fresh strawberries or blueberries to the waffles and mashed banana to the pancakes. Real maple syrup also adds a special touch to breakfast fare.

9. Doctor canned tuna fish with capers and lemon juice, chopped onion, green pepper, and scallions.

10. Frozen pies can stand in for a homemade dessert if you add a scoop of ice cream or your own whipped cream topping and grate some chocolate shavings over the topping.

11. Canned black beans served over brown rice can be a healthy side dish to any meal. To add a special south-of-the-border touch, top with chopped onions and sour cream.

12. Use canned beef stew mixed with sour cream for a quick beef Stroganoff. Serve over egg noodles and sprinkle with chopped parsley.

Common Food Additives Explained

If you're like most consumers, reading package labels has become part of food shopping. Concern over the quantities of preservatives, chemical additives, food colors, and artificial flavors in our foods has made knowing ingredients important. But how many of the additives do you recognize? Do you know if they are safe? An explanation of the most common food additives is given below.

- **Artificial Color.** Over 90 percent of food colors added to food are artificial. Most of these are derived from coal tar, which is produced when coal is heated in a vacuum. When the tar is purified and combined with other chemicals, coal-tar dyes are produced, which supply artificial colors for processing food. These colors are found in baked products, ice cream, sausages, candies, dessert mixes, and beverages.
- **Butylated Hydroxyanisole (BHA).** This additive is a preservative and antioxidant used in almost every processed food containing fat or oil to prevent the fat from becoming rancid. It is added to breakfast cereals, chewing gum, convenience foods, vegetable oil, shortening, sweet potatoes, potato flakes, enriched rice, potato chips, candy, ice cream, ices, and a host of other foods. BHA is a waxy solid and is insoluble in water. It is actually an unnecessary additive, and some brands of vegetable oil and potato don't use it. BHA has been tested and found to cause no adverse effects in animals.
- **Calcium Phosphate (Dibasic and Monobasic).** These phosphates are white, odorless powders used as dough conditioners and firming agents. Dibasic calcium phosphate improves breads, rolls, buns, and cereal flours. Monobasic calcium phosphate is also added to bread, rolls, and buns, as well as to artificially sweetened fruit jelly, canned potatoes, canned sweet peppers, and canned tomatoes.
- **Gum Arabic (also known as Acacia, Acacia Gum, Gum Senegal).** Acacia, the source of gum arabic, is a tasteless, odorless dried gummy extract taken from the acacia tree. It is used as a thickener for candies, jellies, glazes, and chewing gum, as a foam stabilizer in beer and soft drinks, to aid the dissolving of citrus oils in drinks, and to thicken the texture of ice cream. Though it has a low oral toxicity, it has not been fully studied to determine whether it can cause cancer, birth defects, or mutations.
- **Hydrolyzed Vegetable Protein (HVP).** HVP is used as a flavor enhancer in gravy and sauce mixes, beef stew, canned chili, hot dogs, instant soup, and bouillon cubes. It consists of soybean protein that has been reduced by chemical means to amino acids. Though HVP is generally regarded as safe, the FDA has found that commercially prepared baby foods with HVP contain an amino acid that affects the baby's growth. Further studies on HVP's effects on children and adults have been recommended.
- **Niacinamide (Vitamin B3, Niacin, Nicotinic Acid, Nicotinamide).** This nontoxic additive is an odorless powder that plays a role in converting food into energy. Niacinamide is found in prepared breakfast cereals, peanut butter, baby cereals, enriched flours, macaroni, noodles, bread and rolls.
- **Polysorbate 80 (Sorbitan Monoleate).** This substance is added to frozen desserts, breads and doughnuts, artificial whipped cream, non-dairy coffee creamers, pickles, candy, ice cream, and beverages. Though controversial in the 1950s, it has been determined to be safe.
- **Sodium Nitrite.** This chemical is toxic in levels slightly higher than those used in food. Sodium nitrite can combine with certain natural stomach and food chemicals to form nitrosamines, which are cancer-causing agents. Despite these facts, sodium nitrite is valuable because it prevents bacteria growth, which causes botulism poisoning. It unifies the color and improves the taste of cured meats, such as bacon, bologna, hot dogs, sausages, smoked and cured salmon, and meat spreads. The government permits 200 ppm of sodium nitrite in cured foods. However, sodium nitrite is believed to play some role as a cancer-causing agent by many health and nutrition professionals.

If you have played your cards right and encouraged your child to help in the kitchen from the time he was a toddler, it is not a big step to having him prepare meals on his own. If, on the other hand, your child is not familiar with what goes on in the kitchen, let him begin under your tutelage to learn the basic techniques and safety rules he will need to know. When both of you feel he is ready, start with breakfast—his own while you sleep late on a weekend morning or a breakfast the whole family can enjoy—then graduate to lunches and, eventually, dinners.

BREAKFAST

* The easiest—cold cereal and milk—can be tackled by a three-year-old. Or have him spread a banana with peanut butter.
* Soft-boiled eggs and toast require only a timer or a child who can read the numbers on a digital clock.
* Scrambled eggs are easy, too, but a bigger cleanup unless you use a Teflon pan.
* Old-fashioned oatmeal is easy and healthy, whether made with milk or water.
* The *pièce de résistance*—French toast—requires only the simplest skills a five- or six-year-old can master. At these ages, however, you will want to be there to turn the stove on and off.

LUNCH

Have your child begin preparing his own lunches when he starts taking meals to school. The usual fare—sandwiches—is easy; it's the practice and taking on the responsibility that count. Encourage some variety—you can limit peanut butter as an ingredient to once a week. Teach him to make tuna salad and chicken salad from leftovers (you do the cutting up of the chicken).

Once he has gained confidence and competence, have him do a weekend lunch for the family, perhaps with a friend over to share the fun. He could make:

* Open-faced tuna salad sandwiches with melted cheese (A toaster oven comes in handy for this.)
* Pizza—from scratch. He'll have to start an hour and a half ahead of time so the dough can rise.
* Hamburgers
* Ravioli or a macaroni dish
* A spinach, bacon, and mushroom salad
* A chef's salad

DINNER

Coordinating several dishes so that all arrive at the dinner table at the same time is a skill that takes time to acquire. Beginners do better with one-dish dinners, or two dishes—one that bakes while the other is being prepared. Your child will need some practice with you around before he is ready to work entirely alone. Your best bets are:

* Stews that require no browning, such as a beef daube or carbonnade or chicken fricassee (which easily becomes chicken pie)

* Hearty soups—borscht, lentil soup with frankfurters or sausage, bouillabaisse, chicken vegetable soup with rice, pasta and kidney bean soup. Canned stock, frozen vegetables, and cooked meat leftovers can reduce the steps involved and the cooking time.
* Meatloaf accompanied by a salad
* Chicken quarters or pork chops baked on top of a layer of rice and mixed frozen vegetables in canned chicken stock
* Pasta dishes—fettuccine Alfredo, spaghetti with meat sauce, macaroni and cheese
* Casseroles—scalloped tuna or salmon; any cooked meat, vegetable, pasta or rice, and sauce combinations—whatever your (or his) favorites are

TIPS

* Teach your child to handle knives, but let him use them only under your supervision until you are quite confident of his abilities.
* For recipes that call for cut vegetables, cut them yourself ahead of time and wrap them in plastic. Peeled potatoes left any length of time should be kept in a bowl of water. Or buy frozen or canned vegetables that are already sliced.
* Vegetables may be peeled with a peeler—show him how to cut away from his body—or cooked with their skins on.
* Parsley, green onions, chives, and other fresh herbs may be cut with scissors.
* Cheese may be sliced with a peeler or grater. Sliced cheese may be cut with scissors or torn.
* To grate safely, put a rubber band around the item to be grated and keep fingers behind the rubber band.
* Provide very large mixing bowls—there will be less spatter and mess.
* Use wooden spoons for stove-top stirring.
* Teach him to hold the pot handle with a pot holder while he stirs.
* Keep all pot handles pointed to the side of the stove.
* You will decide when your child is ready to turn the stove on and off to do real cooking. For one thing, he needs to be tall enough to see what is in the pots without standing on anything.
* You will decide when your child is ready to move pans in and out of the oven. Provide mitts for him to use.
* Avoid recipes requiring hot oil that might spatter, boiling syrups, or the carrying of heavy pots of boiling water to the sink for draining. Bacon may be broiled in the oven, pasta taken from boiling water with a slotted spoon or a wooden spaghetti fork.
* Select easy recipes you like and simplify them further if you can. Write out your instructions in clear, easy steps on a large sheet of paper he can stick on the refrigerator or a cupboard door.
* Reward his efforts with a good cookbook. Many children's cookbooks are cute and gimmicky and full of recipes for sweets or simple items any child who can read already knows how to make. Among the better ones (with age suggestions, when provided by the publisher) are:

What to Do When Your Mom or Dad Says . . . "Make Your Own Breakfast and Lunch!" by Joy W. Berry (Living Skills), grades K–6

Step-by-Step Kids' Cookbook (Better Homes and Gardens), grades 3–6

Betty Crocker's Cookbook for Boys and Girls (Western Publishers)

Cooking Adventures for Kids by Sharon Cadwallader (Houghton Mifflin)

Easy to Make, Good to Eat by Martha O. Condit (Scholastic), grades K–6

Let's Make Soup and *Let's Make Bread* by Hannah Lyons Johnson (Lothrop, Lee & Shepard), grades 3–5

Clarion Cookbook for Boys and Girls by Eva Moore (Houghton Mifflin), grades 1–3

Kids Are Natural Cooks by Parents' Nursery School (Houghton Mifflin)

Kids' Cooking by Aileen Paul and Arthur Hawkins (Doubleday), grades 3–6

A Cookbook for Girls and Boys by Irma S. Rombauer (Bobbs-Merrill), grades 4–7

You Can Cook: How to Make Good Food for Your Family and Friends by Paula Dunaway Schwartz (Atheneum), grades 5 and up

* If you haven't the time, patience, or interest to teach your child to cook yourself, look around for cooking courses for children offered after school or on weekends at schools and Y's. Choose courses that focus on nutrition and practical skills.

Lunch Box Treats to Tote and Eat

Lunch boxes: Kids love them, moms hate the chore of filling them daily with balanced meals that kids like. It's easiest just to grab the bread and peanut butter, and a piece of fruit, and fill the thermos with milk. What's harder is coming up with new ideas for variety and balance. Why not have some fun and give your kids a surprise, too? Try these:

- Cold leftovers can make splendid lunches: a slice of meatloaf with ketchup, sliced chicken *au mayonnaise*, pasta salad with crunchy raw vegetables, baked beans spread on toast.
- Dress up the fruit: Put an apple on a stick just for a lark. Make fruit kabobs with chunks of pineapple, strawberries, and orange slices. Try something exotic—kiwi fruit or pomegranate.
- Buy a wide-mouth thermos and use it for hot soup or reheated leftovers like macaroni and cheese or stew.
- Raise kids' vegetable quotient with sliced raw carrots, zucchini, cauliflower, and broccoli and a yogurt dip; vegetable kabobs; or tomato juice instead of milk to drink. Stuff celery with peanut butter or ricotta cheese. Make cream-cheese sandwiches with red pepper slices instead of jelly.
- Make tuna salad or chicken salad at night to have ready to spread on bread in the morning.
- Stuff sandwich fillings into pita bread for a change. Or use rolls, bagels, bialys.
- Bake and freeze a batch of whole-wheat banana-bread or zucchini-bread muffins, then occasionally pop one from freezer to lunch box as you assemble lunches in the morning.
- Boost their calcium intake with cups of yogurt, cottage cheese, or homemade tapioca pudding.

Hamburgers are every kid's favorite. Fortunately, they're easy for mothers, too. Here are some hints to make your burgers taste better, look better, and cook better.

1. When making hamburger patties to freeze, make a nickel-size hole in the middle of each patty. This way, you won't have to thaw the hamburger before cooking, and the hole will close up when you cook it. When wrapping burgers for freezing, place sheets of wax paper between each one for easier separation and defrosting.
2. To make perfectly round burgers, press down on the meat with an empty can and trim off the excess.
3. Rather than just forming the patties and cooking them, add some ingredients to your burgers before cooking to make them taste better: a slice of hard-boiled egg in the center; bread crumbs and an egg mixed into the meat; spices such as garlic, salt and pepper, and oregano; minced onion.
4. For a new and different taste, cook your burgers in Worcestershire sauce.
5. Rather than frying burgers, broil them. They'll cook fast, taste better, and save on messy cleanups.
6. Serve your hamburgers topped with fried onions.
7. Marinate your burgers in soy sauce for an hour and broil over charcoal or in the oven for a Hawaiian treat.
8. Stuff your burgers with one (or more) of the following: 2 teaspoons grated or shredded cheese; chopped fresh or canned mushrooms that have been sautéed in butter; sautéed onions; moistened packaged bread stuffing mixed with ½ teaspoon butter.
9. Instead of using hamburger buns, use French or Italian bread, or English muffins. Shape patties to fit. Add cheese, sliced tomatoes, onion, and bottled French or Italian dressing.
10. Add an envelope of onion soup mix to 1 pound of hamburger meat, shape the patties, and fry as usual.
11. Make a pot of chili and top each burger with a scoop or two for added flavor.
12. Top each burger with guacamole dip (made from avocado) for a real Mexican treat.

TAKE-OUT TIMESAVERS

All working moms—and a good many at-home moms, too—no matter how well organized, have days when the cupboard is bare and a trip to the grocery store plus cooking is more than they can manage. Unlike Old Mother Hubbard, however, modern moms have an easy out: calling up or stopping by for take-out food. But is it healthy? Many of the convenient, moderately priced fast foods kids like are high in carbohydrates, animal fats, sugar, and salt, and low in fiber and some vitamins and minerals. To assuage your guilt, pick the healthiest fare available and round out the meal with fresh fruits, vegetables, and other high-fiber, low-fat, low-calorie foods, even if it means an extra stop at a produce stand. Here are some tips:

* **Hamburgers.** Order plain single hamburgers or hamburgers with tomato and lettuce. Skip the French fries and order coleslaw instead. To balance out the meal, drink low-fat milk and serve cantaloupe, apricots, or peaches for dessert.

* **Pizza.** One of the best take-out foods, pizza can provide many wholesome nutrients if you make the right choices. Order whole-wheat crust if it is available. Opt for thin crust over a thick one. Pass up the pepperoni or sausage; ask for red and green peppers instead. A green salad with a simple lemon-juice dressing will complete the meal.

* **Chicken.** Spit-roasted chicken from the deli is a wiser choice than fried. Buy a Waldorf or a "health" salad to provide vitamins and fiber. Have vanilla yogurt for dessert.

* **Tacos.** Soft tacos are lower in fat than fried tacos. Choose bean, cheese, or chicken fillings rather than beef. Take lots of lettuce and tomatoes and an order of guacamole. Finish the meal in typical Mexican fashion with custard.

* **Chinese food.** Avoid the fried dumplings, egg rolls, and barbecued spareribs; have soup as an appetizer instead. Pick dishes with an assortment of vegetables. Ask that no MSG be added to the food. Sliced oranges make a refreshing end to the meal.

* **Fish.** It's hard to get away from fried foods here, unless steamed clams or shrimp or shellfish salads are available. Or make a meal of clam chowder. For side dishes, pick coleslaw and corn-on-the-cob over French fries and hush puppies. Serve fruit for dessert.

Last-Minute Guests

Friends from out of town call unexpectedly; they're just passing through overnight. You'd love to say, "Come to dinner!" But can you pull it all together in time? Of course you can. Impromptu entertaining is fun precisely because it is planned on the spur of the moment. No one expects elaborate preparations or formal elegance. Still, it's nice to have some ideas up your sleeve to make the evening special. Try these:

- On your way home from work you can pick up a steak for quick broiling, a loaf of crusty bread, and fresh greens for a salad. Buy flowers, candles, and colorful napkins if you've none on hand—they'll help make the meal memorable.
- If you need to shop for food, pick a specialty store if it will take less time than the supermarket. Buy something elegant that requires little advance preparation and cooks quickly: whole trout, soft-shell crabs, or fresh pasta.
- Make a meal that will give your guests a part in the work, like a shrimp boil: You boil the shrimp in beer and herbs, and everyone shells his own at the table. Serve a spicy sauce or drawn butter to dip the shrimp in; corn-on-the-cob and a salad can complete the meal.
- Don't always think *dinner*. Invite your friends for dessert and coffee or cheese and wine after dinner. Or, if it's a weekend, have them for breakfast or brunch the next day.
- If time is really short, get a take-out meal from a Chinese restaurant, a pizzeria, or a gourmet deli. After all, you and your friends want to visit—they'll understand if you don't come up with a last-minute home-cooked meal.

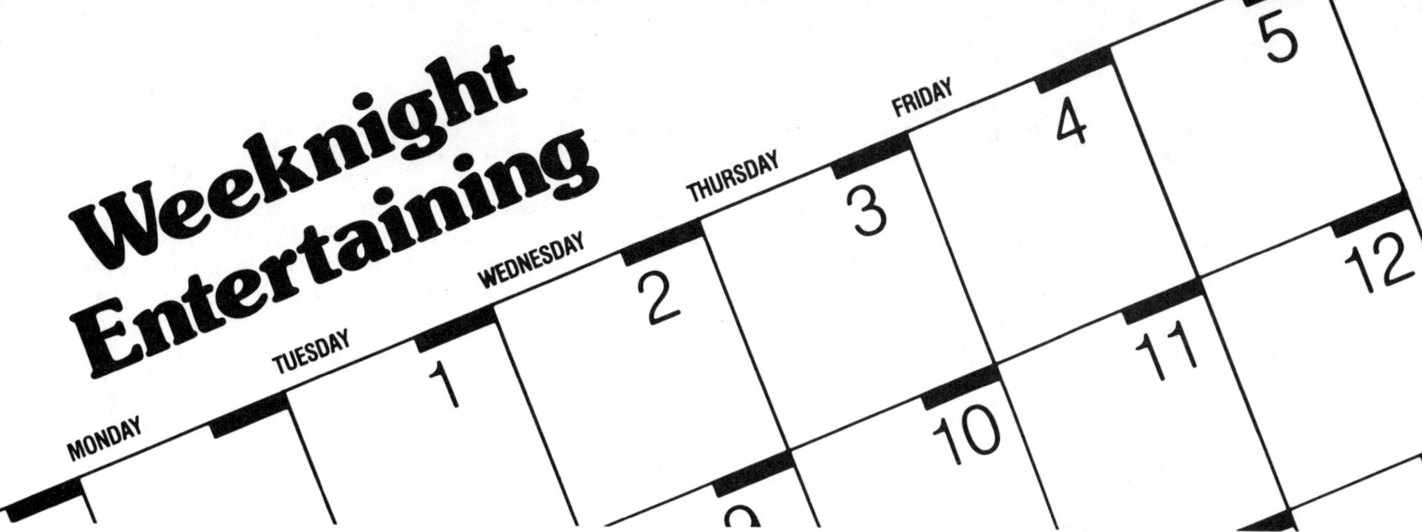

Being a working mom doesn't mean you have to give up entertaining friends at home, but it does mean you have to plan carefully when you do, so that you don't throw your busy schedule completely out of kilter.

Make Entertaining Part of Your Routine

Plan to entertain on a regular basis, say, one evening a month. Decide which evening works best for you, choosing a day that is usually the least stressful at work or that allows the maximum preparation time. An evening early in the week, for example, is often less busy, and you can use the weekend before for shopping or advance preparations. Pick an hour that will mesh smoothly with bedtime routines. You may want your children already tucked into bed, or they may be permitted to come down in nightgowns and pajamas to greet the guests and serve peanuts on the condition that they go quietly up to bed on their own when the time comes.

Limit the Size of Your Parties

Small parties are easier to prepare for, and they allow a real exchange of conversation. A dinner party for four or six is easy to manage. Neither the preparation nor the cleanup is overwhelming, and you will be more relaxed and will enjoy the evening more than if you take on ten or twelve dinner guests at a time. Cocktail parties and after-dinner parties can be larger, but even these are more fun for you and more intimate if you keep the numbers down.

Keep the Menu Simple

A hearty soup or stew in winter, a nourishing salad in summer, a simple roast—ham, beef, turkey, or chicken—or a backyard barbecue can make a good meal to share with guests. Pick recipes you can prepare in advance for some if not all of the dishes to be served. You don't need to plan a new menu for each event: If you come up with a winning combination, use it often—just write down in a guest book who was served what and when. Take advantage of seasonal changes to buy the freshest produce. What could be easier to prepare and draw more raves from your guests than the first steamed asparagus of spring?

Make It Elegant

An understated elegance enhances dining pleasure, and it isn't difficult to achieve if you buy yourself a good permanent press tablecloth and napkins—ones that really don't need ironing—or send your linen cloth and napkins out to be laundered after each dinner. Keep the right number of place settings and the serving pieces of your china and silver where they are easily accessible, with anti-tarnish strips in the cupboard so that you won't have to polish the silver. Or take a more informal route and perk up your everyday dishes and flatware with brightly colored straw mats and matching paper napkins. Either way, don't forget the added impact of candlelight and a centerpiece. Buy candles by the box so that you have them on hand. Grow begonias on a sunny windowsill, and you'll always have a supply of flowers. Or arrange seasonal fruits or vegetables in a basket.

Helpful Books

The Elegant but Easy Cookbook by Marian Fox Burros and Lois Levine (Macmillan)

Ready When You Are: Made-Ahead Meals for Entertaining by Elizabeth Schneider Colchie (Crown)

The After-Work Entertaining Cookbook by Ceil Dyer (David McKay)

The Night-Before Cookbook by Paul Rubenstein and Leslie Rubenstein (Macmillan)

7 Theme Dinners for Sunday Nights

Sunday-night supper is usually a good family time, often a simple soup-and-sandwiches meal after a day's outing. But a more elaborate meal can also be fun, especially if you spend your family day preparing it together. It's a good time to try new recipes, learn about new foods, and teach the kids cooking techniques. To make the learning experience even richer, tie the meal to a theme. Plan to serve dishes from a particular region, from a foreign country, or from a distant time. Let an older child look up information about the place or period to share with the rest of the family. Make a flag or other appropriate centerpiece and simple costumes or accessories to wear. A record or tape could provide the right background music. The library can supply books for after-dinner stories. Here are some ideas (all recipes yield approximately four servings):

1. WAY DOWN YONDER IN NEW ORLEANS

Menu: Shrimp Creole, Rice, Pecan Pie

Shrimp Creole
Preparation time: 30 minutes

2 stalks celery, with leaves
1 medium sweet red pepper
1 medium green pepper
½ pound okra
1 medium onion
1 tablespoon vegetable oil
1 16-ounce can crushed tomatoes
1 pound shelled shrimp

Cut the celery, peppers, okra, and onion into bite-size pieces. Heat the oil in a large frying pan and sauté the vegetables for 10 minutes. Add the tomatoes. Cover and simmer over low heat until the okra is tender, 5 to 10 minutes. Add the shrimp and cook until they turn pink, about 5 minutes, or, if frozen, cook according to package directions. Serve with boiled rice.

Pecan Pie
Preparation time: 15 minutes; baking time: 1 hour

1 cup brown sugar
2 tablespoons flour
1 tablespoon butter
1 cup dark corn syrup
3 eggs, beaten
1 teaspoon vanilla
1 cup pecan halves
1 unbaked pie crust

Preheat the oven to 325 degrees. Mix the sugar and flour; cream with the butter. Add the syrup and eggs; beat well. Stir in the vanilla and nuts. Pour the mixture into the pie crust. Bake until set, 50 to 60 minutes.

2. A NOCHE MEXICANA

Menu: Guacamole, South of the Border Salad, Chicken Enchiladas

Guacamole (Avocado Dip)
Preparation time: 15 minutes

3 ripe avocados, peeled
2 tablespoons minced onion
1 tablespoon chili powder
1 large ripe tomato, chopped
Lemon juice
Tortilla chips

Mash the avocados; stir in the onion and chili powder. Add the tomato and mix until smooth. Sprinkle with lemon juice to prevent discoloration. Serve chilled with crisp tortilla chips.

South of the Border Salad
Preparation time: 20 minutes; chilling time: 1–2 hours

½ cup vegetable oil
⅓ cup red wine vinegar
1½ teaspoons sugar
1 teaspoon salt
1 cucumber, sliced
1 teaspoon chili powder
1 small clove garlic, pressed
2 quarts assorted salad greens
2 green onions, thinly sliced

In a small jar, combine the first six ingredients; cover and shake well. Chill for 1 to 2 hours. Break the greens into bite-size pieces in a wooden bowl. Add the cucumber and onions. Toss with the dressing.

Chicken Enchiladas

Preparation time: 40 minutes; baking time: 18 minutes

2 3-ounce packages cream cheese
1 tablespoon vinegar
⅓ cup sour cream
3 whole chicken breasts, cooked and shredded
1 teaspoon prepared mustard
¼ teaspoon salt
⅛ teaspoon garlic powder
¼ cup ripe olives, pitted and chopped
1 small green pepper, chopped
Tabasco Sauce
Vegetable oil
8 corn tortillas
1 1-pound can stewed tomatoes
1 8-ounce can tomato sauce
2 avocados
¾ cup shredded cheddar cheese

Preheat the oven to 400 degrees. Soften the cream cheese with the vinegar; mix in the sour cream, chicken, mustard, salt, garlic powder, olives, green pepper, and a few drops of Tabasco. Heat about 1 tablespoon oil in a skillet; sauté the tortillas, one at a time, lightly on each side; add oil as necessary. The tortillas should not be crisp. Drain on paper towels. In the same skillet, heat the tomatoes and tomato sauce with 2 tablespoons oil and a few drops of Tabasco. Spoon the chicken mixture into the center of the tortillas. Spoon 1 tablespoon of the tomato mixture over the chicken; roll up the tortillas. Place in a greased shallow 2-quart baking dish. Pour the remaining tomato mixture over the top. Cover loosely with foil. Bake for 15 minutes. Meanwhile, cut the avocados lengthwise into halves; remove the pits and skin. Cut into lengthwise slices and arrange on top of the enchiladas. Sprinkle with cheddar cheese. Return to the oven for about 3 minutes, until the cheese melts. Serve at once.

3. A CHINESE BANQUET

Menu: Egg Rolls with Sweet and Sour Sauce, Oriental Broccoli, Walnut Chicken, Rice

Egg Rolls

Preparation time: 30 minutes

1 tablespoon vegetable oil
½ pound chicken breast, minced
½ pound shrimp, minced
8 green onions, minced
1 cup bean sprouts, chopped
½ cup water chestnuts, finely chopped
1 tablespoon grated ginger root
1½ tablespoons soy sauce
1 pound egg roll skins
Oil for deep frying
Sweet and Sour Sauce (see below)

Heat the tablespoon of oil in a large skillet. Add the chicken, shrimp, and onion and stir fry for 3 minutes. Add the bean sprouts, water chestnuts, ginger root, and soy sauce and stir fry briefly.

To make the rolls, spread 1 tablespoon of the filling along one side of each skin. Fold over the edges of the skin and roll up like a jelly roll, tucking in the ends. Seal the rolls with a little water. Heat the oil in a deep fryer to 370 degrees. Fry the rolls for about 6 minutes, or until the skins are crisp, bubbly, and brown. Cut each roll into three pieces. Serve with Sweet and Sour Sauce.

Sweet and Sour Sauce

Preparation time: 15 minutes

½ cup brown sugar
½ cup cider vinegar
2 tablespoons corn starch
2 tablespoons soy sauce
1½ cups pineapple juice

Combine all the ingredients in a small saucepan. Cook over medium heat, stirring often, for about 10 minutes, or until the sauce is thick and clear.

Oriental Broccoli

Preparation time: 20 minutes

6 medium-size fresh broccoli stalks
Vegetable oil
1 clove garlic, split
1 medium sweet red pepper, thinly sliced (about ½ cup)
3 green onions with tops, sliced diagonally into ½-inch pieces
2 to 3 tablespoons soy sauce
Salt
Toasted sesame seeds

Separate the broccoli flowerets from the stems. Thinly slice the stems, discarding the tough portion of each stalk. In a heavy frying pan, heat enough oil to cover the bottom. Add the broccoli stems, garlic, and pepper. Cover and cook quickly until partially tender, stirring occasionally. Add the broccoli flowerets and onion and cook until tender but still crisp. Season with soy sauce and salt. Garnish with sesame seeds.

Walnut Chicken

Preparation time: 45 minutes

3 large whole chicken breasts, skinned and boned
¼ cup vegetable oil
1 cup walnut halves
1 5-ounce can bamboo shoots, drained
4 tablespoons cornstarch
¾ cup chicken broth
2 tablespoons soy sauce

Cut the chicken into 1-inch pieces. Heat the oil in a large skillet; add the nuts and toast lightly. Remove the nuts; set aside. Add the chicken to the skillet and stir fry over high heat for 3 minutes. Add the bamboo shoots; continue stirring for 2 minutes. Blend the cornstarch with the chicken broth and soy sauce; add to the skillet and mix well. Reduce heat; cover and simmer 4 to 5 minutes until the chicken is tender and the sauce has thickened. Add the walnuts. Serve with boiled rice.

4. ITALIAN PASTA NIGHT

Menu: Fettuccine Alfredo, Tomato and Cucumber Salad

Fettuccine Alfredo

Preparation time: 30 minutes

1 8-ounce package fettuccine noodles
½ cup softened butter
½ cup grated parmesan cheese
⅓ cup half-and-half

Cook the noodles in 8 quarts boiling salted water until tender, 7 to 10 minutes. Drain well. Place the noodles in a heated serving bowl. Add the butter, cheese, and cream a little at a time. Toss gently after each is added. Serve immediately.

Tomato and Cucumber Salad

Preparation time: 20 minutes; chilling time: 1 hour

5 medium tomatoes, sliced
1 cucumber, thinly sliced
1 green onion, thinly sliced
3 tablespoons olive oil
2 to 3 tablespoons red wine vinegar
½ teaspoon salt
½ teaspoon dried oregano, crushed
¼ teaspoon dried basil, crushed
Freshly ground black pepper
1 tablespoon minced parsely

Layer the tomato, cucumber, and onion in a glass bowl. Combine the remaining ingredients and mix well; pour over the salad. Chill for 1 hour before serving.

5. GERMAN BAUERNSCHMAUS

Menu: Pork and Kraut Platter, Potato Pancakes

Continental Pork and Kraut Platter

Preparation time: 3 hours

1 2–3 pound smoked pork shoulder roll
1 2–3 pound boneless Boston-style pork shoulder roast
3 cups water
1 cup dry white wine
1 27-ounce can sauerkraut, drained
2 medium tart apples, cored and cut into 16 wedges
24 prunes, pitted
3 links smoked Thuringer
3 links fresh bratwurst

Place the pork roll and pork roast in a large Dutch oven. Add the water. Cover tightly and simmer for 2 hours. Remove the meat and boil the cooking liquid rapidly until reduced to 2 cups. Add the wine and sauerkraut, stirring to combine thoroughly. Place the pork roll and pork roast on top of the sauerkraut. Add the apples, prunes, Thuringer, and bratwurst. Bring to a boil. Reduce heat, cover, and simmer for 30 minutes. Remove the pork roll and pork roast. Carve into ½-inch-thick slices. Arrange the carved meat with the sausage, sauerkraut, and fruit on a heated platter.

Potato Pancakes

Preparation time: 25 minutes

3 eggs
2 tablespoons flour
1 teaspoon salt
Pinch white pepper
1 tablespoon minced onion
⅛ teaspoon nutmeg
1 12-ounce package frozen hash browns, thawed and shredded
Butter
Applesauce

Combine the eggs, flour, salt, pepper, onion, and nutmeg and mix well. Stir in the potatoes. Heat the butter in a large skillet until bubbly. For each pancake, spoon ¼ cup of the mixture into the skillet; flatten with a spatula. Fry over medium heat until golden brown on both sides, turning once. Serve with applesauce.

6. HAWAIIAN LUAU

Menu: Pineapple Chicken, Diamond Head Asparagus, Rice Mingle

Pineapple Chicken

Preparation time: 25 minutes; baking time: 1 hour, 20 minutes

- 2 broiler-fryer chickens, cut into serving pieces
- 1½ teaspoons salt
- 1 egg, lightly beaten
- 1 6-ounce can frozen pineapple juice concentrate, thawed
- 1⅓ cups fine white bread crumbs
- ¼ cup butter, melted
- 1 3½-ounce can flaked coconut

Preheat the oven to 350 degrees. Rinse the chicken pieces; pat dry with paper towel. Sprinkle the salt over both sides of the chicken. Combine the egg and pineapple concentrate in a pie plate. Combine the bread crumbs with the melted butter in another pie plate; add the coconut and mix well. Coat the chicken pieces with the pineapple mixture, then roll in the coconut mixture. Place in two foil-lined shallow baking pans. Bake for 40 minutes, then reverse the pans in the oven for even baking. Bake another 40 minutes. If the chicken browns before the end of the cooking time, cover loosely with foil and continue to bake.

Diamond Head Asparagus

Preparation time: 25 minutes

- 1½ pounds fresh asparagus
- 3 tablespoons butter
- ⅓ cup water
- ½ teaspoon seasoned salt
- 1 teaspoon soy sauce

Snap off and discard the tough ends of the asparagus stalks. Slice diagonally into bite-size pieces. Melt the butter in a large skillet. Add the water, seasoned salt, and soy sauce. When the mixture boils, add the asparagus and toss lightly. Cover; cook over medium heat for 3 to 5 minutes. Do not overcook.

Rice Mingle Preparation time: 45 minutes

- 3 cups cooked rice
- 2 green peppers, chopped
- 2 pimientos, chopped
- 2 tomatoes, peeled and cubed
- 2 tablespoons chopped onion
- 2 tablespoons chopped parsley
- 1 head Bibb lettuce
- Dressing (see below)

Combine the first six ingredients; toss with the Dressing. Line a serving dish with the lettuce leaves and place the rice salad on top. Chill before serving.

Dressing

- ¾ cup olive oil
- ¼ cup white wine vinegar
- 1½ teaspoons salt
- ½ teaspoon white pepper
- 1 clove garlic, minced

Combine all the ingredients; blend thoroughly.

7. A MEDIEVAL "SOUPER"

Menu: Game Hens with Fruit, Saffron Rice, Blancmange

Game Hens with Fruit Preparation time: 1 hour

- 2 Cornish game hens
- 1 slice white toast
- 1 cup red wine
- ½ teaspoon ground cinnamon
- Pinch cayenne pepper
- ⅛ teaspoon ground nutmeg
- 2 crushed cloves
- 1 teaspoon confectioner's sugar
- 2 tablespoons red wine vinegar
- 15 prunes
- 15 dates
- ½ cup raisins

Roast or broil the game hens. While they are cooking, break up the toast and put it in a saucepan to soak with the wine, spices, sugar, and vinegar. Pit the prunes and dates and cut them into quarters. When the hens are done, cut them into serving pieces and set them aside on a warm platter. Pour the cooking juices into the saucepan with the toast. Add all the fruit and mix well; simmer over low heat for 10 minutes. Pour the sauce over the hens. Serve with boiled rice seasoned with saffron.

Blancmange

Preparation time: 15 minutes; chilling time: 2 hours

- 1¾ cups milk
- 6 tablespoons sugar
- 5 ounces (about 1 cup) almonds, ground (may be ground in the blender or in a mortar with a pestle, in good medieval fashion)
- 1 package unflavored gelatin dissolved in ¼ cup cold water
- Grated and sliced lemon peels

Combine the milk and sugar in a saucepan and bring to a boil. Remove from heat. Sift the ground almonds into the hot milk and add the gelatin. Stir in the grated lemon peel and pour the mixture into a 2-cup bowl or mold. Chill until firm. Unmold and garnish with strips of lemon peel.

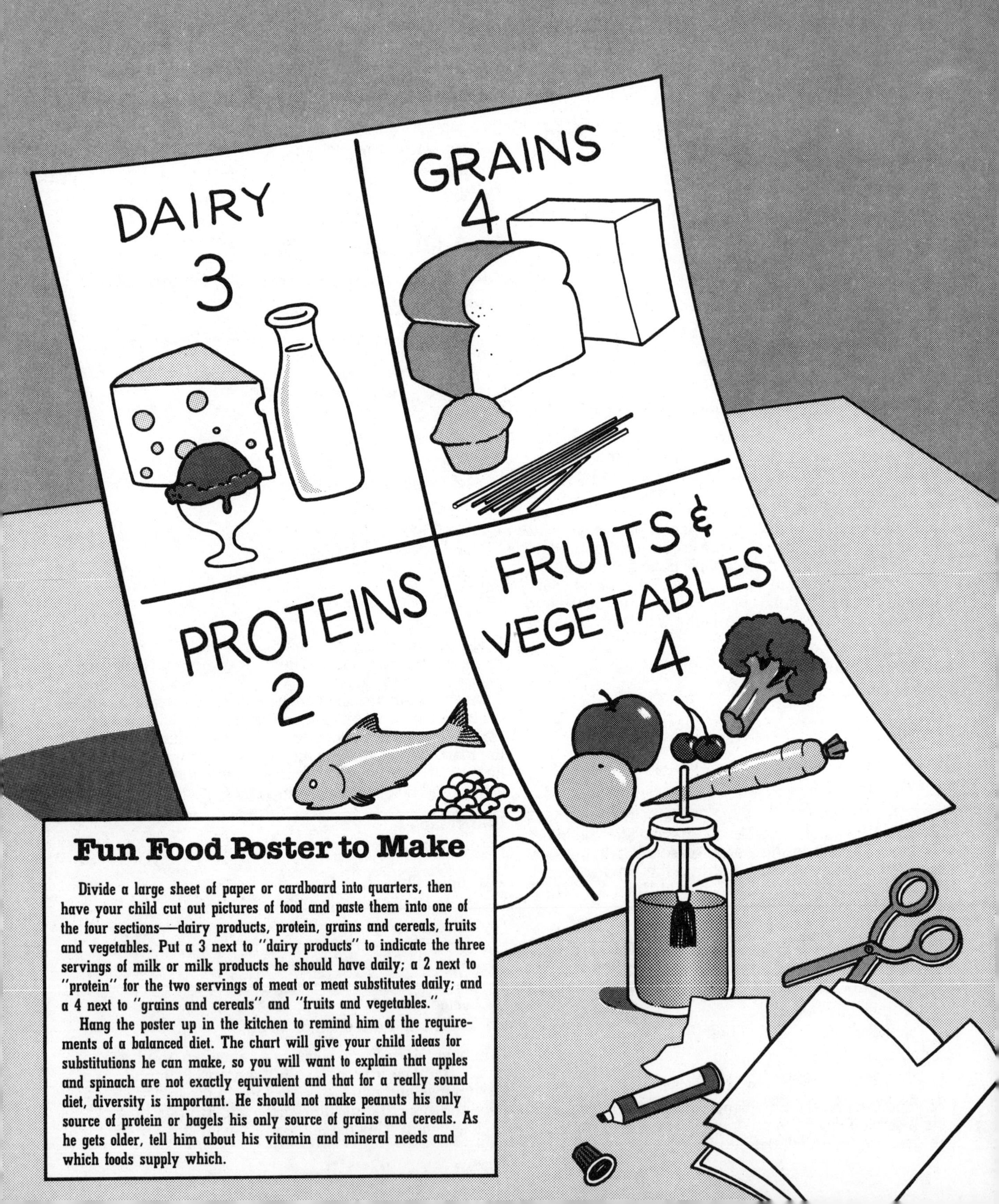

Fun Food Poster to Make

Divide a large sheet of paper or cardboard into quarters, then have your child cut out pictures of food and paste them into one of the four sections—dairy products, protein, grains and cereals, fruits and vegetables. Put a 3 next to "dairy products" to indicate the three servings of milk or milk products he should have daily; a 2 next to "protein" for the two servings of meat or meat substitutes daily; and a 4 next to "grains and cereals" and "fruits and vegetables."

Hang the poster up in the kitchen to remind him of the requirements of a balanced diet. The chart will give your child ideas for substitutions he can make, so you will want to explain that apples and spinach are not exactly equivalent and that for a really sound diet, diversity is important. He should not make peanuts his only source of protein or bagels his only source of grains and cereals. As he gets older, tell him about his vitamin and mineral needs and which foods supply which.

HEALTH

Choosing a Pediatrician

Finding the right doctor for your child is a lot like making a new friend. Your judgment and intuition play a big part in your choice. That doesn't mean the first meeting between you and your child's doctor has to be a hit-or-miss decision. There are some practical steps you can take to find satisfactory medical care for your child.

Seek recommendations. Asking for recommendations from other parents who are satisfied with their pediatricians is a good way to begin, as is asking your obstetrician or other doctors you know. First, think about what is important to you in a doctor. Write down the points that concern you most about the health care of your child. For example, you would expect to choose a doctor who is willing to answer your questions, not one who rushes patients in and out of the office, striving to keep up with a hectic schedule. And you will surely want a doctor who is responsive to phone calls, whether your child suddenly develops symptoms of some illness or a more serious emergency occurs. It is also wise to select a pediatrician who shares your views on raising children.

Interview several doctors. When you have the names of a few doctors, call their offices for appointments to interview them. Make it clear to the receptionist in each office that you are coming in for an interview only—without your child. Find out if you will be charged for a consultation or a regular office visit. There can be a difference. The purpose of the appointment from your end is to get some idea of what kind of treatment your child will be given. Prepare yourself by bringing along a list of questions to ask the doctor. If your child has special health problems, allergies, or disabilities, you'll want to know if a particular doctor is prepared to offer complete medical care.

Consider your own needs as well. You may be a very protective mother, who would insist on bringing your child to see the doctor for any health problem that *you* consider an emergency. Make sure the doctor is willing to respond to that need. Anything that is of importance to you should be explored during this interview.

Investigate credentials. There are a number of ways to tell if a pediatrician has proper credentials:
Licensing: Look for a state license displayed on the wall of the pediatrician's office. This is your assurance that she has been graduated from an accredited medical school. Many states are now also demanding proof of Continuing Medical Education (CME) credits earned as a requirement for license renewal.
Board Certification: Physicians who have been certified by their specialty board have acquired a certain degree of knowledge and training in a particular area. A general practitioner isn't going to provide your child with the same specialized care as a pediatrician.
Academic Affiliation: A doctor who is affiliated with a major teaching hospital or medical school is likely to be competent. To earn that affiliation, she has undergone a screening process and a review by her professional peers.
Reputation: If the pediatrician has been recommended to you by several people, or by a professional medical organization, she is probably beyond reproach. However, even that may not be enough if *you* don't "like" her.

Check availability. If you're going to need to see the doctor often or even if you expect to bring your child in for just routine examinations, it helps to choose a doctor who is available to her patients. Some physicians are so involved in teaching or research that they devote little time to seeing patients. Getting an appointment with them means weeks of waiting time. Check to see if the doctor you choose has arrangements made for someone to cover for her when she's not available.

Establish hospital affiliation. Make special note of this. Your doctor's hospital affiliation refers to the hospital where your child will be admitted if the need ever arises. Make sure in advance that this hospital is satisfactory to you.

Be sure you are compatible. It may be a small point, but if you don't feel at ease speaking with a doctor, there's a good chance your child won't feel comfortable either. Does the doctor treat you like an intelligent person or a nervous mother? Competence and certificates mean little if you must deal with a doctor you don't trust or with whom you cannot communicate.

12 Ways to Keep Kids Healthy in Winter

Not only is winter the season for riding sleighs, building snowmen, and singing Yuletide carols, it's the season for catching sore throats, coughs, colds, and flus, all of which take their toll on your child. Is there any way to avoid them?

Unfortunately, until a cure for the common cold is found, there isn't much you can do, but you can lessen the severity and the duration of illnesses by following a number of tips.

1. Dress your child in layers. Whether he's going to school or outside for a snowball fight, it's important to insulate him from the cold by dressing him in layers of clothes that will retain body heat and repel the cold.
2. Give your child a multivitamin daily. By insuring that he receives all the necessary vitamins and minerals every day in a supplement, you can better protect against illness. Even if he does come down with a scratchy throat or cold, in all likelihood the illness will be less severe because of the vitamins.
3. Provide a balanced diet. It's hard to watch your child's eating habits when you're not around, but by educating him early on about the importance of a proper diet, and by stocking kitchen cupboards with nutritious foods, you can help him develop good eating habits that will last a lifetime. Tips for breakfast: Keep instant oatmeal around, teach your child how to fry an egg, keep a hand-held orange juice squeezer handy for him to use. For lunch: Cut and package vegetables and fruits so he will be more likely to take them along for lunch, prepare hot soups that can be kept steaming in a thermos until lunchtime, insist that your child eat a hot meal at school two days a week. For dinner: Prepare foods that are high in protein and vitamins.
4. Install storm windows and caulk all windows and entrances in your house to guard against drafts.
5. Buy your child wool sweaters rather than acrylic ones. Man-made fibers may cost less than natural fibers, but they also do less to guard against the cold. Teach your child to dress himself warmly in winter. Wool socks are an important component of winter dressing. Teach him to change out of any damp or wet clothing, no matter how comfortable he says it feels.
6. Keep your child home from school at the first sign of sniffles to prevent a mild cold from developing into something more serious. It's even advisable to keep him home an extra day to prevent the illness from reoccurring.
7. Check all boots. Make sure they are waterproof and don't have any holes.
8. Provide your child with mittens. Gloves do less than mittens to keep hands warm. Reduce the likelihood that they'll get lost by attaching them to coats with small clips that are sold for that purpose.
9. Make sure your child wears a head covering when he goes outside. Eighty percent of body heat is lost through an uncovered head. Buy a coat with an attached hood.
10. To keep other members of the family healthy when one person is sick, sterilize eating utensils after use. Teach your child to cover his mouth when he sneezes, and also to discard all used tissues immediately.
11. Treat your sick child with extra doses of vitamin C. Many pediatricians recommend extra vitamin C, believing it can help speed the natural recovery process.
12. Learn the symptoms of frostbite. In the mildest forms, body extremities (fingertips, toes) feel cold, then painful, then numb. Tell your child to come inside quickly if he experiences any of these symptoms. In more severe cases, the layers of skin leading to the muscle tissue get frostbitten and will feel hard and doughy to the touch. In the most severe cases, the affected person may become incoherent, lose consciousness, and go into shock. Take your child to a doctor immediately if severe symptoms occur.

Do's and Don'ts for Treating a Fever

Fever generally indicates that the body is reacting against infection. It is part of the body's defense mechanism against the invading virus or bacteria, and for this reason some physicians feel that the fever may actually be beneficial in fighting disease. The fever itself is not dangerous unless it is greater than 106 degrees Fahrenheit or 41.1 degrees centigrade: Above that point it may be harmful to the brain. When your child is running a fever, your job will be to monitor its progress and minimize its potentially damaging effects.

DO find out what your doctor recommends for treating fever: Doctors differ in their procedures. A good time to ask is at the two-month checkup, when your baby will be given his first DPT inoculation and stands a good chance of having a fever in reaction to it.

DO report any fever in an infant to your pediatrician at once—other than an expected reaction to a shot.

DO observe an older child who is feverish for other symptoms of illness. Call the pediatrician if a fever above 101 degrees persists for more than two days, or if a low-grade fever lasts more than a week.

DO keep close track of the fever during the "watching" period and throughout your child's illness by taking and recording his temperature approximately every four hours.

DO keep your child cool by dressing him in light pajamas or other clothing. Contrary to popular belief, loading him down with blankets in an effort to "sweat the fever out" doesn't do the child any good and can raise the fever even higher. Also, keep the temperature of his room comfortably cool.

DO give your child plenty of liquids, whether he feels like taking them or not, as fevers have a tendency to leave children dehydrated. Feed your child any kind of liquid—water, fruit juices, soda, soup. Even sucking on ice or popsicles helps—this is the best means of introducing liquids if the child has vomited.

DO let your child bathe in lukewarm water, unless he feels chilled. A cool washcloth on the forehead or wherever he wants it can also be soothing.

DON'T give an alcohol bath, as the fumes may cause side effects.

DON'T force your child to eat or prohibit him from eating when he wants to. The old adage about starving a fever is plain nonsense. Let your child's appetite decide.

DO allow your child to play quietly in his room or around the house. Bed rest is not required, but strenuous activity should not be encouraged.

DON'T give aspirin unless your pediatrician specifically recommends it. Because aspirin may make an illness such as Reye's syndrome worse, many doctors routinely prescribe acetaminophen (Tempra, Tylenol) to reduce fever.

DO measure fever medications carefully and record the time and the amount given at each dosing. Be aware of the symptoms of medication overdose: Rapid deep breathing or complaints of ringing in the ears may indicate an adverse reaction to the dosage.

DON'T ignore high fevers. If your child's temperature reaches 103 degrees or higher and your efforts to lower it have no effect, call the doctor for advice.

DON'T necessarily miss work when your child has a mild temperature. Have your sitter take his temperature at regular intervals, and ask her to call you if it rises.

DO keep your child home from school or day care. Even a low-grade fever may be a sign of contagious infection. Keep your child home for twenty-four hours after his temperature returns to normal to be certain the illness is indeed over.

When Your Child Gets Sick at School . . .

Of all the tugs at a working mom's conscience, the image of your child sick when you are not around creates the worst sort of guilt. But you'll worry less about what will happen if you prepare yourself in advance. Here are some things to keep in mind:

1. Know what kind of health staff and facilities your child's school has and what the school's policies are regarding sick children.
2. Give the school emergency information and authorization forms before school starts. List on these cards your telephone number at work and your husband's, as well as the names of *two* friends, relatives, or neighbors who do not work and are willing to take on the responsibility of picking your child up from school if she is ill. Keep all information on these cards up to date.
3. Ask the school to permit your child to lie down in the nurse's office when she is not feeling well, until the school day ends. Be sure that the school nurse knows that you work.
4. Sign a form permitting the school staff to administer aspirin or acetaminophen when necessary.
5. Be sure the school can reach you. If your work takes you away from the telephone, your co-workers should know where to find you. If necessary, use a beeper or a telephone answering machine or service you can call to ask for messages.
6. Have a list of emergency backup help: three or four people who can be available weekdays on short notice. Look for retired or unemployed people, at-home moms of school-age children, college or nursing-school students, people who work on flexible or part-time schedules.
7. Make contingency plans at work. It may mean asking a colleague to cover for you if you need to leave the office. She should know your job well enough, and you hers, so that you can fill in for each other. Or you may want to organize your working materials so well that in a pinch co-workers can find important papers or follow your instructions by phone.
8. Call your pediatrician after you have talked to the school nurse and gotten a full account of the symptoms. If it's a "watch and see" situation—as many childhood ailments are at the start—and you have an important meeting or deadline, you might want to call on someone else to pick up your child at school and stay with her until you can get away or a backup sitter can take over. Ask to speak to your child and let her know who will be coming for her; reassure her that you will be home soon.
9. Tell your boss you are needed in an emergency. Show your commitment to your job by offering to take work home with you or to do extra work when you return. See that you have all bases covered at work before you leave.

Sun Sense

Before vitamin D was added to milk, sunbathing was the popular way to give children a dose of this necessary vitamin. In recent years, however, we've been warned about the hazards of skin cancer from too much sun. But that doesn't mean we have to avoid it altogether. By following sensible precautions, your child can still enjoy a moderate amount of sunshine without suffering serious effects.

Sunburn Risk

A variety of factors determine how the sun will affect your child's skin:

1. **Geographical location:** The nearer you are to the equator, the more direct are the sun's rays. That's why the sun's rays in Florida are several times stronger than in the northeastern part of the United States.
2. **Altitude:** High altitudes offer less protection from the sun because there is less atmosphere through which to filter dangerous ultraviolet rays before they reach the ground.
3. **Time of day:** The sun burns more strongly at noon, when it is directly overhead, than early in the morning or late in the afternoon.
4. **Medication:** Some medications make you more susceptible to sunburn. Check with your doctor if your child is taking any medication, as it may cause a photosensitive reaction.
5. **Complexion:** While almost all skin is susceptible to sunburn, very light-skinned children, particularly blonds or redheads, can tolerate much less exposure to the sun than darker-complected children.

Sun Lotions—"SPF" Explained

The aim of a suntan lotion is to help you stay in the sun longer without burning. It's important to buy a product that will screen out ultraviolet rays. The best sunscreens contain a chemical called PABA (para-aminobenzoic acid) or benzophenone. In 1978 the FDA required that a suntan lotion's sun protection factor (SPF) appear on all sunscreening products. The letters SPF plus a number tell you the amount of protection a product provides from the sun's burning rays. The higher the number, the greater the protection. For moderate protection, an SPF of 4 or 6 is sufficient. However, if your child is fair-skinned, a higher SPF may be necessary. To figure out how long it is safe for your child to stay in the sun, multiply the SPF number by the amount of time he can usually stay in the sun without protection before his skin starts to turn red. The largest SPF number is 25, and it's considered a complete sunblock because it doesn't allow any of the sun's rays to pass through. For infants and very young children, a sunblock of 15 or more is recommended by most pediatricians.

Exposure

To avoid sunburn, it's necessary to apply the sunscreen to all exposed areas of the body and to reapply it after swimming or perspiring.

If you're planning a trip to the beach, it's a good idea to allow your child's skin to get used to the sun before exposing him to several hours of it all at once. Begin by letting him play in the sun in his bathing suit for 15 minutes. Increase the exposure by 5 minutes on five successive days. By the sixth day, he should be ready for an outing at the beach, provided you apply protective lotion to his skin and keep a T-shirt or beach jacket on him during the midday hours.

Sunburn

Too much sunlight will cause any kind of skin to burn. When the skin is burned, tiny blood vessels at the surface dilate to produce a scorched look. There are three types of sunburn:

1. **Mild:** There will be some reddening of the skin. Dust the area with talcum powder to soothe and cool.
2. **Moderate:** The skin is redder and may be slightly swollen, tender, and possibly itchy. Blisters and peeling may result. Apply wet dressings of gauze dipped in a solution of baking soda and cornstarch—1 tablespoon of each per 2 quarts of cool water. A lukewarm bath can help take the sting out of the burn.
3. **Severe:** A severe burn may be accompanied by chills, fever, and bad blisters, which can become infected. Consult your pediatrician in such cases. Your child should drink plenty of liquids to replace all the moisture lost. Give him salty foods to replace salt lost from dehydration, and make sure he rests indoors in a cool room. Give a form of acetaminophen to ease the pain.

Your Child's Teeth

Every mother eagerly looks forward to her baby's first tooth. But can you recognize the first signs of its coming? Babies begin teething as early as four months of age. Excessive drooling is often the beginning of teething, along with increased finger sucking and gum rubbing, poor appetite, wakefulness, crankiness, mild fever, and diarrhea. The following treatments may provide some relief for your suffering little one:

* Use baby Tylenol to reduce fever.
* Treat drool rash by using only soft cloths to wipe up saliva, not tissues or paper napkins.
* Apply a soothing salve to affected areas at baby's bedtime.
* Give baby a cold carrot stick or teething ring to chew on.
* Massage painful gums gently with your fingertips.

Between six months and a year, incisors, the sharp front teeth used to cut food, start to appear; molars grow in somewhere from twelve to eighteen months, and when your baby is nearly two, the "eye" teeth or canines come up. The two-year molars normally show—you guessed it—around the age of two.

Baby teeth begin to fall out when kids are six or seven years old, usually in the same order in which they arrived. At that stage, they'll begin to be replaced by permanent teeth, a process that continues until children are about twelve years old.

Care of Teeth

Baby teeth provide the foundation for permanent teeth. They reserve the space for adult teeth to grow in and allow for the development of the jaw and facial bones. Even though baby teeth will be shed, they still need careful attention. Breastfeeding contributes to proper jaw alignment because the sucking action affects the jawbones. Breast-fed babies also tend to have healthier teeth because of the nature of mother's milk and the natural rinsing action during breastfeeding.

As soon as your baby's teeth come in, avoid giving milk or juice in a bottle at bedtime. During sleep, less saliva is produced, and bacteria can develop in the mouth, producing decay acids that erode the protective enamel on the teeth. Teeth at this stage can become brittle and fall out prematurely.

If your child is a thumb sucker, try to break the habit by the age of three. After that age, sucking imposes pressure on the front teeth and can cause buckteeth, poor jaw alignment, swallowing problems, and even speech impairment.

Introduce fluoride early, and follow your dentist's or pediatrician's advice on proper use. The aim of good dental hygiene is to keep plaque from forming. Begin the after-meal brushing habit early. A sugar-free diet is best, but it can be hard to stick to. Brushing after meals helps remove sugar from between teeth if a child has been eating sweets.

Your child should begin to have regular dental checkups at two years of age. This will introduce proper brushing and flossing early, as well as lessening feelings of fear so often associated with going to the dentist.

The Big Brush-Off

The problem with trying to get children to brush their teeth is that kids can't see any immediate visible benefits to brushing. However, as we all know, the consequences of poor oral hygiene are all too apparent later on in the form of cavities, stained teeth, receding gums, and periodontal problems. Your job is to make your children understand this and to teach them good brushing habits early on. Here are some tips to help you along:

1. Let kids pick the toothpaste they like the taste of. Just make certain their choice contains fluoride and not a lot of whitening agents that will only strip teeth of precious enamel.

2. Some children **are** willing to brush their teeth—the problem is getting them to brush properly. If you suspect your child isn't brushing correctly, stand in the bathroom and watch. As a good example, you can brush your teeth with her until she catches on.

3. Let them choose their own brushes. They come in different colors and different bristle grades, from hard to soft. You can even have your child's brush engraved with her name. Contrary to what we were told years ago, it's now believed that softer brushes are better than hard ones. If you think it will help, bring home an electric toothbrush. The novelty of it could encourage brushing.

4. Bring home a Water Pic. Dentists have sung the praises of such devices since their introduction into the marketplace. They're fun to use, and they flush out pieces of food that toothbrushes can leave behind.

5. School your child in the benefits of flossing. Flossing helps prevent the accumulation of plaque. Have your child watch you floss, or instruct her as she attempts to floss for the first time. Explain that her gums might bleed so it won't frighten her if it happens.

6. Get into the habit of taking your child to the dentist every six months. The dentist will be best able to instruct your child on how to brush her teeth the correct way. Beware: Not all dentists concur on the subject of the correct brushing procedure. Some believe up and down is the correct way, while others stress the back and forth, horizontal method.

7. Try to restrict your child's intake of candy and sweets. An occasional treat (chocolates are better than hard candy) should be followed by a thorough brushing.

8. Your child should get into the habit of brushing at least twice a day—after breakfast and before going to sleep. If she hasn't picked up the habit yet, continually ask whether or not she has brushed her teeth. She'll soon grow weary of your questions and will take it upon herself to brush regularly.

9. Buy disclosing tablets at your local pharmacy, to pinpoint where plaque is building up on teeth and where your child should spend more time brushing. After brushing, your child chews the harmless red tablet. Her whole mouth will turn light red. The spots on the teeth that weren't brushed well enough will be left with dark red stains, and she will know to concentrate on those spots next time. By brushing again she can get rid of the dye. It's a fun way to learn how to brush better.

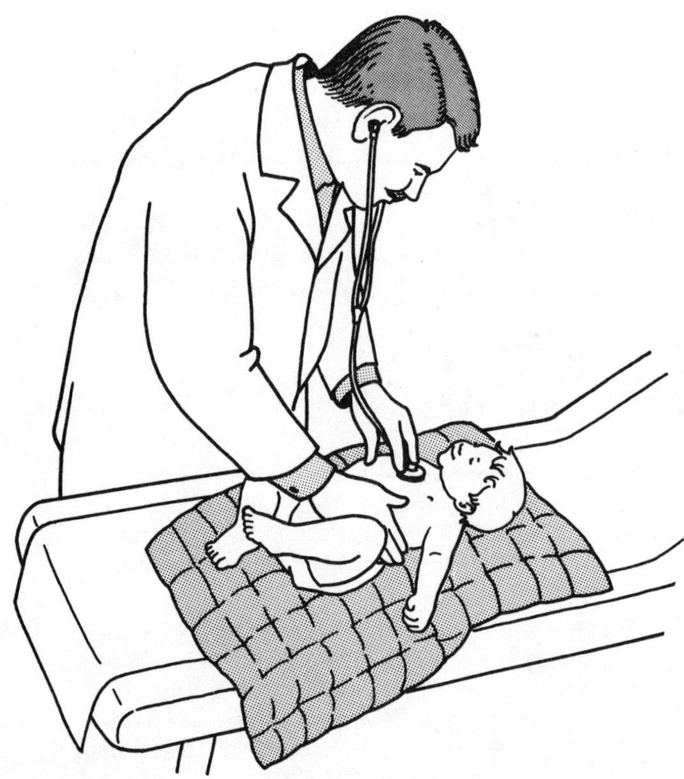

Baby's First Visit to the Doctor

What to Ask, What to Expect

You and your spouse will have met your pediatrician at a prenatal visit, your baby will have been checked by her in the hospital, but the first time you, the doctor, and your baby will come together will probably be four weeks later when you take him in for his first checkup. Anxious first-time moms are apt to fear the doctor will be evaluating them as parents and will give them poor marks for a less-than-picture-perfect baby. (That funny rash on his chin, the waxy stuff behind his ears, the toenails that won't grow—surely they will count against you!) Fortunately, the doctor's knowledge of one-month-old infants is solidly grounded in real experience, not diaper commercials, and her desire is to help parents promote the health of their children, not to carp or criticize.

What to Expect

The doctor will weigh and measure the baby, check his eyes, ears, nose, and mouth, feel the soft spot of his head, listen to his heart and lungs with her stethoscope, feel his abdomen for abnormalities of the liver or spleen, test his reflex responses, and examine his overall development. She will ask you about his eating and sleeping habits and his activities when awake.

You will undress the baby and put him on the examination table for the weighing and measuring; for the rest of the examination, the baby may be on the table or in your lap if he needs soothing.

The first visit will not include an injection; the first immunizations are usually administered at two months.

After the doctor has finished her examination, recorded the information, and compared it to her findings at her last examination before the baby left the hospital, she will discuss his progress with you, answer your questions, and prepare you for what to expect in the month to come, advising you of any necessary changes in care.

What to Ask

Save your questions until after the doctor has finished her initial examination and talked to you about the results. What she has to say will most likely relieve some of your worst fears and cancel out the need for such queries as, "Is he getting enough to eat?"

Bring a list of questions with you; it's hard to remember on the spot all the little worries you've been having, especially when the doctor reassures you smilingly that your baby is thriving under your splendid care. Don't be embarrassed or fearful of taking up the doctor's valuable time; all concerns are worth asking about. Why does he spit up so much? How can I get that scaly stuff off his scalp? When will he sleep through the night? Why does he cry so much? What's best for his diaper rash? Breastfeeding problems are in the pediatrician's domain, too; she can advise you on the proper care of your breasts, expressing milk for feedings when you are away, and other concerns you may have.

Add any questions that occur to you during the examination; it is helpful to know what the doctor looks for and why. Most of all, don't hesitate to tell her if you do not understand something she has said. You, after all, are the one ultimately responsible for the baby's day-to-day care; the doctor's instructions must be crystal clear.

If after you get home you remember something you forgot to ask or a new question pops into your head, don't hesitate to call back during her telephone hour: That's what she's there for.

Checkup Guide

You and your baby's doctor will get well acquainted during the first three years of your baby's life, for you'll be taking him to see her frequently for checkups. Checkups accomplish a great deal. They provide records from which your doctor can evaluate your baby's growth and developmental progress, a regular schedule for administering immunizations against childhood diseases, a means of detecting health problems and abnormalities, and valuable guidance for parents in anticipating problems and promoting the health and safety of the child.

A typical examination will include the following:

1. The child will be weighed and his height measured. By comparing past weights and measurements with the current ones, the doctor can establish the child's individual pattern of growth. Deviation from this pattern may be an indication of illness before other symptoms develop.

2. Various instruments will be used to check the child's eyes, ears, nose, and throat for signs of illness. The ophthalmoscope and the otoscope light up and magnify the interior of the eyes and the ears; a flashlight and a tongue depressor help the doctor see the tonsils and throat. She will also look for the appearance of healthy teeth on a regular schedule.

3. In infants, the normal closing of the fontanels will be checked. The sides of the neck will be felt to see if the child's lymph nodes are tender or swollen, a sign of illness or infection.

4. With the stethoscope the doctor will listen to the child's heart to find out how strongly and steadily the heart is pumping and whether the valves are functioning properly. She will listen to his lungs to detect any constriction of the air passages or accumulation of mucus.

5. By pressing the abdomen, the doctor checks for abnormalities and finds out if any areas are tender or sore.

6. The doctor will observe the movement of the arms and legs and will check the child's reflex responses, in some cases by tapping certain tendons with a rubber hammer. She may ask an older child to walk across the room so that she can tell whether his spine is developing normally.

7. The doctor will then ask you a variety of questions to find out about the child's nutrition and daily routines. She will also ask whether your baby smiles, rolls over, sits up, pulls himself up to standing, walks alone, or says words—all guideposts in assessing his development.

8. Specific screening tests to detect problems may be performed, depending on the age of the child and the risk of the disorder being tested. Many doctors perform annual hemoglobin and hematocrit determinations, urinalysis, and skin tests for tuberculosis. Children over three will have their blood pressure taken and their vision and hearing checked.

9. The doctor will prepare you for issues coming up in the months ahead. For example, when your child is approaching the crawling stage, she will advise you to childproof your home, post the number of the local poison control center on your telephone, and buy syrup of ipecac. Topics such as starting solid foods, giving vitamins, weaning, dental care, and toilet training will be discussed, along with your questions and concerns.

10. Inoculations—when required—are usually administered at the end of the visit, since communication between you and the doctor will most likely be called to a halt by your child's need for immediate solace.

How to Help Your Overweight Child

More than strict dieting to lose weight, overweight kids need to change their eating habits and activity levels sufficiently to maintain their weight until their bodies grow enough to make that weight right for them. Lynn Perton, former Chief Nutritionist of Pediatric Ambulatory Care at St. Luke's–Roosevelt Hospital Center in New York City, advises parents of overweight children: "Look at the life-style you are developing for your child." By examining the causes of the problem, she helps families find what changes need to be made. Are snacks providing more calories than meals? How is the child spending money on the way home from school? Are sedentary or lazy ways becoming habitual? Is food regularly offered as solace or reward? Reorienting family attitudes and habits, with parents setting a good example themselves, is the most important factor in helping a child thin down.

Develop a Strategy

If your child is looking pudgy, check first with his pediatrician and let her advise you whether he is indeed overweight. Often children gain weight just before a growth spurt; the extra fat is then used up by the sudden addition to their height. Your pediatrician may be able to help you develop a weight-maintenance plan or may recommend a nutritionist who will.

Discuss Dieting with Your Child

If your child is old enough to be taking responsibility for his own snacks and some meals, talk about his weight problem with him. He is doubtless already aware of it. Let him know that you will help all you can but that it will be his job and that it won't be easy.

Revise Your Shopping List

Stop buying ice cream, cream cheese, sour cream, whipping cream. Skip bacon, sausage, tuna canned in oil, spareribs. Omit fruit canned in heavy syrup, fruit drinks, fruit roll-ups; cut down on supplies of dried fruits and fruit juice. Eliminate frozen vegetables prepared in cream or cheese sauces and all kinds of potato and corn chips, cookies and pastries, soft drinks and candy. If these items are simply not in the house, it will be easier on everyone.

For children under two, whole milk is important. For older children with weight problems, buy skim milk. If your child really doesn't like skim milk, compromise with low-fat or 2% milk. Or have him try buttermilk—he may like it.

Stock up on fresh fruit, vegetables, unsweetened cereals, tuna canned in water. Buy meats low in fat, especially fish, veal, and chicken. Look for skim-milk cheeses.

Alter Your Cooking Habits

Your cooking habits will change next. Bake or boil potatoes instead of frying or mashing them. Steam—don't cream—vegetables. Boil eggs; don't fry or scramble them. Broil or bake fish and chicken.

When you think of a high-calorie dish he likes, look for a low-calorie substitute. Chicken or turkey franks contain less fat than beef or pork frankfurters. Fill celery with cottage cheese instead of cream cheese. Baked apples make almost as good a dessert as apple pie. Ice milk is lower in calories than ice cream.

Change Your Eating Rituals

Serve meals *and snacks* at regular times. Never let a child skip a meal, especially breakfast.

Serve all food in one place. Don't allow your child to eat while he does anything else, like watching television or chatting on the phone with friends.

Prepare smaller portions. Consult your pediatrician or a good nutrition book on the amounts your child needs. If the right portions look terribly small to you, use smaller plates.

Encourage your child to eat slowly and chew each mouthful well.

Dilute fruit juices with water or seltzer. Better still, offer a piece of fruit instead—it takes longer to eat and is more filling. Serve thirsty children water.

Between meals, put away all food in cupboards or the refrigerator, where it won't be as tempting.

Deal Sensibly with Treats

Don't expect your child to forgo all treats. He should not have to suffer at birthday parties or when invited out. His friends' parents, however, can be asked discreetly to help him by not overfeeding him when he visits.

Reward your child with praise and attention, not food.

Encourage Exercise

Help the whole family develop a more active life-style. Plan family outings that will include walking, running games, swimming, bicycling, or other sports. Change transportation habits—walk to school instead of riding the bus; use stairs instead of elevators. Take family "constitutionals" after dinner. If your child is interested, let him choose the activity that appeals to him most—karate, swimming, dancing, gymnastics, team sports, whatever—and sign him up for regular classes after school or on weekends. Or give him a chinning bar, a jump rope, a punching bag—any simple sports equipment he can enjoy using at home.

Have Realistic Expectations

Don't look for quick results. Habits don't change overnight, and rapid weight loss is not your goal anyway, for it could hamper normal growth and development. Weight loss, if any, should be slow.

And be aware of differences in body build. Not everyone can or should look like Twiggy. Your child's bone structure will probably resemble that of his parents and grandparents: It is his genetic inheritance.

What Shots, When?

Vaccines stimulate the body's own natural way of fighting infection by introducing small amounts of a particular bacterium or virus (sometimes treated to make the germs less toxic) so that the body can produce its own antibodies against it. The immunity acquired by this means may last years or even a lifetime. Immunizations against several diseases that once killed small children are now routine and should be given to every child to protect him. These include diphtheria, measles, mumps, polio, rubella, tetanus, and whooping cough. They are given on a regular schedule to ensure the best continuous protection. Here is a list of what vaccines and inoculations your child will be given, and at what age.

Diphtheria, Pertussis, Tetanus

Immunization is given in a series of three injections, each containing vaccine against all three diseases. The first shot is administered at two months, and the others are spaced at one- or two-month intervals thereafter. Boosters are given at fifteen to eighteen months and at four to six years of age. DPT shots often cause a reaction: A mild fever and soreness around the injection beginning several hours later and lasting one or two days are common, as is a hard lump where the shot was given that may last for several months.

Further immunizations against pertussis are not necessary after age six. Additional diphtheria and tetanus boosters (DT) are recommended by the American Academy of Pediatrics every ten years, although many physicians feel a five-year interval is safer. A tetanus booster is also given if the child is badly injured in an environment that might harbor tetanus germs—typically any place horse or cow manure has been—to ensure the best protection.

Trivalent Oral Polio Vaccine

A tasteless vaccine that is administered orally with a dropper, OPV is made up of the three types of virus known to cause polio. It is usually given at the same time as the DPT shots. Children who have a low resistance to infection may require the inactivated polio vaccine (Salk vaccine). Physicians differ about the necessity for further boosters. If, however, you are traveling with your child to an area where polio is common, a booster is a good precaution.

Measles, Mumps, Rubella

A combined immunization against these three diseases should be given soon after the child's first birthday, usually at around fifteen months. It is believed to provide lifelong protection. A reaction in the form of a mild case of measles sometimes occurs a week after the inoculation and lasts one to five days.

Immunizations against other diseases are usually necessary only when the child has been or may possibly be exposed to the disease, for example, if he has been bitten by a rabid animal or if you will be traveling with him in an area where a disease such as cholera, plague, smallpox, typhoid fever, or yellow fever is endemic. Check with your doctor well ahead of any trip you plan with your child. He will have up-to-date information on what vaccines are required for which areas of the world.

AGE	VACCINE
2 months	DPT, OPV
4 months	DPT, OPV
6 months	DPT, OPV
15 months	MMR
18 months	DPT, OPV
5 years	DPT, OPV
15 years	DT

First Aid

10 COMMON MEDICAL EMERGENCIES AND HOW TO HANDLE THEM

All the childproofing and careful supervision parents provide cannot totally prevent accidents and medical emergencies from happening, and we need to be prepared to deal with them. All parents should learn first aid and resuscitation techniques, and discuss emergency procedures with their children's physician before any emergency occurs. Here are ten of the most common medical emergencies and what you can do to help.

1. **Bleeding.** Some bleeding can be beneficial, as it helps carry dirt and germs out of a wound. Teach your child not to be afraid of it. Usually it stops quickly when you start to clean a cut. More copious bleeding can be stopped with pressure. Press directly on the wound with a clean cloth or gauze pad, and elevate the wounded part of the body above the heart. Pressing on a pressure point above the wound—that is, closer to the heart—can also help.

For nosebleeds, pack the nostril with tissue, or press the nostril firmly between your thumb and forefinger until the bleeding stops—3 to 10 minutes.

Any bleeding that continues for more than 15 minutes requires immediate medical attention.

2. **Cuts and Abrasions.** Cuts deep or large enough that the skin gapes open and deep puncture wounds should be treated by a doctor. If a piece of skin and some flesh have been cut off, take the piece with you to the emergency room in a plastic bag of salty water or ice.

Smaller wounds should be cleaned carefully in water and bandaged if necessary to keep the area clean. Change bandages that get wet, and remove bandages overnight to let air promote healing.

3. **Poisoning.** Call poison control or your doctor *immediately*. Give the age of the child, the exact substances swallowed—name of product, maker, and contents listed on the label—and if known, the amount ingested. You may be told to induce vomiting with syrup of ipecac or be directed to a medical facility. Take the poisonous substance and its container with you. Do not just follow the advice on labels or in first-aid manuals—it may be outdated.

4. **Burns.** Recognize how serious the burn is. Burns are classified into three categories:

* First-degree burns, which affect the outer skin only, turn the skin pink or red and will look white when pressed.
* Second-degree burns go deeper. These make the skin moist or blistered and are painful to the touch.

* Third-degree burns leave the skin white, dry, or charred and may be painless at first because the nerve endings have been destroyed.

All third-degree burns and any extensive second-degree burns—especially around the face or joints—should receive medical attention right away.

Smaller second-degree and first-degree burns should be cooled quickly with cold water or ice and kept immersed or covered with cold, wet cloths until the pain diminishes. Be careful not to break any blisters. Call the doctor if signs of infection—fever or pain and swelling—develop.

5. Shock. Always watch for signs of shock when a child has been badly injured or burned. If he becomes very pale, confused, trembling, or nauseous, and his hands and forehead are cold and moist, have him lie down. If his head has not been injured, put his head lower than the rest of his body. Get medical help.

6. Choking. Know the signs of choking:

* The child can neither speak nor breathe.
* He will turn blue from lack of oxygen.
* He will lose consciousness.

Because it is difficult for adults to apply the Heimlich maneuver correctly to children, many physicians recommend first trying to dislodge the obstruction by turning the child over across your leg and slapping him smartly between the shoulder blades. If four whacks do not do the trick, sit him up and, reaching around from behind the child, apply a quick upward thrust of pressure to the upper abdomen between the navel and the rib cage. For infants, use the index and middle fingers of both hands; for older children, two hands clasped together.

7. Bumps, Sprains, Fractures, Dislocations. Wrap bad bumps and sprains with towels to hold an ice pack against the injury, elevate the injured part, and have the child lie down and rest.

Summon medical aid if the child shows signs of shock, or if he becomes unconscious or acts strangely after a head injury.

Much pain and swelling may indicate a fracture or dislocation. Immobilize and support the injured part with a splint or sling, and take the child to the hospital.

Never move a child if you suspect spinal injuries; call for an ambulance.

8. Bites and Stings. Wash human and animal bites thoroughly under running water and soak several minutes in warm, soapy water. Call the pediatrician for further advice. Animals will need to be checked for rabies, and in either case, the wound will need to be watched for infection.

The stings of bees, hornets, wasps, and yellow jackets are painful but not dangerous if the child is not allergic to the venom. Remove the stinger (if any) with tweezers, wash the area, and apply cold compresses and calamine lotion.

Watch for allergic reactions: Hives, itching and swelling away from the stung area, nausea, or difficulty in breathing call for prompt medical advice. A child who is sensitive to bee venom will be given an emergency sting kit and instructed in its use.

9. Croup. Croup is common in very young children and often strikes in the middle of the night. Usually the child has a mild cold, perhaps a fever. One warning sign is a cough that sounds like a seal barking. Then the child awakens making harsh noises as he tries to breathe. Take him into the bathroom and turn on the hot faucet of the shower. Try to calm him. In most cases the steam will relieve the problem and the child will go back to sleep. Put a vaporizer in his room and stay in or near his room that night and the next, as the condition may recur.

If the steam treatment does not improve his breathing, or if he begins to turn blue from lack of oxygen, call the pediatrician and take your child immediately to the emergency room of the nearest hospital.

10. When Breathing Stops. If there is reason to suspect choking, treat the child for this first. If not, begin mouth-to-mouth resuscitation immediately:

* Check his mouth and remove any foreign matter.
* Place the child on his back and tilt his head back to open the air passage.
* Open his mouth and put your open mouth over his. Pinch his nostrils shut with your fingers. If the child is very small, cover both his mouth and his nose with your mouth.
* Blow hard until his chest rises.
* Stop blowing, remove your mouth, and let the air come back out. You should hear it being exhaled and see the chest fall.
* If his chest is not rising and falling, an obstruction may be blocking the air passage. Check the mouth again. Treat for choking. Then try blowing air into the lungs again.
* Continue the breathing and exhalation, blowing your breath into the child's mouth every four or five seconds, more frequently for an infant, until breathing resumes. It may take a long time. Help should definitely be summoned.

Tips for Taking Care of Kids' Hair

No More Tangles

Snarls and tangles, yowls of protest: The daily hairbrush hassle is on. The only thing worse is the weekly shampoo—you'd guess it was Chinese water torture to judge from the screams. Not to mention the agony of haircuts. But unless your kid is into the Kojak look, it's a fact of life you've got to deal with. Children's hair is much more easily damaged than adults' hair; their scalps are tenderer; and their egos, gender identity, and need for autonomy are all bound up in the issues of hair care and styling. No wonder it's difficult. Here are some strategies:

1. When brushing the back of a child's hair, stand in front of her and have her hug you. Kids love hugging. It will help take her mind off what you are doing, and what's more, if it pulls, she can let you know by squeezing instead of screeching.

2. A spray conditioner to take tangles out of wet hair is equally effective on dry hair and will also combat excess static electricity in fine hair.

3. Always use a wide-tooth comb when disentangling hair; start with the ends and work gradually upward to the scalp.

4. Baby shampoos will not sting kids' eyes, but most are too alkaline for kids' fragile hair. Choose a mild shampoo and rinse well. Finish up with a good conditioner.

5. To help a child who hates having her hair washed:

* Prop up an unbreakable mirror at tubside so she can enjoy the crazy hair-dos she can make with the suds.
* Have her hold a favorite washcloth over her eyes while you rinse.
* Get in the bathtub with her and let her lie back with her head in your lap while you do the washing and rinsing.
* Take a shower with her and let her imitate you as you wash your hair.
* Give her a chance to do as much of the job as she can. It's less scary for her if she is making the decision to pour the water over her own head.

6. After the final rinse, pat hair dry with the towel: Rubbing only tangles and breaks hair. Avoid blow-drying, if possible, as it dries out the ends.

7. Short hairstyles with bangs are the easiest to keep looking neat, but not all children love them. If your daughter wants longer hair, help her pick a style that follows the way her hair falls naturally. Or suggest a "punk" style that is short all over except for a few longer strands down the back. Keep any hairstyle trimmed every two months. Trim bangs when they reach the eyebrows.

8. To avoid hairdresser and barbershop trauma:

* Trim hair yourself if you are adept at it and can amuse your child with water play or some other absorbing activity while you do it.
* Patronize hairdressers who specialize in children's hairstyles and provide toys, TV, and children's magazines to look at and balloon rewards after the ordeal is over.
* Find a hairdresser who will come to your home and do the entire family in an evening.

9. Keep long hair in place while adding pizzazz with fancy barrettes, snazzy headbands, and trendy clips she can arrange herself. Save more elaborate do's like braids for weekends when you have more time. When arranging long hair, avoid rubber bands, as they break and damage hair; to allow better circulation in the scalp, keep pigtails loose and shift the part frequently.

10. Don't forget the role of diet in growing healthy hair. Plenty of water, fresh fruits and vegetables, and adequate protein are as important as gentle care and frequent grooming in making your child's hair shiny and beautiful.

EMERGENCY

When Your Child Gets Sick While You're Away

Nothing is more frightening for a working mother than the thought that her child might need emergency medical care when she is not there. Here are some ways to minimize that possibility—and what to do should it occur.

PREVENTION

Guard against emergencies by:

* Childproofing your home
* Teaching your child traffic safety
* Always using car seats and seat belts in your own car and insisting that anyone who drives your child anywhere have her safely buckled in
* Teaching your child to respect the dangers of water, fire, heights, strange animals, sharp objects
* Learning what behavior to expect at different ages, especially the dangers toddlers are likely to get into, and warning caretakers of what to expect
* Making sure that neither you nor your caretakers ever leave babies or small children unattended, especially in high chairs or in the bathtub, or leave children at home or in a car alone until they are old enough to take care of themselves
* Buckling your child into her stroller every time she gets in
* Familiarizing your sitter with your household safety rules, for example, what appliances your child is permitted to operate herself

BE PREPARED FOR EMERGENCIES

Accidents will happen. Prepare yourself and your child's caregiver by taking the following measures:

1. Buy a good handbook with illustrations of emergency procedures, and keep it near where you leave instructions for baby-sitters. For example:

A Sigh of Relief by Martin I. Green (Bantam Books)

The Babysitter's Handbook by Barbara Benton (Morrow)

Both of these books have a handy emergency index on the back cover, with arrows that facilitate opening the book in a hurry to the page you need.

2. Paste a label on every telephone in your house, listing the numbers of your child's doctor and the local poison control center. Post a baby-sitter's card listing these and other important numbers in a prominent place near a frequently used telephone. Numbers on it should include: your office, your husband's office, nearby relatives, neighbors, your children's schools, the hospital your pediatrician is affiliated with, the local police precinct, the fire department, a plumber, an electrician, a taxi service.

3. Have your child's caretaker go with you to the pediatrician's office when your child is having a routine examination so that she can meet the doctor and know where his or her office is.

4. Tell your child's caretaker which hospital the pediatrician is affiliated with, how to get there, and where the emergency entrance is. Leave money to pay for a taxi.

5. Be sure your doctor has your telephone number at work and your husband's.

6. Keep your medicine cabinet well stocked with first-aid essentials.

7. Make up a formal statement authorizing emergency medical treatment for your child in case she is injured and you cannot be reached. It should have:

* the names of both parents and their daytime phone numbers
* the doctor's name and phone number
* the name of a friend or relative (or the caretaker) whom you authorize to call the doctor, designate a hospital, and give permission for necessary medical treatment
* a statement that if none of the above can be reached, the pediatrician on duty at the hospital may provide or obtain necessary medical care

Both parents should sign the form. Have it notarized, and give a copy to the person in charge of your child in your absence.

8. Make copies of all emergency information and the authorization for emergency medical treatment so that you will have them ready for a new or substitute sitter.

9. When you are traveling, take important phone numbers with you and give day and night phone numbers where you can be reached to everyone who will be helping look after your child while you are away, including the parents of friends she may visit and her school.

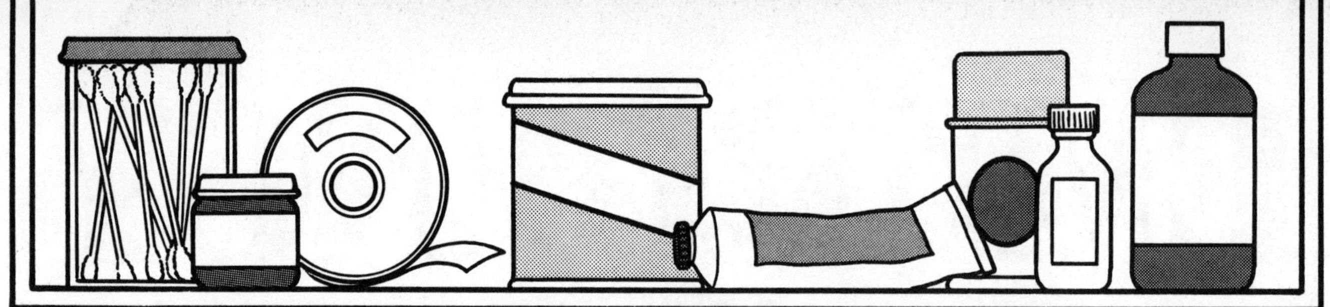

Working Mom's Medicine Chest

Working mothers often have anxieties where their children's health is concerned, but a well-stocked medicine chest can help relieve some of the worry about minor scrapes and bruises, sniffles and sprains, especially if they happen when you're not around.

Here's a list of basics to keep on hand for those unexpected accidents and illnesses. Make sure that your caretaker knows where everything is and that all medicines are kept securely locked away from children. Check your medicine cabinet periodically to see that everything is in good supply and that you are not keeping medicines beyond their expiration dates.

First-Aid Supplies

Absorbent sterile cotton
Adhesive tape (1″ wide)
Band-Aids in assorted sizes
Cotton balls
Cotton swabs
Elastic bandages
Eye cup
Heating pad
Ice bag or ice pack
Sterile gauze pads (3″ x 3″)
Sterile gauze roll (1″ wide)

Instruments

Oral thermometer
Rectal thermometer and lubricant
Scissors (blunt end, for cutting bandages)
Tweezers (for removing splinters)

Medications

Acetaminophen (adult and child dosages)
Alcohol
Anesthetic spray (for sunburn and minor cuts and scrapes)
Antibacterial ointment (for surface cuts)
Antidiarrhea medication
Aspirin (adult and child dosages)
Burn ointment
Calamine lotion (to treat insect bites and poison ivy)
Cough syrup
Decongestant (adult and child dosages)
External analgesic cream (the best contain mentholatum and are rubbed into the skin to treat muscle sprains)
Nose spray or drops
Oral anesthetic ointment (especially for teething babies)
Peroxide (or any mild antiseptic solution for cleansing cuts)
Petroleum jelly
Sunscreen (for children a number 15 provides the most protection)
Syrup of ipecac (or any emetic to induce vomiting in case of accidental poisoning)
Vicks Vaporub (or something similar to apply to the chest as a decongestant)
Zinc oxide ointment (for skin irritations)

HOUSEKEEPING

How to Hire Cleaning Help

Many working moms find themselves overburdened if they do all the cleaning themselves, especially if the space is large and there are small children underfoot. They would be delighted to pass along their chores to a handy little robot that lives under the stairs, emerges to clean while everyone's out, and keeps the house in spotless order. Until such devices are invented, however, it's a good idea to settle for human help.

How Much Help Do You Need?

Hiring cleaning help does not necessarily mean hiring a full-time maid to do everything. The important thing is to identify which jobs you'd like done by someone else. Working out a cleaning schedule will help you decide what you can manage yourself and what will require outside help. Hiring a cleaning woman one day a week is often the best arrangement: She can take on all the weekly tasks and usually get the monthly tasks done, too, by doing a few each week; you will be in charge of daily upkeep and the semi-annual cleanups.

Another alternative is to have someone come in every morning for a few hours to do the daily chores, clean one room thoroughly, and wash some laundry. Then one Saturday morning a month, the family could tackle the monthly tasks, particularly the sorting and discarding that are hard to delegate.

If it's the heavy-duty stuff that gets you down, bringing someone in one afternoon a week to do all the floors and bathrooms may make the difference. Or perhaps your home can get by with your daily maintenance and a cleaning service that will do a thorough job on all the rooms every two weeks.

Knowing exactly what you want done will help you select the right person for the job.

Where Do You Find That Person?

Depending on the help you are seeking, ask friends; read bulletin boards in neighborhood Laundromats and supermarkets, and put up your own want ads there; look in the Yellow Pages for cleaning services and employment agencies that provide domestic help; call a college or university in your town to ask about students available for part-time employment. The possibilities are numerous. Tell everyone you know what you are looking for—your baby-sitter, for instance, may know someone looking for work. If you live in an apartment building, talk to the doorman, the superintendent, and cleaning women you see in the elevator or doing laundry in the basement. If you live in an isolated area, ask at the post office and local stores.

How Much Will It Cost?

Cleaning help invariably costs more than child care—often twice as much, when figured at an hourly rate. Friends and neighbors can let you know the going rates; your interviewees will have their own demands. If you think you've found the right person, meeting his price—if it is not completely out of line with what you expected and if you can afford it—is much the best way to get off on a good footing. Whether you pay by the hour or by the job should be decided right off; the important thing, however, is whether the job is done to your satisfaction, not how long it takes someone to do it.

Fringe benefits are best worked out at the beginning. As an employer you are obliged to pay Social Security taxes and file quarterly statements with the IRS. Federal unemployment tax is required if you pay the worker more than $1000 in a calendar quarter. Once-a-week workers are usually given one sick day a year, two days of paid vacation, and one paid holiday a year.

Getting the Most Out of Your Help

Establish a professional relationship from the start. Your new employee is just that—an employee, not a servant. Friendliness, courtesy, and tact will help build good relations between you. Show him how you want everything done the first day, and then let him work in peace. Good management techniques are as valuable here as at work: Make your requirements perfectly clear, be tactful in pointing out mistakes, and praise work well done.

50 PROFESSIONAL HOUSECLEANING TIPS

If there is one thing no woman—working or not—wants to spend time doing, it's housecleaning. Unfortunately, for most of us it's a fact of life. But the next time cleaning day rolls around, try some of these professional tips to help minimize the effort and maximize the results.

1. When mildew forms anywhere, wash it off with vinegar.

2. To clean yellow bathtub stains, wash the tub with a solution of salt and turpentine.

3. To get at dust in hard-to-reach places, cover a yardstick with a sock and secure it with a rubber band.

4. Wipe away tiny scratches on glass by polishing them with toothpaste.

5. To remove candle wax from wood surfaces, use a blow dryer to soften the wax, then wipe it away with paper towels. Clean the area with a mixture of vinegar and water; dry thoroughly to prevent water marks.

6. Save old toothbrushes for cleaning silverware, combs, and typewriter keys.

7. Make chemically treated dustcloths by dipping cheesecloth in a solution of 2 cups water and ¼ cup lemon oil. Let dry before using.

8. Waxing the inside of ashtrays makes them easier to clean.

9. Cover scratches on finished wood with liquid shoe polish. Or rub shelled walnuts or pecans over the wood. The oil in the nuts will cover scratches.

10. Glass in picture frames will gleam if cleaned with eyeglass tissues. (Avoid using liquid cleaner, as it can seep under the edges of the frame and stain the picture.)

11. To clean deeply carved frames, use an empty, dry plastic squeeze bottle and pump it to blow dust out of crevices.

12. If book pages get wet, sprinkle them with talcum powder or cornstarch until the moisture is absorbed. Shake or brush the powder away.

13. Gold will gleam if you mix 1 teaspoon cigarette ash with some cold water to form a paste. Rub the gold with a soft cloth dipped in the paste. Rinse and buff dry with a chamois cloth. (You can substitute baking soda for ashes.)

14. Remove stains from ivory or plastic piano keys by rubbing with a damp cloth dipped lightly in baking soda (do not let the soda fall between keys). Wipe clean with a fresh cloth; buff dry.

15. To clean lamp shades: Wash in the bathtub with detergent and warm water; rinse off with a spray hose. Let water drip off, then wipe with a soft terry towel. Use a blow dryer to speed drying. Note: This method is good only for shades *sewn* onto frames; if they are *glued* on, have them dry cleaned.

16. Telephones can be cleaned with a paper towel moistened with alcohol.

17. To clean a chandelier, make a solution of 1 part denatured alcohol and 3 parts water. Cover the floor or table under the fixture with newspaper. Use a ladder to reach the crystals. Submerge each crystal in a bowl of the liquid for a few moments, swishing back and forth to clean. Let air dry.

18. Get rid of stale cigarette or cigar smoke odor by leaving a dish of ammonia or vinegar in the room overnight. Alternatively, dampen a towel with diluted vinegar and wave it throughout the room.

19. If candle wax drips on a tablecloth, hold an ice cube against the wax till it's brittle. Pry off with a dull knife or fingers.

20. When candlesticks accumulate wax, place them in the freezer. When wax freezes, it will easily peel off.

21. Scuff marks can be removed from floors with a pencil eraser or fine, dry steel wool. Rub crayon marks off the floor with toothpaste or silver polish.

22. Wash walls starting from the bottom up to prevent water trickling down, which leaves hard-to-remove dirty streaks.

23. To loosen transparent tape from walls without spoiling paint or wallpaper, place a warm iron and a protective cloth over the spot. It will soften and loosen the tape's adhesive backing.

24. Old nylon stockings make good cleaners for rough-textured walls. (Sponges tear and leave hard-to-remove pieces in cracks and crevices.)

25. Make a paste of cornstarch and water to clean grease stains off washable wallpaper.

26. To clean grease spots from nonwashable wallpaper, place a blotter over spots and press with a moderately hot iron. Repeat if necessary.

27. Use plain vinegar to remove water spots and streaks from windows.

28. Clean corners of windows and hard-to-reach places with a toothbrush or cotton swab.

29. Newspaper as a window wiper makes glass shine and leaves a residue that is more resistant to dirt than plain glass is.

30. Get rid of grout scum by making a paste of 3 cups baking soda and 1 cup water. Scrub with a sponge or toothbrush.

31. Car wax will make ceramic tile shine. Apply, leave on 10 minutes, and buff.

32. Make glass shower doors sparkle by cleaning with a sponge dipped in white vinegar.

33. Eliminate carpet odors by sprinkling with baking soda before vacuuming.

34. Prevent static shock from carpets by spraying lightly with 5 parts water mixed with 1 part liquid fabric softener.

35. If your shag rug has gone flat, spring it back to life with a lightweight bamboo yard rake.

36. An easy way to wash blinds is by wearing cotton gloves and using your fingers to clean the slats.

37. If your child has taken to the sticker craze, rather than letting him mar the walls, hang a large, clear plastic adhesive-backed sheet on a door or wall. When he tires of them, stickers will peel off without damage.

38. To eliminate static from the TV screen (it acts as a dust magnet), wipe the surface with a damp paper towel dipped in fabric softener.

39. Repair worn spots or tears on your ironing board cover with iron-on patches.

40. Trash cans will not be overturned by neighborhood dogs if you drive two stakes or broom handles into the ground and slip the trash can handles over them.

41. To keep steel wool pads from rusting, store them in a clay flowerpot saucer. Clay absorbs moisture and prevents rusting.

42. To keep the vacuum cleaner cord from retracting while in use, clip a clothespin to the cord after pulling it out to the desired length. Adjust as necessary.

43. Perspiration odor in clothes will disappear if treated with vinegar before laundering.

44. Clothes will dry quickly indoors if you place a fan on a table about 3 feet from the clothing and turn it to the highest speed.

45. Sticky starch will come off your iron if you run it while heated across a piece of aluminum foil or paper sprinkled with salt. Note: Don't try this on Teflon-coated irons or you'll ruin the surface.

46. If you wash an ironing board cover, fasten it back on the board while it is still damp, for a better fit.

47. When painting a room, line the paint tray with a large plastic bag before pouring in the paint. When finished, just lift off the bag and toss it out.

48. Remove varnish stains from hands with Spray 'n Wash. Rub hands, then wash with soap and water.

49. To unclog a vacuum cleaner hose, insert a straightened wire hanger with a small hook on the end into the hose. Work back and forth. To make sure the hose is free of debris, drop a coin through it.

50. Raw egg that has dried on the floor can be cleaned off by sprinkling with salt. Let sit for 15 to 20 minutes, and it can be swept up with a broom.

Cleaning Checklist: What to Do When

Housework is a lot like dieting: Everyone loves the results but everyone hates doing it. But, as with dieting, cleaning is successful only if it becomes habit. By listing the jobs that need to be done daily, weekly, monthly, and twice yearly, you can make a schedule of tasks for yourself and your helpers to guide your efforts in the chronic battle against household entropy.

Daily

Daily tasks should aim at keeping up appearances: Neatness and order can create a pleasant illusion of cleanliness.

☐ Make up beds.

☐ Wash dishes after every meal, or rinse them off and load them in the dishwasher, then run it at the end of the day.

☐ Wipe off eating surfaces and counters after every meal.

☐ Straighten up clutter.

☐ Take garbage out.

☐ Sweep up visible dirt, crumbs, ashes, etc., with a dust mop, a damp mop, or a carpet sweeper.

Weekly

Generally, every room needs cleaning once a week, whether you distribute the rooms through the week by doing one every day or set aside a block of time for the whole house.

☐ Thoroughly vacuum all carpets and rugs, including doormats, with a good beater brush.

☐ Dust furniture and other surfaces.

☐ Dust windowsills, or wipe them with a damp cloth.

☐ Wash mirrors.

☐ Clean the bathroom(s).

☐ Vacuum and mop all washable floors; wax linoleum and rubber tile, especially in heavily trafficked areas.

☐ Spot-clean walls and woodwork to remove spatters and dirty fingerprints.

☐ Clean all kitchen surfaces and appliances, especially stovetop burners and toasters.

☐ Change sheets and towels.

☐ Do laundry.

Monthly

Monthly jobs are the easiest to put off, for they are even more unpleasant than the daily and weekly ones and they never seem urgent until they've become horrendous, which they will if you let them go too long. It's a good idea to work these chores into the weekly cleaning schedule, doing a few each week.

☐ Defrost (if yours is not frost-free) and clean out the refrigerator.

☐ Clean the oven.

☐ Wipe kitchen cabinet and pantry shelves.

☐ Sort toys, discarding broken toys that cannot be mended.

☐ Vacuum refrigerator coils and the lint collector on the dryer.

☐ Wash the kitchen exhaust fan or vent and the top of the refrigerator.

☐ Clean light fixtures.

☐ Dust blinds.

☐ Wash doormats.

☐ Clean and oil butcher block with mineral oil.

Semi-Annually

Semi-annual jobs are biggies, many of which cannot be slipped easily into the daily or weekly schedule: Extra time should be set aside, perhaps a weekend, with all the family pitching in. Spring and fall are the logical times for these undertakings.

☐ Wash curtains, bedspreads, and washable rugs.

☐ Turn mattresses and wash dust ruffles and mattress covers.

☐ Launder or replace shower curtains.

☐ Wash windows and install screens (or storm windows).

☐ Clean out closets, putting winter (or summer) clothes away and taking out summer (or winter) things. Put anything not worn for the entire season in a stack to go to the thrift shop.

☐ Discard or take to the thrift shop outgrown clothing; toys, books, and magazines you do not need; and any household objects or furniture you never use.

☐ Dust books.

☐ Polish silver, brass, or other metal ornaments and fixtures.

☐ Clean out the medicine cabinet.

☐ Organize pantry shelves, discarding stale spices, condiments, and packaged foods.

☐ Wax fine furniture and wooden floors.

☐ Take stock of what major jobs need doing, and make a schedule for getting them done: painting; refinishing floors; cleaning drapes, carpets, or upholstery; making repairs; replacing worn sheets, towels, rugs, or mats; washing blinds and shades, walls, and woodwork.

KIDSTUFF

Where to Put It All

Kids accumulate stuff faster than pack rats. From the first flood of baby gifts and boxes of hand-me-downs that loving relatives and friends shower upon us, we are beset by the problem of Where to Put It All.

There are three kinds of stuff to worry about: what gets used every day; what gets used only occasionally but is needed right then when the time comes; and what gets used a lot at certain times and rarely at other times. It all has to be accessible, and you have to know where it is.

For clothing you need:

1. High closet shelves, a stepladder to reach them, a good light in the closet, labels, and boxes. These boxes need to be sturdy and have tops that are easy to take off. Buy them at the dime store or ask for paper boxes from your local copying service. All out-of-season clothes that still fit and all hand-me-downs that don't yet fit can go into these boxes. Sort the clothing by season and size, and label each box clearly. Keep a packet of labels and a felt-tip marker on the same shelf. You'll be surprised how often you'll be writing new labels.

2. Low shelves in the closet or on a storage wall, plastic boxes from the dime store—both shoe-box size and sweater size—and more labels. These will be drawers for a child from eighteen months to five or six years old. The smaller boxes will hold socks, underpants, undershirts, tights; the larger ones, pajamas, overalls, pants, skirts, T-shirts, sweaters, and tops. Adjust the shelves so that the boxes just fit and your child can reach them all. (Save the box tops in a bag on the high shelf—you don't need them now.) Draw a picture and write the name of what is in each box on the front.

3. A chest of drawers for an older child—his clothing is outgrowing the boxes. Still, keep dividers in the drawers to separate socks from tights and underpants from undershirts. Labels on the drawers will let you, him, sitters, and housekeepers know where everything goes.

4. A closet rod low enough for the child to reach. You can install one quickly by hanging a broomstick from an adult-height rod. Shorten the ropes as your child grows.

5. Hooks, hooks, and more hooks. Putting clothes on hangers can be difficult for a small child. He should have the option of hanging shirts or pants on hooks. Robes, pajamas, raincoats, jackets, and hats can all live on hooks.

6. Bins, baskets, or plastic milk crates on low shelves for shoes and boots.

Usually it is simplest to keep boots, jackets, snowpants, and all in-season outerwear near the front door rather than in a child's closet. A colorful string bag can be hung on each child's coat hook to hold mittens, caps, earmuffs, mufflers, and leg warmers.

For toys you can use:

1. High shelves for displaying special toys, heirlooms, or collections belonging to an older child.

2. Low shelves for toys played with frequently, with heavier toys on lower shelves and stuffed animals and lighter toys higher up. Shelves with a lip will keep toys from falling off. On these shelves use:

* small bins or plastic washbasins to hold toys with small parts

* a puzzle rack to stack wooden puzzles neatly

* labels or drawings to show where things belong

3. An open toy chest or basket. No matter how much carefully planned shelf and cabinet space you have, there always seems to be a need for the unstructured space of a toy chest. Avoid the hazards of pinched fingers and worse by dispensing with a lid. Add casters for convenience in collecting toys over a wide area.

4. Hooks. Dolls and stuffed animals can hang from cup hooks attached to the bottom of a high shelf or mantle or on the back of a door if you sew a loop of ribbon or a curtain ring to their heads or backs. Lego pieces can be hung in a drawstring bag that opens into a round play mat. Special hooks on a Peg-Board can hold tennis rackets, hockey sticks, and other sports equipment.

5. Shallow bins on casters that fit under the bed. These can hold dress-up clothes or a model train set.

6. Deep shelves—at least 15 inches—to hold board games and jigsaw puzzles. Put the shelves close together so that the boxes won't be stacked too high. These shelves will need to be out of reach of small children.

7. A recycling closet. Put away toys that your child isn't using. He may not be through with them and will be delighted to see them again in a few weeks. When you take a toy out again, put something else away. Toys from this closet will be called into action on rainy weekends or when your child is sick. Use it to store toys you are planning to take on a trip—they will be more appreciated if he has not seen them for a while. It can also hold holiday items and books for special occasions.

Decorating Ideas for a Kid's Room

A kid's room should be a cheerful, safe, practical place with open area to play in, good storage facilities, easy surfaces to clean, and cozy space for resting and sleeping. You cannot "decorate" it once and for all; it will need to change as the child does to meet her different needs. But you can set the stage so that these changes will be easy.

1. Pick bright colors that are likely to have long appeal: Primary colors against a white background are a good start. Let items that will change anyway—quilts, cushions, toys, and posters—provide most of the color.

2. A vinyl or other washable floor surface is a must. It can be made softer and prettier with an inexpensive washable cotton rug. Anchor it securely with a good rubber mat.

3. Use washable semi- or high-gloss paint or vinyl wallpaper.

4. Opaque window shades and curtains with a thermal backing will insulate the room in winter and block out evening and early-morning light in the spring and summer. Your child—and you—will sleep better.

5. Buy or build furniture that can be converted to other uses later. That precious pink cradle with dotted swiss curtains will hardly last six months before something bigger and safer will be required. A sturdy crib can be used two or three years, and some models can be converted to youth beds. A changing table can become a dresser or a desk—or vice versa with a vinyl-covered foam pad temporarily attached on top.

6. Bunk beds are a wonderful spacesaver in a room shared by siblings. Get the kind that convert easily to single beds in case your space requirements and their tastes change. And be sure they are safe:

* The framework supporting the upper mattress must not come loose under any circumstances.

* The lower part of the guard rail must be low enough that even by pressing on the mattress a head could not get caught under it.

* The lower bunk should never be used by a baby or a child under two, as there is a danger of her getting trapped between the bunk and the wall.

7. Fold-up beds or futons are other popular spacesavers. The children can sleep safely near the ground, then roll up their beds out of the way for daytime play.

8. Bean-bag chairs are fun and practical. Children love playing on them and do not outgrow them as quickly as they do small chairs.

9. Floor space is in many ways more useful than a play table and chairs. Children can spread their work and games out more, and the space can accommodate more children. Nothing rolls off, and there's no question that it all has to be picked up when playtime is over.

10. A folding card table or a fold-down plywood table attached to a wall can be used for projects that need several days' work. A cloth sewn to fit over it with cut-out windows and door will make a playhouse that is easily stored. An older child—by age five or six—will want a regular desk.

11. Provide adequate lighting, especially in work areas and by bedsides. Small, inexpensive lamps in cheerful colors will appeal to your child longer than cute nursery lamps. Teach small children to handle them carefully, and keep cords out of sight behind furniture. High-intensity and other lamps with metal shades can burn a child easily and are best hung on a track on the ceiling. Have a switch near the door and a night light so that you can check on your youngster easily during the night.

12. Reserve some wall space for creative expression. Line a wall with cork for pinning up posters and artwork. Buy a blackboard or use chalkboard paint on a large piece of plywood, the wall, or the back of a dresser or bookcase that juts out into the room.

13. Plan lots of storage space right from the start. Adjustable open shelves both 12 inches and 24 inches deep allow for the greatest flexibility. You will also want cabinets and drawers at least 24 inches deep.

14. Use the ceiling for hanging large, colorful decorations—a mobile, a kite, a piñata, an inflatable globe. Plants are also safest hanging from the ceiling.

Getting Kids to Help with the Housework

The plants haven't been watered, the dust is an inch thick on the piano, there's a week's supply of cookie crumbs under the kitchen table—and housework is about the last thing you have time for. You also don't have money to hire a maid every week. Don't despair! You have an untapped resource living right there in the mess with you—those little people who helped create it—your children.

Now is the time to introduce them to the joys of housework—and if you're clever, you may even find they actually *enjoy* helping. Here are a few tips to get you started on the road to domestic order.

FOR YOUNG CHILDREN—START EARLY

Get your children in the habit of helping while they are still small. Very young children love to help. Find something for them to do and put them in charge of that job. A two-year-old can fill the paper-napkin holder from a large bag of napkins on a shelf he can reach. He can put dry food into the dog's dish if it is in a stable container he can open easily and if he has a large scoop. A three-year-old can unload the unbreakable dishes from the dishwasher if they are stored on a low shelf; he can also help set and clear the table. Don't be too fussy about how well these tasks are done, and be generous with your praise.

MAKE IT FUN

If he gets bored with a task, suggest something else—sorting silverware, opening or closing the curtains, folding washcloths, matching socks, or, if he's handy at pouring, watering the houseplants. The main thing is to keep his interest up and to introduce the idea that families work together.

Even a pre-schooler can learn to pick up after himself, but you will need to work alongside him and provide all the incentives you can. Say something like: "Let's count the blocks as we put them away"; "Find all the toys made of wood (plastic, metal)"; "You put the red and blue blocks away, I'll do the yellow and green ones." Also, set a timer to race against. Try singing: "A Spoonful of Sugar Makes the Medicine Go Down"; "Way Down

Yonder in the Paw Paw Patch" (the toys can be the paw paws you pick up together); "All By Myself" (name the tasks being done); any familiar tune with words made up to describe what you are doing or what wonderful thing you will do when you are finished. Or play some lively recorded music.

GIVE PRAISE AND REWARDS

★ Gold stars on a calendar or chart of daily tasks. ★ A small box of raisins. ★ An extra story at bedtime or right after the task. ★ A big hug. *Remember:* With small children you may occasionally spend more time doing the chore with them than you would if you did it yourself. But resist the temptation to take over. Eventually they'll become adept, and their sense of competence will be greatly enhanced by working on their own. And as they get older you'll have a far easier time getting them to help.

FOR OLDER CHILDREN— MAKE RULES

Specific rules can be set by the time a child is six. Discuss with him why his help is needed, and let him choose tasks he prefers as far as possible. Be reasonable and fair about what he can do. He should be responsible for all of his own things—books, toys, clothing (getting it to the hamper, folding it and putting it away after the laundry's been done). Expect at least one additional daily chore, even if it's a small one—emptying wastebaskets or setting and clearing the table. Add to the responsibilities as children get older. Teach them to cook, to sew on buttons, to do all kinds of household cleaning. Make each step of the process clear. Do it with them, then watch them do it. Write down a list for each child and post it where he will see it.

APPRECIATE THEIR WORK

Give gold stars (if they still have appeal) or some other show of appreciation, and be generous with your praise. Resist the temptation to redo a less than perfect job. Avoid bribes and rewards—save them for when you need something extra done.

ENFORCE AND RENEGOTIATE

Any punishment for tasks not done should be agreed on *in advance.* The loss of some privilege, docking TV time or allowance often works best. Whatever the punishment, it must be inescapable.

Renegotiate your work "contract" as different interests and skills develop. Rotate chores nobody loves. If children really understand the need for their help and are encouraged and praised so that they feel proud of their contribution, and if the lines of communication are kept open, punishments should not be necessary.

FOOLPROOF FILING

When the bills come in, the receipts pile up, and the dry-cleaning tickets are more likely to get lost than traded in for clean clothes, it's time to set up a more efficient way of dealing with those tiny but necessary scraps of paper. Clearly, piling them all in one drawer or leaving them on the kitchen table isn't the answer. Try organizing with the following items:

1. **File Cabinets.** By investing in a two-drawer file cabinet, you can pull together your world of paper scraps. Along with the cabinet, purchase a box of file folders and plastic tabs. Mark each folder with a separate subject. Some examples of folder subjects you'll need are: dry cleaning and laundry tickets, credit-card receipts (broken down further into the names of department stores and credit-card companies), postage and mail supplies, utilities and household bills, warranties, leases, theatre or ballet tickets—almost any piece of information that you don't want to lose and need to have at your fingertips. By keeping your files in alphabetical order with letter tabs, you can find items at the touch of a finger. To prevent a filing backlog, get into the habit of filing things as they come to you.

2. **Paper Holders.** If you have no room for a file cabinet, these desk items—consisting of a wooden base with a metal pin sticking out vertically from the center—make excellent small receipt holders. You can designate one for dry-cleaning receipts, one for bills, and so on. Your larger documents, such as warranties, can be filed in manila envelopes, which can be purchased in an office-supply store.

3. **Plastic Desk Organizers.** These are sold in office-supply stores and come in various sizes and shapes. You'll want to stick with the slotted design, which can hold different categories of information in each slot. As bills come in, write on the back of the envelope when the bill is due. Every two weeks, sort through the organizer for bills and pay those that are about to come due. Write the date paid on the front of the envelopes, and put them in a folder or manila envelope used exclusively for paid bills. It's best to separate the bills according to type for easy reference, should you need to go back to a specific bill in the future. Designate each organizer for a different purpose and keep like papers in their correct organizer.

4. **Cardboard Magazine Holders.** Sold in some department stores and stationery stores, these holders make good paper containers because they can hold many scraps and they readily fit on any shelf. Assign each holder a category and then arrange them on the shelf in alphabetical order for easy access. Go through the holders once every few weeks to stay current. To make holders attractive for storing on open bookshelves, cover them with fabric or brightly colored contact or wrapping paper.

5. **Gift and Shoe Boxes.** Before you toss out old shoe and gift boxes, consider their use as storage containers to help file papers. They can also be covered with fabric or paper, or even decorated with paint and stickers by the kids.

By utilizing one or a combination of these methods, you will be able to organize papers that have eluded you for years.

8 WAYS TO STOP IRONING—STOP IRONING? YES! IT CAN BE DONE. HERE'S HOW:

1. Send out cotton shirts, linen tablecloths and napkins, anything else that *must* be ironed.

2. Buy permanent press. Read laundry labels carefully before buying any garment. Test fabrics by wrinkling them in your fist.

3. Don't overload the washing machine; rinse with cold water, and take clothes out when the cycle is finished.

4. Dry clothes on the permanent press cycle or at a low temperature.

5. Take clothes out of the dryer as soon as they are dry. Hang up blouses, slacks, shirts, dresses, and skirts right away, or, if you are in a hurry, at least spread them out quickly over the dryer door.

6. If clothes have been left in the dryer too long, dampen a terry-cloth towel and add it to the load of wrinkled clothes. Run the dryer another five minutes.

7. Blot washable curtains with towels and hang them up to dry. Pleats may be "pressed" into curtains by folding them while they are still wet and holding the pleats with trouser hangers as they drip dry.

8. Use vinyl placemats and paper napkins for daily meals, straw placemats and permanent press napkins for more gracious dining. Individual napkin rings for each family member can save on laundering cloth napkins.

JOB NOTES

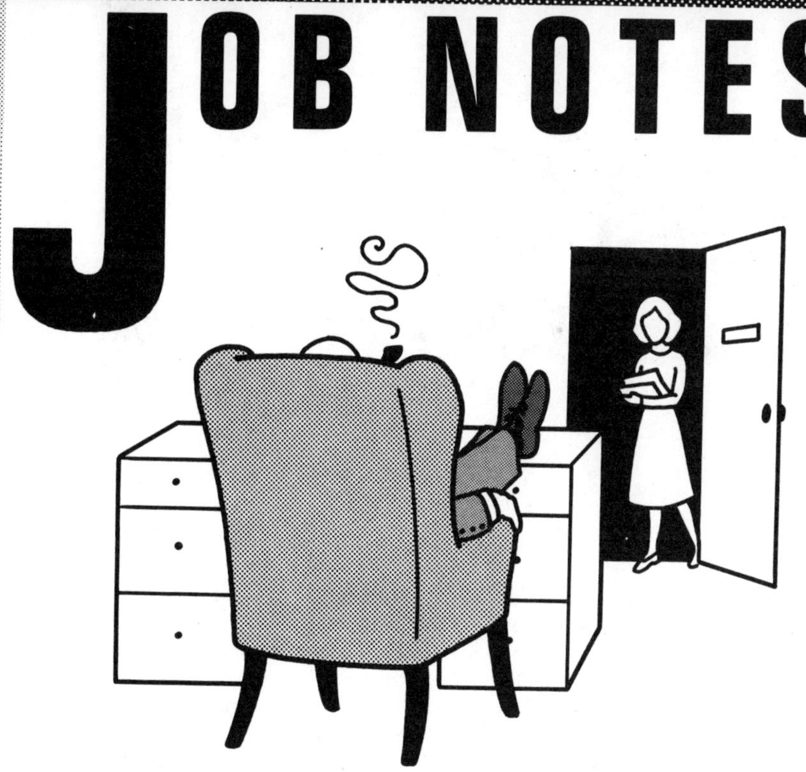

How to Deal with a Difficult Boss

Bosses come in all sizes and shapes and with a wide variety of personalities. Some are supermanagers, who make directions clear, corrections kind, and work a joy. They bring out the best in you and then praise you for it. But most bosses are ordinary folk—or worse. What do you do when you're stuck with someone particularly difficult to deal with? He or she controls your paycheck, the work you get to do, and sometimes even your chances of future employment: How do you cope?

Take stock. Go over all the advantages and disadvantages of your job: salary, job security, how it contributes to your career goals, fringe benefits (child care, if any; insurance), commuting distance, overhead costs, the stress of dealing daily with your boss. Weigh these against the chances of finding another job with similar advantages, and decide if the job you have is worth your making some adjustments.

Figure out what bothers you most about her. Try dealing directly with that problem.

* If she is not communicating clearly, ask questions, leave memos, suggest a meeting to go over specific issues. You have a right to know what is expected of you and to have your performance evaluated regularly.

* If she is on your back about every little thing, go over with her just what your responsibilities are—in writing if necessary—and ask her to give you the space and time to complete a job before she checks on you again. Prove you are capable of working on your own.

Try to see her point of view. Is she overworked, insecure, unhappy with her position? Are there ways you can help her improve her performance? Often a little sympathy and ego-building on your part will ease the strain. Bosses are human, too. Be tactful and discreet in making suggestions for changes.

Keep your sense of humor. You're probably not the only one suffering. Shared privately with co-workers, office jokes can go a long way in alleviating the stress of working for a temperamental boss. Or entertain your family with reenactments of her incredible behavior—you'll find yourself laughing, too.

See your job in its proper perspective. Work is only part of your life. You can gain satisfaction from many other activities. At work, focus on what needs to get done. Don't let the boss's inordinate demands or lack of support get you down. Just do your best. Praise yourself for doing so well.

Change jobs. If the going is really rough and the stress at work is carrying over to your home life, quitting may be the only answer. Before you do, you might want to take one last risk to change the situation: Talk to your boss's boss about the problems you have had. She may have suspected something was wrong and may take appropriate action. Or she may stand behind your boss. Quitting is hard, especially if other job prospects have not yet materialized, but the feeling that you are taking control of your life will help to make it seem worthwhile.

CANCELLED

HOW TO SURVIVE BEING FIRED

Few blows can strike harder than a dismissal notice from your boss. You've put time and effort into your work; you've surmounted criticism from well-meaning relatives and friends, maybe even your husband and children; you've organized your life to meet all your responsibilities as wife, mother, and worker. It has not been easy. Now you are out on your ear. How do you begin to pick up the pieces?

• Focus on what needs to be done. Don't get lost in the welter of emotions that will come over you. Channel your anger to constructive uses.

• Ask for severance pay. Be firm. You are going to need it. Two weeks' pay for each year of service is the usual amount offered; ask for more.

• Ask for the continuation of insurance benefits.

• Keep your office as long as you can, and use it as a base of operations for your job search.

• Take full advantage of any outplacement service and references offered.

• Apply for unemployment compensation.

• Hold on to your child-care arrangements if you can possibly afford to, or reduce them only slightly and temporarily. You are going to need the time to pull yourself together and initiate the search for another job.

• Start looking for work right away. Follow up all leads. Call the competition. Talk to friends, former employers, anyone who has offered you a job in the past.

• Use spare time to analyze what went wrong and to rethink your career goals. Read *What Color Is Your Parachute?* by Richard N. Bolles (Ten-Speed Press). Look for other helpful books on employment in your field.

• Try job counseling. Look first for free counseling services offered by libraries, Y's, university placement centers, professional organizations you belong to.

• Keep up your professional relationships, memberships in business associations, and other ties to work.

• Take a temporary job if money is tight. If you let your child-care and household help go, you will be removing yourself from the job scene and will have even less time to look for work. Temporary jobs, on the other hand, put you on the inside and can develop into permanent positions.

• Set some time aside for play—alone or with family or friends. A week's vacation or even a weekend mini-vacation or an afternoon's hike can help relieve the stress of job loss and of looking for work.

• Give yourself a present that will help keep you going: a special bath oil you can use in a relaxing bath every evening, a bud vase for your desk and flowers to put in it every morning—something to remind you that life can be beautiful and that you do care about yourself.

• Keep a diary. Use it to work out your feelings about what has happened and to chart your progress as you cross your personal desert. Go back through it regularly.

• Talk to your spouse and friends about your anxieties. Let them know you need extra loving care. Your children will respond, too, if you tell them frankly when you are tired and discouraged.

• Don't give up. You are not in fact falling off the world, although it may feel that way at first. One door closes and another opens. It may even turn out to be for the best—but you've got to stay in there plugging to find out.

Should You Fight to Keep Your Job?

If you are represented by a union and if you have been treated unfairly, there is a good chance you can get your job back. If job prospects in your field are slim, you may want to take this route. It has disadvantages: It may be a long uphill battle that will take a lot out of you emotionally, and you may again find yourself working for the same boss, who will do everything he can to make life unpleasant for you and fire you again first chance he gets. It can be a great personal victory for you, however, and may prevent others from being treated as unfairly as you were.

Let's Organize!

How to Set Up a Day-Care Center Where You Work

With more mothers working, 500 out of 5 million companies in the United States now offer on-site day-care for employees' children. The advantages range from peace of mind for working mothers with pre-school children to more productive workers for employers. Since such projects are often initiated by employees, here are some guidelines you'll need.

1. Gather all the information you can to support your position. Take a survey of the number of employees who would benefit from the project, the number of children to be cared for, the kind of day-care program that would best serve the children, the needs and preferences of the parents, the variety of services to be offered (part-time or flexi-hours, for example), and the benefits to the company.

2. Licensing requirements for day care vary from state to state, so do thorough research on regulations that would affect your establishment. Requirements range from minimum indoor and outdoor space for activities to the size of the staff in relation to the number of children to be supervised. This information can be obtained from the State Department of Human Resources or Social Services.

3. Physical space is a major consideration. Will the company need to renovate a present site or add space to it? What about toilet facilities? Is there room for large play equipment?

4. Prepare a budget that includes the cost of equipment, the number of staff to be hired, what their salaries will be, and carrying expenses such as supplies, food, etc.

5. You will need to decide on a philosophy that will guide the educational and personnel policies of your company's center.

6. If the day-care center is incorporated separately, is not run for profit, and opens itself to the community as well, your company can file for tax-exempt status. If the center is established as a profit-making, wholly owned subsidiary and operates at a loss, your company will receive a 100 percent deduction.

7. Decide early on what health practices are important to your group. Will children be given inoculations and an annual physical checkup? Is a nurse or physician available on a consulting basis? How will you handle emergencies?

8. Will the company absorb the costs, or will each employee using the facility be expected to pay for her child? Or will it be a cost-sharing arrangement between employee and employer? Most day-care centers charge between $25 and $100 a child for each week's care. Offer your company several options so that this point doesn't become a stumbling block.

9. When you've worked out all the details of your plan, approach management with a sound written proposal, supported by a petition signed by the majority of employees, whether or not they have children. It helps to develop an ally in upper management to push your cause. Present your proposal to someone trustworthy, preferably someone who will also benefit from an on-site day-care center.

10. Keep in touch with management after presenting your proposal. Establish a deadline for a response from management. If you get a firm refusal, request an explanation. Don't be discouraged. Bring the subject up again and again. Most day-care centers succeed because employees persist.

The most recent and complete listing of companies offering on-site day-care centers is available in a book titled* Employer Supported Child Care. *It can be ordered from Auburn House Publishing Company, 14 Dedham St., Dover, MA 02030; (617) 785-2220. It costs $16.95.

8 Ways to Make Your Job Fit Your Needs

Have you ever thought that your job could be done just as well at home—and in less time? Though the forty-hour week is still the standard, some companies are experimenting with choices for their employees that would have been revolutionary only a few years ago. Why not explore the possibilities?

1. Flex-Time: As workers' needs become more individualized, some companies are showing more flexibility in arranging schedules. Flex-time permits variations in starting time, in departure time, and even in the number of days a worker is on the job. You can still put in a thirty-five-to-forty-hour week, but not on a regular daily basis. One option is to work four days of the week for ten hours a day. Another is to do some of the work at home and some at the workplace.

2. Permanent Part Time: Although it can be hard to find a part-time job that offers the same rewards as full-time work, there may be a way of turning your present job into a part-time commitment. Professionals, nurses, secretaries, writers, industrial workers, and sales persons are some of the best candidates for arranging working hours that break the nine-to-five routine. In some cases you may have to sacrifice a few of the benefits, such as accumulating seniority, job security, health insurance, paid sick leave, and vacation. However, many companies are now willing to meet employees halfway and make adjustments in benefits.

3. Job Sharing: This is a good option for teachers and office workers. It involves any two people sharing the responsibilities of one full-time job. The salary and benefits are equitably divided in half. For the employer there are several advantages: A wider range of employee skills is garnered, and in emergencies one partner can cover for another. For the employee, the system reduces stress because the job tasks are shared with someone else. Additionally, part-time work can be done in a job that normally doesn't lend itself to a part-time schedule.

4. Working at Home: Computers have opened up this option, since they allow workers to stay in contact with the workplace via computer and phone. Some companies, including Atari and Lanier, have already started allowing employees to work at home. In fact, some industry analysts predict a second industrial revolution that will make the home a center for employment.

5. Freelancing or Consulting: Hiring yourself out as a consultant or freelancer brings a freedom to your work schedule that's not available elsewhere. When you don't have to report to a desk every day at a specific time, you are free to deal with your family's needs. However, when you're called in on an assignment, you must be able to arrange for your child's care immediately. Beware of freelance jobs that simply mean full time with no full-time benefits. The advantages of freelancing should be a higher per-hour wage and the freedom to work your own hours.

6. Temporary Work: Though not conducive to climbing the career ladder, taking on temporary jobs is one way to allow flexibility in your schedule, especially right after your baby is born. Temporary positions can last anywhere from one day to one week to one year. The stipulation is that it's a temporary job that will end on a designated date. Temporary agencies can help you find work, or you can make arrangements with your present employer to work on a temporary basis.

7. Half and Half: Dividing time between home and office is another way of dealing with your family life. Work you do on your own (writing reports, calling clients, etc.) can be accomplished at home, and the work that requires the presence of other people or equipment (attending meetings, working at a machine) can be done when you are at your workplace.

8. Bringing Baby to Work: Before you gasp in horror, realize it has been done. The benefits are enormous: You can breast-feed your baby and help develop that important bond while still spending time on your job. Before bringing this up with your employer, think of some strong arguments for your case. Suggest trying it on a trial or part-time basis to find out if it can work.

JUST FOR YOU

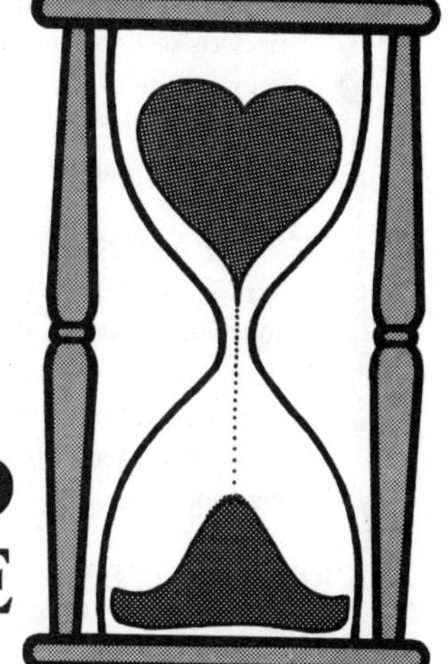

12 WAYS TO FIND MORE TIME WITH YOUR MATE

The biggest complaint most working mothers have—next to not having enough time for themselves—is not having enough time with their husbands. The key to spending more time with your mate is *planning*—don't expect those wonderful times together just to happen. Here are a dozen ideas guaranteed to keep you and your favorite man happily in touch with each other despite your job.

1. Arrange for a baby-sitter to put your children to bed one night a week and go somewhere together, even if it is only for a short time: Take a walk, have dessert and coffee at a pleasant café, drop by the house of friends you've been meaning to see, visit a museum that has evening hours, go ice skating.

2. Make a date for lunch. Keep your rendezvous secret from your work colleagues, and let everyone think it is an important business appointment (in a way it is). Make it somewhere you haven't been together before. Try to arrange your schedules so that you can do this once a month.

3. Invite your children's friends over for dinner from time to time, then orchestrate return invitations so that all your children are invited out at the same time. Surprise your husband with a candle-lit dinner for two at home.

4. Give another couple with children, who get along well with yours, a weekend off by taking their kids from lunchtime on Saturday until Sunday afternoon. When your turn comes to leave your children with them, visit a nearby city, go to a country inn, do all those things you did together on weekends before children, or just stay home and relish the quiet together.

5. Teach your children to respect privacy. When your bedroom door is closed, it means you do not want to be disturbed, although they may knock if there is something important that they need you for. Take advantage of this rule when you and your mate want to be alone together.

6. A time set aside regularly in the evening—when your children are doing their homework or watching television—can give you and your husband a chance to talk together in a different room. (Take the telephone off the hook.)

7. Plan an early-morning activity for your children on Saturday or Sunday, and enjoy breakfast together in bed.

8. Use the local playground or nearby park for picnic suppers in summer. The children will eat and run off to play while you and your husband have a quiet supper for two.

9. Arrange with your boss to take an afternoon off from work, and have your husband do the same. Then the two of you can go to a movie or matinee, or perhaps spend the afternoon at your favorite department store, with each of you buying some new clothes.

10. Take a family vacation to a resort that has organized activities for children. Your travel agent will have suggestions.

11. Enroll in a class, club, or sports activity you can enjoy together regularly—a square-dance club, a bowling league, tennis lessons, a French bread-making class.

12. Look for unexpected times when you and your husband can spend just a few minutes with each other—like taking a shower together in the morning or getting up half an hour earlier and having a quiet cup of coffee before the kids awake. Scheduling brief interludes like this can sustain your relationship until you can find a day or an evening to be by yourselves.

TIRED FEET

Any job that requires you to stand or walk for long periods of time can take its toll on your feet. Although you might not be aware of how much you use your feet, the pain at the end of the day is enough of a reminder. Here are a number of ways to help your feet cope.

IF THE SHOE FITS . . .

Proper foot care begins with wearing shoes that fit. This sounds easy, but most of us are caught up in shoe fashion, rather than shoe fit, and cart home pair after pair of uncomfortably stylish shoes. Though 3-inch heels may *look* better, shoes with sensible 1-inch heels will prove more wearable and cause your feet less pain.

KEEP THE FEET

Some lessons in basic foot care:

1. Keep toenails cut short to prevent ingrowth, which results from pressure against the front of the shoe. The best time to cut nails is right after bathing when they are soft and pliable.

2. After a particularly tiring day, come home and soak your feet in very warm or hot water and Epsom salts.

3. Keep the heels of your feet from cracking in cold weather by applying cream to the area.

4. In warm weather, use talcum powder to absorb moisture and reduce friction.

5. Never wear shoes without socks. Besides providing a breeding ground for athlete's foot, you're exposing your feet to the risk of blisters.

6. Whenever possible, wear socks that are mostly cotton—70 percent cotton to 30 percent nylon is an acceptable ratio. These socks will help your feet breathe.

7. Have your husband (or a professional) massage your feet. Some believe that certain points on the feet correspond to body parts and by relaxing these parts you'll release tension in the body.

PAINFUL PROBLEMS

1. *Corns:* These are caused by tight or short shoes. Find out which pair or pairs are responsible and toss them out. If you have high arches and insteps, you're more prone to corns on the tops and tips of your toes.

There are a couple of ways to treat corns. One method is to use an emery board, instead of a pumice stone, a few times a week. Avoid using corn pads or corn drops with salicylic acid. Although it works quickly, the acid usually burns the good skin surrounding the corn as well. Furthermore, the acid is dangerous for diabetics and others with impaired circulation.

2. *Calluses:* Calluses are found on the balls and heels of feet and can be smoothed down with an emery board or pumice stone. Very thick ones should be removed by a podiatrist. If the callus starts to reform, occasionally rub it with an emery board after bathing. For long-term management, avoid high-heeled shoes, which force the weight of your body onto the balls of your feet.

3. *Blisters:* Small and painless ones can be left alone to heal. Large blisters should be washed with alcohol and popped to speed recovery and help prevent infection. Make a small slit in the blister with a razor blade that's been sterilized in boiling water. Press out the fluid. Though the procedure sounds painful, the pain is minimal since the blistered skin isn't connected to any nerve endings. Clean the area with an antiseptic and cover with a gauze square taped down around the edges. At night, take the bandage off and expose the blister to air to help it heal faster.

4. *Athlete's Foot:* Though we tend to think of this as a man's malady, women get it just as often. There are different forms of the fungus, which can easily spread to other parts of the body by mere physical contact. To treat the itching, scaling, and cracking between the toes, the antifungal liquids or creams available from the drugstore are most effective. Apply powder afterward to help keep feet dry.

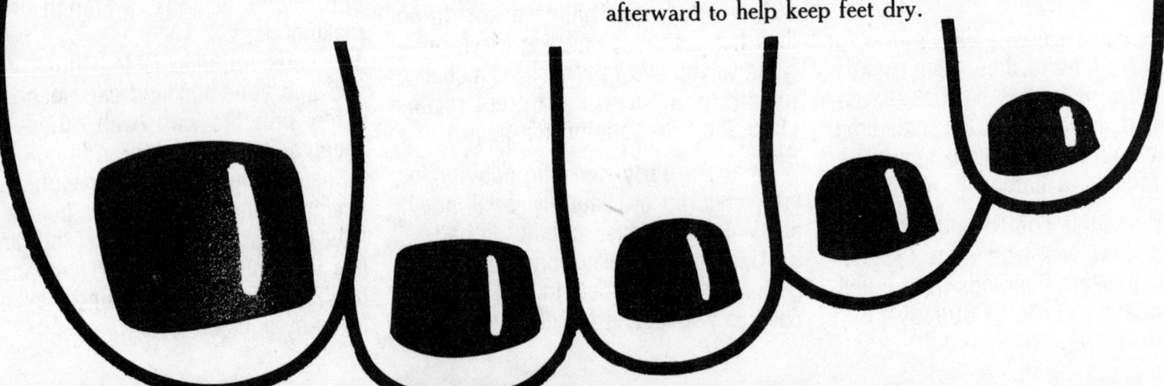

6 Things to Do on Your Lunch Hour

You've probably spent a good many lunch hours shopping. But have you ever thought about using that time for other tasks—some of them more useful and even entertaining? Here are some ideas to consider when eating or shopping have lost their appeal.

1. Join a health club that has a branch near your office, or go to the local Y for lunchtime classes. Many of them offer aerobics, swimming sessions, and yoga groups—and at hours convenient for the working person. If nothing is available in your area, find a quiet, private spot in your workplace to exercise. Set aside one or two lunch hours a week, pretending you actually have an appointment. After spending a few lunch hours this way, it will become a "health" habit you won't want to break because you'll feel and look better on and off the job. Invite a few co-workers to join you. You may be starting something big!

2. How many times have you promised yourself to see an art exhibit at a gallery or to stop in at the museum located not too far from your job? What could be more relaxing in the middle of the day than to stroll over or take a short ride to see something beautiful? Many such places have mini-gardens or benches on the property. Nibble on a sandwich you've brought along before or after you take in the exhibit. You'll go back to work feeling relaxed and ready to face the rest of your workday with less tension.

3. No time to go to the library? Lost your card? Lunchtime is one of the best times to take care of that. There's bound to be a library not too far away where you can get a new card if you need one. Then begin to catch up on those best-sellers you haven't yet read, the ones everybody talks about. You need to go only every week or two. But keep reminders about due dates so you don't run up fines for overdue books.

4. All those letters you mean to write but never find time for finally can be taken care of if you spend one lunch hour a month on your correspondence. You'll be in the good graces of your faraway relatives and out-of-town friends once more.

   Write at your desk during your lunch hour, find a quiet place in a restaurant while you are eating, or pick a private corner in an employee lounge where you work. To start yourself off, buy pretty stationery and some pens with different shades of ink to suit your writing moods.

5. Find a reliable dry cleaner and shoe repair near where you work, and drop your things off during lunch. Many services will have your clothing or shoes ready in a few hours, so you can pick them up on the way home or the next day. Then you won't have to rush home feeling tense because you're afraid you won't beat the stores' closing time.

6. Designate a bill-paying lunch hour (you'll only need to do it once or twice a month) to catch up on your "personal business." You can do this on a park bench during nice weather. Carry your checkbook, bills, receipts, envelopes, and stamps to work in a large brown envelope. You can use any extra time to balance your checkbook or go over bank statements and credit-card bills.

Best Catalogues for Busy Moms

Catalogues open up a whole new world of shopping for the busy working mother. Now you can choose what you and your family need—everything from cosmetics to foodstuffs—without moving off your living room couch.

Gathered here are some of the best catalogues from which to shop, broken down into categories. Some stores will even save you money on brand names, in addition to saving you time.

Books - General

Barnes & Noble, 126 Fifth Avenue, New York, New York 10011

Free 72-page catalogue listing hard- and soft-cover books on almost every subject. Publishers' overstocks are sold at discounts of 80 to 90 percent.

Strand Book Store, 828 Broadway, New York, New York 10003

A variety of catalogues is offered: Strand Specials, Review Specials Half-Price, Art Books, and Rare and Unusual Art Books. Newly published books are 50 percent off, and the store specializes in rare and out-of-print books.

Books - Children

Children's Book and Music Center, P.O. Box 1130, Santa Monica, California 90406-1130

The 96-page catalogue is $1 and lists phonograph records and books. They carry about 25,000 titles from all major publishers.

Nursery Books, 4430 School Way, Castro Valley, California 94546

The 24-page catalogue costs $1 and lists a selection of books for all ages, including cloth books for babies from four to six months old.

Clothing - Children

Esprit, 950 Tennessee Street, San Francisco, California 94107

The famous Esprit line has been tailored to children's and preteen sizes. The 16-page catalogue is $2.

Youngland, 30 N.W. 23rd Place, Portland, Oregon 97210

Youngland offers top name-brand children's clothes in sizes infant through 14. Their 32-page catalogue is free.

Clothing - Maternity

Lady Madonna, 36 East 31 Street, New York, New York 10016

The large catalogue is free and offers maternity clothes for the office, swimwear, and sportswear.

Mother's Work, P.O. Box 40121, Philadelphia, Pennsylvania 19106

The 20-page catalogue includes swatches of fabrics and costs $3. This store offers a full line of business suits and dresses as well as lingerie and sleepwear.

Clothing - Mom and Dad

Cable Car Clothiers, 150 Post Street, San Francisco, California 94108

The 64-page catalogue is free and lists a complete selection of clothing for men and women.

Land's End, Land's End Lane, Dodgeville, Wisconsin 53533

The 112-page catalogue is free and offers traditional sportswear for men and women.

Cosmetics

Beautiful Visions, Inc., 810 South Hicksville Road, C.S. 4001, Hicksville, New York 11802

Free 48-page catalogue listing famous-name cosmetics at a savings of 40 to 75 percent below wholesale.

Boyd's Madison Avenue, 655 Madison Avenue, New York, New York 10021

Send $2 for the 32-page catalogue listing hard-to-find imported toiletries and cosmetics.

Gifts

Neiman-Marcus, P.O. Box 2968, Dallas, Texas 75221

The famous Neiman-Marcus catalogue is 134 pages and costs $3. It sells a number of spectacular gifts (his and her Shar-Pei puppies, for example).

Abercrombie and Fitch, 400 South Edward Street, Mount Prospect, Illinois 60057

The 36-page catalogue is free and offers an abundance of gifts, including Leica binoculars and safari outfits for men and women.

Housewares

Bernie's Discount Center, 821 Sixth Avenue, New York, New York 10001

The 16-page catalogue offers the latest name-brand appliances at cost, plus 15 percent.

The Company Store, 1205 South Seventh Street, Lacrosse, Wisconsin 54601

The 16-page catalogue is free and offers down products at 50 percent less than retail.

Hoffritz, 515 West 24 Street, New York, New York 10114-0041

The 40-page catalogue is free and offers a wide variety of cutlery items.

Conran's, 145 Hugenot Street, New Rochelle, New York 10801

Contemporary designs in furniture from Europe are offered in their free 16-page catalogue.

Laura Ashley, 55 Triangle Boulevard, Carlstadt, New Jersey 07072

The 104-page catalogue is $4 and lists items available for interior decorating, including fabrics, wallpapers, and lamp shades.

Epicure, 65 East Southwater, Chicago, Illinois 60601

Over 160 kitchen utensils are offered in Epicure's free 32-page booklet.

Mail-Order Houses and Department Stores

B. Altman & Co., 361 Fifth Avenue, New York, New York 10016

The 117-page catalogue is free and offers fashions for the whole family as well as jewelry and home accessories.

Harrods, Harrods British Publications, Inc., 11-03 46th Avenue, Long Island City, New York 11101

The 200-page catalogue is $5.50, and yes, the store is still in England. The items offered include perfumes, clothing, gourmet food, luggage, and toys. A great way to shop.

J. C. Penney Co., Inc., P.O. Box 2056, Milwaukee, Wisconsin 53201

The 1334-page catalogue costs $2 and offers everything a big department store is known for.

Macy's, Catalogue Department, 151 West 34 Street, New York, New York 10001

The largest store in the world puts out three catalogues over a three-month period for a cost of $3.

Sears Roebuck and Co., Sears Tower, Chicago, Illinois 60684

Sears' 1400-page catalogue is every child's dream at Christmas or Hanukkah. Everything you could possibly need for the family is inside.

Meats

Amana Society Meat Shop, Amana, Iowa 52203

Smoked ham, sausage, and bacon that have been processed by an old-fashioned method are available from their free 14-page catalogue.

Signature Prime, 143 South Water Market, Chicago, Illinois 60608

A free 6-page brochure lists the corn-fed cuts of beef that Signature Prime supplies to the better American clubs, hotels, and restaurants. Also offered are seafood, lamb chops, veal, and turkey.

Toys

Childcraft, 20 Kilmer Road, P.O. Box 500, Edison, New Jersey 08818

A selection of sturdy toys, furniture for children, and teaching devices is offered from this company, known for quality. The 52-page catalogue is free.

FAO Schwartz, 5th Avenue at 58th Street, New York, New York 10151

The 24-page catalogue is free and lists the entire sampling of one of the greatest toy stores in the world. Life-size stuffed animals, a two-story dollhouse, and child-driven cars are just some of the delights available.

ROUTINES TO UNWIND AT THE END OF A BUSY DAY

At the end of your work day you deserve a break before plunging into the work that inevitably greets you when you walk in the door. Your family will also prefer a more relaxed mom at dinnertime. Arrange for extra time between work and home, arrange for time to yourself after arriving home, or plan an activity with your children that will help you unwind. Here are some suggestions:

1. Enroll in an exercise class after work.
2. Learn a method of meditation that works for you—take 15 or 20 minutes to meditate either in your office before going home or in a church on the way home.
3. Make an appointment to get a massage, a facial, or a haircut on your way home.
4. Stop for a half-hour swim after work.
5. Go jogging or bicycling at the end of the day—alone or with anyone in your family who wants to join you.
6. Take a good novel with you to work and read it on the bus on the way home. If you drive or walk, take time to stop and read a chapter on a park bench or at a café.
7. If you usually take the bus or subway, walk a part of the way home.
8. Buy flowers on the way and arrange them when you get home.
9. Take a warm bath first thing after you get home, then slip into something comfortable.
10. Give yourself a mini-facial: Massage cream into your skin and rinse off with warm washcloths, splash with cold water, and put on fresh makeup.
11. Take half an hour to practice the piano or whatever instrument you used to play when you were a kid. Or start a new instrument such as a recorder and practice it.
12. Either lie down alone in your room or cuddle with your children on the living room sofa or carpet.
13. Take the children outside for a fifteen-minute rope-jumping session.
14. Sit down with your feet up and drink a big glass of orange, vegetable, or tomato juice while you listen to everyone's news.
15. Do simple yoga exercises with the children on the living room floor:
    * Roll your head slowly, first one direction, then the other.
    * Rotate your shoulders slowly, first forward, then backward.
    * Bend over from the waist and hang quiet-

ly for a full minute, then slowly roll up one vertebra at a time.

* Stretch your arms out behind you, hands clasped, lifting them as high as you can while bending forward at the waist.

* Raise your arms slowly above your head while breathing in, stretch them out and exhale as you bring them down. Then jog in place or do a few minutes of jumping jacks.

16. Lie down on the living room floor and let your children give you a backrub.

17. Freshen up with spray-cologne kept cool in the refrigerator before you start fixing dinner.

Some DON'TS:
DON'T turn on the TV set.
DON'T go through the mail—save it for after dinner.
DON'T do grocery shopping on the way home unless there are pleasant, uncrowded places you can shop along the way.

Lunchtime Fitness Exercises

Do you talk about how you need to exercise but can never seem to find the time to do it? There *is* a way to fit in an exercise routine despite a busy home and work schedule. By combining on-the-job body toners with exercises that can be squeezed in during spare minutes, you'll find those excess inches gradually dwindling away.

Try these during your lunch hour, coffee break, or between work assignments. If you have your own office, shut the door. If not, spend a few minutes in the rest room or employee lounge. The following exercises can all be done while seated in a chair. Do each exercise the number of times recommended, but gradually increase the number each day to fit your schedule.

Upper Arm Toner

1. Extend your arms directly in front of you.
2. Raise your arms overhead in a wide "V." Crisscross your arms, back and forth scissor-like, 25 times, and then extend your arms out to the side with palms down.
3. Keeping your arms straight, turn palms up to the ceiling and back to the floor, 25 times, ending with palms down.
4. Bring your arms behind your back and clasp hands and try to raise your arms slowly, 5 times, over the back of your chair. Release and let your arms hang loosely by your side.

Lower Back Release

1. Sit up in your chair and raise your arms above your head while inhaling.
2. Collapse forward over your legs until your head hangs over your knees. Rest your hands on your feet. Exhale and relax all your muscles. Raise yourself and repeat 5 times.

Waist Whittler

1. Sit up in your chair. Grasp the right edge of the seat with your left hand.
2. Curve your right arm over your head and bend to the left as far as you can without pain.
3. Reverse the positions of your arms and alternate sides for a total of 10 bends on each side.

Back Stretch

1. Sit in a chair with your back straight. Grasp the front edge of the seat with both hands. Let your head and shoulders slump forward.
2. Without letting go of the seat, arch your back and sit up tall with your head high. Repeat for a total of 4 times.

Stomach Muscle Toner

1. Lean diagonally back against the chair and grasp the front of the seat with both hands. Raise your legs to form a V with your torso. Bend your right leg at the knee and straighten your left leg while pointing the toes on both feet.
2. Straighten your right leg and bend your left leg, reversing your original position. Alternate for a total of 10 repetitions.

Shoulder Relaxer

1. Sit on the edge of your chair with your feet flat on the floor. Take a deep breath while you raise your shoulders up to your ears (or as far as you can). Exhale slowly while you lower your shoulders and relax. Repeat 5 times. This movement will get the kinks out of your back and shoulders.

How to Accomplish Things You Don't Have Time For

Getting done everything you need to do in the brief span of twenty-four hours a day sometimes seems impossible. Just attending to the necessities of work, household, and child care can become so overwhelming that it's easy to give up on acomplishing anything extra, pursuing a hobby or a sport, even socializing with friends. But all work and no play not only makes Jane a dull girl: It makes her a prime candidate for burnout. Here are some time-saving tricks for getting done all those things you would really like to do but never seem to have time for.

1. Do a little at a time. Many tasks lend themselves to chunks rather than stretches of time. Getting those dining-room curtains made may be easier if you set up a card table where you can leave the work out and do it in half-hour chunks instead of waiting for a free weekend.

2. Don't be inflexible about your plans. If something comes up at the last minute or you remember a chore that must get done, alter your schedule to fit it in. Don't let your appointment book rule your life.

3. Let your friends know the best times to call you; out-of-town relatives in the habit of popping in to see you can be asked to telephone in advance so that you can set aside time to do something together. Use a telephone answering machine or service if necessary to avoid interruptions when you are busy.

4. Learn to delegate tasks to others—on the job and at home. Train your assistant or secretary to take over less important tasks; ask for a summer intern to help out. Hire

help for odd jobs. Get the kids to run errands. Give evening baby-sitters a little extra pay to do mending or ironing after the kids are asleep.

5. Carry work with you—a small packet of stationery or postcards, a paperback novel you'd like to read, a knitting or embroidery project—for those odd moments you're caught waiting for someone.

6. Double up on errands. If there's a good bakery near your children's shoe store, when you take them for shoes, pick up extra bread or rolls to store in the freezer. Schedule dentist appointments for yourself and the kids on the same day.

7. Do two things at once whenever you can. Wash dishes or straighten up your desk while talking on the telephone; brush the dog while watching TV. Use playground time to catch up on reading or portable chores. For example, you can get your mending done if you keep a bag with needles and scissors next to the playground toys and fill it with articles of torn clothing and the requisite thread and buttons.

8. Provide shelves near the front door where you can put items you need to take with you when you go out: shirts for the laundry, clothes for the cleaners, items to be returned to a store, shoes to repair, letters to mail, books to go back to the library. If you put a note on the items, other family members will know to do the errand when they go out.

9. Keep a notebook in your purse to make a list of nonurgent tasks that you can sneak in when time allows: books or games you've read about and would like to buy, supplies needed for a crafts project, ideas for gifts for family or friends.

10. Open charge accounts with stores that will take phone orders and deliver: Department stores, grocery stores, drug stores, cleaners, and liquor stores will often do business this way. Catalogue shopping can save time, too.

11. Use commuting time to advantage, whether by working, reading for pleasure, planning your day, listening to educational tapes, or relaxing.

12. Figure out your best work times and do the most important jobs at those times. Plan work to fit your own biological clock. If vacuuming helps you wind down before going to bed, do it then.

13. Make minor decisions quickly. Don't waste time on unimportant or unnecessary trivia. When you find yourself running out of time, take stock of all you have been doing for the last few days and see where you can eliminate time-wasting activities.

14. When embarking on any project, set a realistic deadline for yourself—whether in hours, days, weeks, or months—and see that you meet it. Longer projects will need to be broken down into manageable units, each of which will have its own allotted timespan.

15. "Don't put off until tomorrow what you can get done today," goes the old saying. Procrastination is a great time-waster. Jobs you find yourself constantly putting off should probably be delegated to someone else; if this is not feasible, then attack these jobs first and reward yourself when they are done.

How to Pamper Yourself When You're Sick

Mothers don't have time to get sick—especially not working mothers. So when illness strikes, the temptation is to keep right on working, muddling through and being heroic. But nothing could be worse for your health and your morale: You're likely to end up sicker still and resentful of all the demands made on you. If you really feel ill, call in sick at the office, get help for the kids and the household—your emergency baby-sitters, your husband, your best friend, whomever you can recruit—and get to bed. When they realize you are serious, your family and friends will gladly pitch in. Let them take over. Your task is to take care of yourself. Do for yourself just what you do for the kids when they are sick: Stock your bedside table with necessities—tissues, medication, a thermos of juice or tea—and entertainment. Relax and enjoy the chance to rest and heal. Sleep all you can; the rest of the time you can:

1. Read all those old magazines or that stack of clippings you've been saving, or try a novel or a mystery.
2. Listen to the radio or your favorite records. You'll have time to hear an opera right through—or the whole Ring cycle for that matter.
3. Catch up with friends through long telephone visits or letters.
4. Bring down fever and freshen up with a lukewarm bath and splashes of your favorite body cologne.
5. Treat yourself to your favorite fresh fruits, juices, milk shakes, and other nourishing foods—or childhood favorites your mother used to give you when you were sick: bouillon and crackers, chamomile tea, strawberry Jell-o, baked custard.
6. Turn on the TV and watch the daytime soap operas you never get to see or the old syndicated sit-coms you loved as a child.
7. Finish knitting that sweater you started umpteen years ago for your oldest that will now fit your youngest.
8. Bring the family photo album up to date.
9. Cheer yourself up by wearing your prettiest nightgown.
10. Have the kids in for individual visits when you feel up to it and if contagion is not a danger. A toddler will appreciate the chance to play quietly at your bedside; an older child may enjoy chatting at length about her activities and concerns.

If a high fever continues for more than two days, or if other symptoms warrant it, get prompt medical attention. Heed the doctor's advice, and be as careful about taking your medication as you are about your children's taking theirs when they are sick. They need a healthy mom.

Don't get up and go back to work as soon as the fever disappears. Give yourself a day to recuperate—and that means not taking over household and child-care responsibilities yet either. But do share your convalescence with your children by playing card or board games, reading to them, or watching a favorite TV program together. They will be delighted to have mom back; you'll be glad to see them, too.

SAFETY

Car Safety

A federal regulation that went into effect in January 1981 requires that all children under the age of four be strapped into car seats. The car seats also must have passed a test under crash conditions to ensure their safety and effectiveness.

Car seats not only protect children in automobile accidents, they also prevent accidents by restraining children who may be too active in the car and may distract the driver.

Depending on the age of your child, there are several styles of car seat that comply with federal regulations:

- INFANT SEAT: Used from the time your baby rides home in the car from the hospital until she weighs up to 20 pounds. To be effective the seat must face backward and should be placed in the back seat.
- CONVERTIBLE SEAT: Can be placed backward or switched forward for toddlers. It can be used from birth to 40 pounds.
- TODDLER SEAT: Protects a 20- to 45-pound child by strapping her in with a safety harness.
- SHIELD SEAT: Allows a toddler more freedom of movement than the harness.
- BOOSTER SEAT: Uses a harness strap anchored at the top for a 20- to 65-pound child.

Here are some safety tips provided by the American Automobile Association:

1. Never hold an infant in your arms while riding in a car. In a vehicle traveling 30 miles per hour, the impact of an accident would throw a 10-pound infant forward with a force of 300 pounds. Also, the adult holding the child would virtually crush him while being thrust forward by the impact of the crash.
2. Most accidents occur at low speeds within 25 miles of home. Don't relax the rules when driving near the home. It's not worth taking the risk.
3. The safest seat in a car is the center back seat. However, you should place a car seat there only if a seat belt is installed for that space. The passenger seat, next to the driver, is often referred to as the "death seat." A child's safety seat should not be used there.
4. When your child outgrows the car seat, a seat belt must be used. You can set a good example by wearing yours. In some states, such as New York and New Jersey, anyone traveling in the front seat without a seat belt is subject to a fine.

Following these safety tips can save your child's life. Can you afford to ignore them even for just a drive around the block?

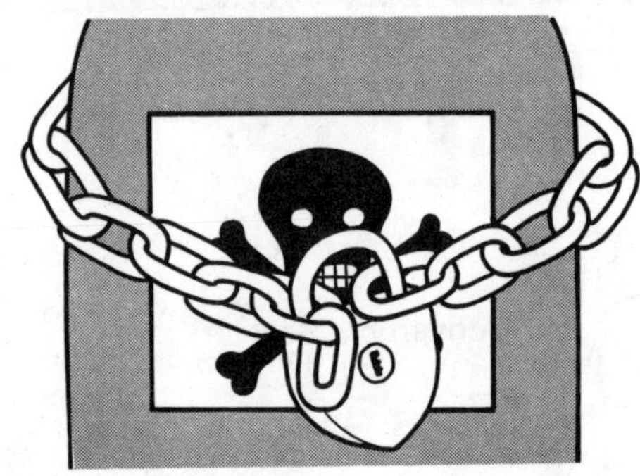

Childproofing Your Home

Toddlers are inquisitive and delight in touching things and investigating new territory. The trouble is that they can't differentiate between safety and danger. You cannot assume that you or another responsible adult will always be there to stop your child from hurting himself or that you can teach him in a few days what's safe and what isn't and trust him to adhere to your guidelines. He will need to learn to respect plenty of "no-no's," since you can't remove every source of danger in his world—but you will only encourage timidity and dependence or rebellion if you fill his life with them. So don't take chances—his life itself may be at stake. Childproofing is your best recourse.

As soon as your child can crawl or move around in a walker—often as early as five or six months—start planning a safe environment for him to explore. Get down on his level and examine your home from his point of view. Search out potentially dangerous items and places that might prove tempting to his eager curiosity. Most homes are full of hazards. Are there dangling cords or tablecloths he could tug at with disastrous results? Are there unstable pieces of furniture he could pull over on himself when trying to help himself stand up? Are there small objects he could taste and choke on? Are there open electrical outlets to poke at or wandering extension cords to grab and bite?

Start by moving all breakables out of his reach and, if possible, out of sight so he won't think of trying to climb up to get them. In low cabinets and drawers containing items you don't want him to get into, install plastic spring locks that can be easily opened by adults but are too tricky for most small children to work. Really hazardous materials, of course, should be kept under lock and key. Use easily accessible cabinets to store unbreakable objects you don't mind him playing with, such as pots and pans and plastic dishes. Bookcases and record shelves can be temporarily blocked off with pieces of Masonite screwed or taped to the shelves, or simply turned around backward until the child is old enough to learn to leave them alone.

Then check all the following:

Medications

Keep them out of reach in a cabinet only adults can open. Ask for safety caps when you buy any medicine. Don't take medicine yourself in front of your child. Get rid of unused medicines by flushing them down the toilet. Be sure overnight guests do not leave medicines where your child may find them, and ask grandparents and other people whose homes your child visits to do the same.

Poisonous Household Items

Keep laundry and dishwasher detergents, bleach, ammonia, and all other regularly used household cleaning agents in their original containers on high shelves. Cigarettes, vitamins, cosmetics, and liquor should also be kept out of children's reach. Less frequently used poisonous items are best kept locked up. Among the most dangerous substances are rat and insect poisons; alkaline cleaners for ovens, toilets, and drains; cleaning fluid; lighter fluid; furniture and floor polishes; metal polish; shoe polish; wax remover; mothballs; turpentine; paint thinners; gasoline; benzene; kerosene; plant sprays. Get rid of any of these items if you don't really need them, and dispose of used containers safely. Marking all toxic substances with "Mr. Yuk" stickers, available from your local Poison Control Center, can help youngsters learn to avoid them.

Poisonous Plants

Hundreds of common household and garden plants have poisonous leaves, flowers, or berries, among them dieffenbachia, philodendron, English ivy, hyacinth, daffodil, oleander, azalea, rhododendron, laurel, and the holiday trio: poinsettia, holly, and mistletoe. Your local Poison Control Center can answer your questions about any particular plants you own. You're safest bet is to do without plants entirely or keep them out of reach and sweep up any leaves or berries as they fall.

Rugs

Tack down scatter rugs or use rubber matting under them to make them slip-proof.

Furniture

Tape foam padding over sharp corners of tables, remove and store glass tops safely away, remove hardware that protrudes from low drawers and cabinets. Put away small tables or plant stands that are easily toppled.

Stairs

Install safety gates at the top and one or two steps from the bottom of all staircases. Provide carpeting and a low handrail to help your child learn to use stairs safely, and practice with him going up and down.

Bathtubs

Make yours slip-proof with a good rubber mat. Turn down the thermostat on your hot water heater to between 120 degrees and 125 degrees Fahrenheit to prevent accidental scalding, and always test the water before letting a child get into it. Never leave a child alone in the bathtub for even one second. Bath mats with non-skid backing help prevent falls on slippery wet floors.

Windows

Install window guards on all windows above street level.

Electrical Hazards

Plug unused electrical outlets with plastic safety caps. For outlets that are in use, there's a special outlet cover to prevent a child from pulling the cord out; however, since plugged-in electrical wires carry current in them even when the lamp or appliance is not in use, it is best to keep all wires out of reach and out of sight behind heavy furniture and to unplug all small appliances immediately after using them. Don't leave lamp sockets empty.

Dangerous Tools and Household Objects

Knives, scissors, power tools, matches, cigarette lighters, razor blades, small coins, pins, needles, buttons, beads, plastic bags, curtain and telephone cords, exposed springs, guns and ammunition, knitting needles, you name it—anything sharp, capable of producing a flame, small enough to swallow, long enough to strangle on, or dense enough to suffocate on must be stowed safely away out of reach. Gradually, very gradually, your child will learn to use all of these things properly, some sooner than others. In the meantime, you will need to devise your own safe storage systems.

Personal Safety Habits

Develop safe cooking habits: Keep pot handles turned away from the edge of the stove, and use back burners for frying and boiling. Don't leave a burning cigarette anywhere, and avoid smoking in your child's presence. Don't let your child climb up into your lap when you are having a cup of hot coffee or tea, and don't put a hot drink down near the edge of a table. Keep tabs on what your child is doing, and keep him from wandering off to other rooms where you cannot supervise him by using gates in doorways or putting doorknob covers on the doorknobs. Keep wastebaskets above his reach, and be careful where you dispose of trash. Run a quick safety check of your home every day.

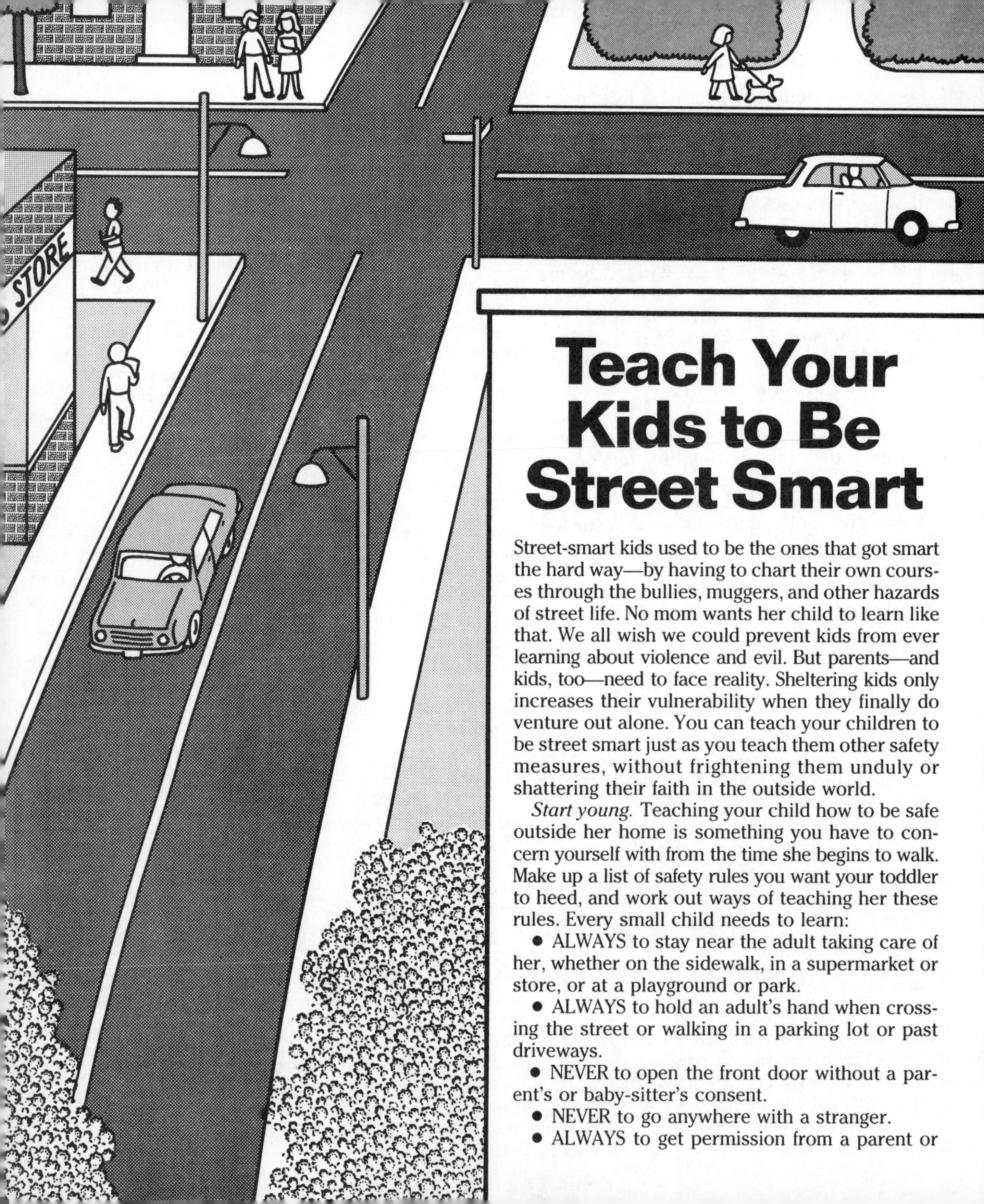

Teach Your Kids to Be Street Smart

Street-smart kids used to be the ones that got smart the hard way—by having to chart their own courses through the bullies, muggers, and other hazards of street life. No mom wants her child to learn like that. We all wish we could prevent kids from ever learning about violence and evil. But parents—and kids, too—need to face reality. Sheltering kids only increases their vulnerability when they finally do venture out alone. You can teach your children to be street smart just as you teach them other safety measures, without frightening them unduly or shattering their faith in the outside world.

Start young. Teaching your child how to be safe outside her home is something you have to concern yourself with from the time she begins to walk. Make up a list of safety rules you want your toddler to heed, and work out ways of teaching her these rules. Every small child needs to learn:

- ALWAYS to stay near the adult taking care of her, whether on the sidewalk, in a supermarket or store, or at a playground or park.
- ALWAYS to hold an adult's hand when crossing the street or walking in a parking lot or past driveways.
- NEVER to open the front door without a parent's or baby-sitter's consent.
- NEVER to go anywhere with a stranger.
- ALWAYS to get permission from a parent or

baby-sitter before going anywhere with someone she knows.

- What to do if she gets separated from whoever is taking care of her: Stay put. Call, scream, or cry loudly (chances are her guardian is not far away and will hear the cries). Look for a uniformed security guard or policeman and tell him or her her name and that she is lost. Don't go anywhere with anyone not in uniform who offers to help.
- To say NO to adults who hold her or touch her in ways she is not comfortable with.

Inculcate these rules. Your child will learn these rules only by constant repetition, consistent enforcement, patient explanation, and frequent example.

- Define the word "stranger" many times. Make pointing out strangers a game when you are out together. Explain that strangers are people we don't know, so we don't know if they are good people or bad people.
- Take her to your local police station. She will get to see the police dogs or run the siren on a police car. It will reinforce the lesson that police are friendly and helpful and teach her to recognize police uniforms.
- Begin to teach traffic safety by asking the child to watch the pedestrian signs and to tell you which way to look for cars. Play games when walking or driving that will increase her awareness of traffic rules.
- Talk about her fears, her daily activities, her relationships, especially to adults and older children. Respect her feelings. Do not ask her to be friendly with people she dislikes.

Prepare your child to go out alone. As your child gets older, think of all the things she will need to know when she goes out by herself:

- Her address and phone number with area code
- Her parents' phone numbers at work
- The safest route to take to where she is going
- How to cross streets safely
- Where to turn for help—friends' houses, storekeepers, police and fire stations, the post office
- Where there are public telephones in your neighborhood and how to call for help
- To refuse any offers from strangers, whether of candy, money, or rides
- Not to answer requests for directions. People needing directions should ask an adult.
- To walk confidently and purposefully
- Not to flaunt her money or possessions
- Not to keep all her money in one pocket or wallet
- That there is safety in numbers—on the sidewalk, at playgrounds, in public restrooms, at the movies
- What to do if she is being followed—cross the street, walk in the opposite direction, go into a store and ask for help
- What to do if she is asked for money—stay calm, give up the money or other possession, get a good look at the mugger so that she can describe him later, report the incident to the police immediately afterward

She cannot learn all these things the night before she walks to school alone for the first time. Teach them gradually. Play lots of "what if" games to find out if she can recognize and avoid dangerous situations and to prepare her to cope with an attack or assault.

Let go gradually. You will decide when she is ready to walk alone to a friend's house, to a store, or to school, depending on the safety of your neighborhood. Increase her independence little by little. Her first ventures out alone might be to a friend's house on the same side of the street or to a small store around the corner. Have her begin crossing the street with you but without holding your hand, then alone while you watch. Send her on an errand with a friend her age. Don't let her prod you into allowing her more freedom than you think she can handle; don't push her if she is reluctant. Get together with other parents of children her age in your neighborhood to discuss the safety measures they take and to plan ways you can coordinate your efforts to make your kids street smart.

Helpful Books

Private Zone by Frances Dayee (Warner Books)
Safety Zone by Frances Dayee (Warner Books)
How to Raise a Street-Smart Child: The Complete Parents' Guide to Safety on the Street and at Home by Grace Hechinger (Facts on File)

WHEN AND HOW TO LEAVE YOUR CHILD ALONE

One of the nicest—and yet scariest—moments in parenthood is the first time you walk out of your house and leave your child home without a baby-sitter. You relish the new-found freedom while quaking with new-found fears. You're glad your daughter is learning to take care of herself, but you're scared there's something crucial you've forgotten to tell her. Staying home alone is a big responsibility for a child, and for both your sakes, you'll want to be sure both of you are well prepared to take this step.

When Is My Child Ready?

No one can tell you what age your child must be before she may stay home alone after school or when you go out at night. You need to decide this for yourself. Affirmative answers to the following ten questions are a good sign she may be ready:

1. Does your child like the idea of staying home alone?
2. Does she know how to use the telephone?
3. Does she communicate well with adults?
4. Can she lock and unlock the doors by herself?
5. Is she always careful and obedient about safety rules—not handling matches, not climbing on furniture, not using knives or tools she has been told not to use?
6. Does she react calmly when things go wrong—not going to pieces over an accidental spill or a broken toy?
7. Is she good at following instructions and solving problems?
8. Does she tell you spontaneously about everything that happens in her life?
9. Do you have a close relationship?
10. Do *you* think she is mature enough to take care of herself and get help in dealing with any emergencies that might arise?

However willing and mature she is, the answers to three other questions are going to influence your decision:

1. Does your house have adequate security?
2. Do you consider your neighborhood safe?
3. Is there an adult your child knows who lives nearby and will be available to assist her in an emergency?

When you've decided your child *is* ready, test your assumptions by leaving her alone at home for a short period. Walk the dog. Go get groceries. Have coffee with a friend. Discuss with her how she felt, what she did while you were out. If you were both comfortable, start preparing her for the time she will be home alone after school and, sometime further down the line, when you are out for the evening.

1. Have a fire drill. Teach your child fire safety rules—not to try to put out a fire, but to leave the house and call the fire department from a pay phone or alarm; not to open a hot door; not to use elevators; how to "stop, drop, and roll" if her clothes catch fire; the best exits to take.
2. Make a list of emergency phone numbers and phone numbers of adult friends. Go over with her whom to call for help and whom to call for companionship. Have her call you at work as soon as she gets home from school every day.
3. Make a list of rules for her to obey whenever you are not at home: which friends are allowed to visit (if any), what appliances she may and may not use, what activities she may and may not pursue, where she may and may not go in the neighborhood, what time she must be home.
4. Review basic first aid. Make a first-aid kit and store it where she can easily reach it. She should also have access to an authorization form for emergency medical treatment, which you have signed and had notarized.
5. Teach her to be careful not to let strangers know she is home alone:
   * She should keep her house keys out of sight in her book bag or pocket or inside her clothing.
   * She should never open the door to strangers.
   * She should never reveal to anyone calling on the telephone that you are not home; she should simply say, "My mother is busy. If you will leave your name and number, she will call you back."
6. Teach her to look carefully as she enters the house to be sure nothing is awry and to leave immediately if she suspects an intruder has been—and may still be—there.
7. Act out what to do in a variety of situations she might have to deal with. Self-reliance courses (such as those developed by some chapters of national organizations like the Camp Fire Council and the Boy Scouts of America) and books and pamphlets addressed to children can reinforce your advice and help build her confidence. Recommended are:

   By Yourself by Sara D. Gilbert (Lothrop, Lee & Shepard)

   In Charge: A Complete Handbook for Kids with Working Parents by Kathy S. Kyte (Knopf)

   Prepared for Today, published by the Boy Scouts of America

   The Official Kids' Survival Kit: How to Do Things on Your Own by Elaine Chaback and Pat Fortunato (Little, Brown and Company)
8. Plan ways she can use her time to keep boredom and loneliness at bay—snacks, homework, chores, projects, games and activities. Make a list of suggestions of things to do that she can consult when she runs out of ideas.

SINGLE MOMS

Coping with the "Daddy Lets Me" Syndrome

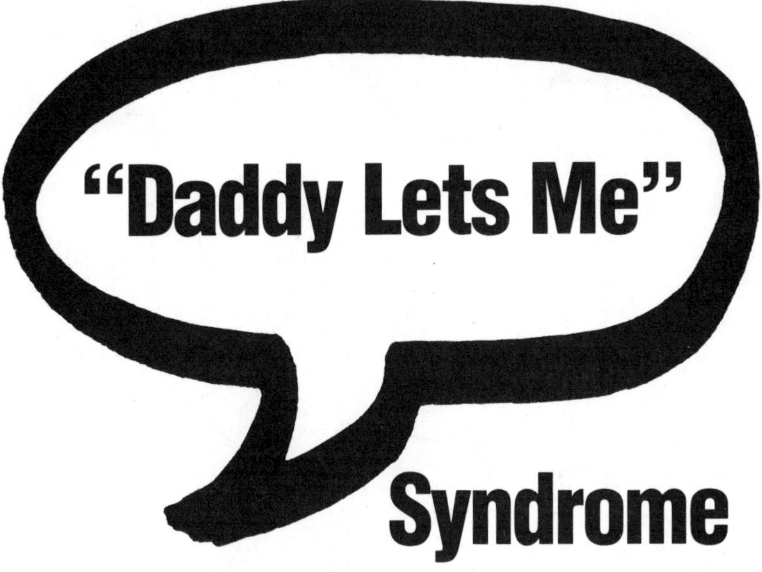

All parents face the problem of dealing with differences in child-raising methods, but it becomes exacerbated when the parents are not communicating well with each other. Kids are very quick to take advantage of this situation. The divorced mom with custody of her children has the hardest time of all: Not only does she find herself bearing the entire burden of disciplining the children at a time when it is particularly needed, but her ex, feeling deprived and angry, may take revenge by actively undermining the structure she is trying to build. How to cope:

1. Resist the temptation to compete. If you play the same game and grant them privileges you would not ordinarily agree to in hopes of winning their loyalty or irking your ex, you will only encourage further manipulation on their part. No one wins this game.

2. Be frank with your kids. Without rancor, simply explain that you and daddy do things differently. You do not think ice cream before dinner is a good idea. Explain why. Don't try to explain his motives or say, "That's why we're divorced!" Just tell them you expect them to follow your rules when they are with you. Remind them that they are used to different approaches to discipline. Their teachers, for example, expect them to follow certain rules in school that are not required at home.

3. Keep communication lines open. You and your ex don't need to talk about anything else in your lives, but you do need to talk about the children. Establish a regular time, convenient for both of you, when the children are not around, to set up schedules, to let him know about the children's activities, to discuss problems and iron out difficulties. He will feel less angry and left out if he knows more about what is going on and is included in decisions affecting the children.

4. Make it less easy for him to be the spoiler. If your ex-husband sees the children only for Sunday outings, make him take over more custodial responsibility by encouraging overnight visits or visits at your home when you are out. Suggest that he see the children in more natural child–parent situations, perhaps have them over to his place even if it is small and give them chores and responsibilities there.

5. Don't be reluctant to seek outside aid. Professional counseling or family therapy can provide support for you, make suggestions for improving communication between you and your ex, analyze problems, and teach practical ways of changing destructive patterns of behavior.

When There's a New Man in Your Life . . .

It hasn't been easy. The man you married is gone. You've been juggling job and children, your grief and theirs. The last thing you expected was for that nice man at work to stop by your desk and invite you for a cup of coffee. He's getting divorced, he says; maybe you'd like to go out to a movie with him? But what will you tell the kids?

1. Say nothing. Your first date is a momentous occasion for you, but one they need know nothing about. After all, you are likely to be meeting and dating other men, too. There is no need for them to meet every man in your life; there is time enough for that if a more serious relationship develops. Tell the children you have a meeting (you do), and meet him at the movie theater or a coffee shop. And you're old enough to come home alone.

2. Easy does it. Begin to tell your kids about your new friend if you continue to date him and it seems that your friendship will last. He needn't be a marriage prospect, although he might be. Bring the matter up casually, and let them know a little about him and how much you enjoy knowing him. Pique their curiosity. Let them ask when they will get to meet him. Involve them in the decision to invite him to dinner one weekend.

3. Arrange a meeting. The first meeting works best if it is casual, short, and relaxed, possibly on some neutral turf.

* Choreograph a "spontaneous" meeting. Have him "run into" you when you are somewhere with the kids—shopping, the library, church. Introduce everyone and chat briefly, then go your separate ways. That will give the kids a chance to react and to voice their reactions to you, not him.

* If he works in your office, take the kids one day to see where you work, then introduce him along with your other co-workers.

* Have him drop by for a short visit at home—not when you are going out on a date afterward. Just you, him, and the kids—this is no time for any outside opinions. If he has kids, too, then you can meet them at a separate, similar gathering (no need to create new sibling rivalries yet).

4. Involve him in your family life. Play it by ear. Depending on their reactions either to the news that you are dating someone or to him after they have met, plan the best ways of involving him in your lives.

* Pick situations that will not mimic the role your former spouse played. Have him for dinner, but seat him in the guest's chair, not where your husband sat. Take him along to watch your daughter's basketball game, but not if her father was always her best fan. He has his own skills, talents, and interests: See where these can mesh with what you and the children enjoy doing.

* Listen to any complaints. Your kids will doubtless feel that compared to their father, this new man doesn't measure up. Just listen.

* Don't push him on them. If they take an intense dislike to him, play it cool. Keep dating—he's *your* friend, after all—but don't plan to include him in all your family time. Vary the scene: Spend time alone with each child and time with them without him. You can let them know that you are disappointed they don't like him but that you still like him a lot. Unless their jealousy is excessive or your choice has not been a good one, they'll come around.

* Don't flirt or otherwise flaunt your relationship with him in front of the kids. Be friendly and discreet. You want them to like him, not to see him as a rival for your affections.

5. Staying overnight. An occasional overnight visit is probably best treated the way you would handle the overnight stay of any guest—male or female. Let him sleep in the guest room or on the couch. Regular visits are another matter: If you and he are deeply involved yet not ready to live together or marry, you will need to tell your children that he will be living with you some of the time. Explain it as a kind of trial marriage, something couples do to help them decide whether they can get along well enough to make a more permanent commitment.

6. Living together. The decision to live together is apt to be easier for children to understand and come to terms with than frequent, irregular sleep-overs. Especially if they've been through the pain of divorce, they can sympathize with your wish to live together before remarrying; they don't want any more big changes. You can help them counter any teasing or criticism they get by reaffirming to them the reasons for your decision. Be open and honest with everyone else about your relationship, too. It will help your children if they see your friends accept your living arrangements.

7. Remarriage. You've carefully prepared the kids for the new man; he's no longer new. They know him well and like him. You and he have decided to marry. Suddenly they come up with a lot of objections, for marriage is another ball game. Listen and be patient. Include them in your plans and decisions. Give them a say in any changes in living arrangements. Have them take part in the wedding ceremony; after all, they are getting married, too. It will give them an active role in the new family unit.

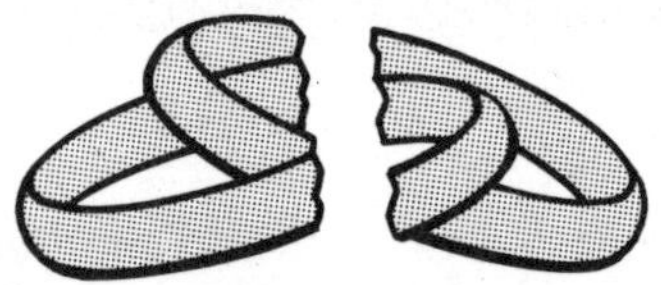

How to Cope with Your Ex-Husband

Getting a divorce—even one that fits Oscar Wilde's quip about divorces being made in heaven—isn't an easy step. You may be delighted or depressed—or a little of both—by the departure of your spouse, but either way, major adjustments lie ahead. One of the hardest is finding a new footing for dealing with the man you loved enough to marry and have children with.

Emotional Divorce

Legal divorce can be accomplished pretty quickly these days, but emotional divorce usually takes much longer. If you are still in love with him or if you still care enough about the hopes and dreams you had for your life together to hate him for dashing those dreams, then you are not really emotionally divorced. Every meeting, every exchange, will be difficult, loaded with open or barely concealed fury. Until you deal with your own inner turmoil, face up to your own contribution to the failure of the marriage, and accept your new single status as the springboard to a new life, the going can be rough. During this period of adjustment, you will need all the self-control you can muster. To help speed this process, it's best to keep contact to a minimum and limit communication as much as possible to issues having to do with the children.

- Avoid asking him to do little chores he used to do, like moving heavy furniture or fixing a leaky faucet, even if he is willing. Finding other sources of help and becoming more independent yourself are important goals for you.
- Be realistic in your expectations—don't imagine he will be more helpful and supportive as an ex-husband than he was as a husband.
- If communication becomes antagonistic, written notes may be necessary for a time. Or use your lawyer.
- Don't come between him and his children; help and encourage him to meet his responsibilities toward them. But don't use the children as an excuse for frequent phone calls or conferences. Learn to make your own decisions about how to handle behavioral problems.
- Don't be offended by his criticisms; if you think they are unfair, ignore them. Arguing back can only lead to further acrimony.
- Friendly visits or dates only prolong the ordeal of emotional divorce. They can be very destructive when they re-open old wounds that time has begun to heal. Some couples seem to need these encounters to remind them of why they got divorced, but it's not a good idea to encourage them.
- Keep your emotional distance by not getting involved in his personal problems or telling him about yours.

TRAVEL

Air, Bus, and Train Travel Tips

Traveling with kids by public forms of transportation entails many of the same hassles as traveling by private car—and a few more. Negotiating children and luggage through crowded airports or bus or train stations, waiting when journeys get delayed, and keeping behavior sufficiently under control so as not to disturb other passengers are added to the burdens of finding amusing pastimes and coping with motion sickness. But there are some pluses. The novelty of the experience can create enough excitement to extend the kids' good humor beyond its normal bounds, and even buses and planes allow more freedom of movement than the family car. And—in most cases—bathroom facilities travel right along with you. Here are some suggestions for happy traveling:

1. Reserve seats ahead whenever possible. Let airlines know that you are traveling with children and what their ages are. Some airlines still have bassinets that attach to the bulkhead for small infants, but you need to arrange for them in advance. Airplane seats at the front of the coach section usually offer the most legroom—which becomes space for small children to play on the floor.

2. Ask for priority in boarding, or if seats are reserved, wait until other passengers are on board; it will save standing in slow-moving lines.

3. A lightweight diaper bag with a shoulder strap is essential when traveling with an infant. You'll need diapers, ointments, wipes, a small blanket, a change of clothes, a bib or two, small toys, teething biscuits, and any food he will require.

4. Dress children in bright, easy-to-spot colors to help keep track of them in crowds. If you put siblings in similar outfits, even strangers will help keep them together.

5. A harness may be useful to keep tabs on an active toddler; be sure to accustom him to it first.

6. For children three and under, a lightweight folding stroller can come in handy if there are long corridors to traverse in getting to the plane or train. If the child wants to walk, you can always use it to wheel your carry-on bags.

7. When traveling to a different climate, pack and check boots, hats, gloves, and coats for the whole family in one soft bag. You will have fewer carry-ons to worry about. When you arrive in the colder place, you can button everyone into an overcoat when you retrieve your luggage at the baggage claim. Fold up the empty bag and tuck it into another suitcase.

8. Give each child a small bag he can tote himself (but be prepared to take it if he gets tired). Fill it with a favorite small toy or two, a pad and pencil, a small activity book, or some stickers or stamps. A zipper will help everything stay in the bag.

9. Be prepared to entertain small children. Some kids are lulled to sleep by the sounds and motions of travel, but others are so curious about the new environment that they won't sleep even if you travel at night or naptime. Take books to read—the paperback Beatrix Potter, the Nutshell library, or the small paperback versions of Richard Scarry's books are all lightweight, little, and popular with kids; several will fit into your purse or the child's tote bag.

10. Bring munchies and beverages—especially on airplanes for takeoff and landing, when changes in air pressure bring discomfort or even pain to small ears. (Few airlines these days offer gum or mints!) Babies should be given a bottle or breast-fed during takeoff and landing so that their swallowing will even out the pressure on both sides of the eardrum. Food is also important in case of delays, since the meal is usually postponed right along with the flight. Fresh fruit, unsalted nuts, granola bars, and packaged juices, however bulky and heavy to tote, will save the day.

Traveling with Kids: the Pros & the Cons

There are all kinds of travel: long trips and short trips, seashore vacations, holiday weekend getaways, business trips, family visits, travel abroad, camping, and cruises. Parents making any kind of travel plans are always faced with an additional decision: Should we take the kids? Some parents would never dream of going anywhere without them, as if they were permanent attachments; others would never dream of taking them along. Both groups are missing out on a lot, for travel can be both wonderful family time and wonderful escape-from-family time. So when you think about taking the kids on a trip, consider the following:

The Pros

1. You won't have to arrange for someone to take care of them, and you won't worry about them while you are away.

2. You can get a kid's-eye view of other cities and foreign countries, discovering parks and playgrounds, children's museums and zoos you wouldn't otherwise see.

3. Kids love most tourist attractions—climbing monuments and bell towers, watching folk dancing, taking boat and train rides, clambering over old ruins, or walking through elegant palaces. Even a two-year-old can be awed by the Swiss Alps or the rose window at Chartres.

4. Traveling with children does not necessarily mean you will have no time alone. Bonded baby-sitters are available in most major resorts and cities of the world.

5. Travel provides excellent opportunities for sharing in your children's education. They'll be learning about other cultures and foods, new climates and landscapes; they'll get geography and history firsthand, as it were; and the best part is, you'll be learning it all together.

6. A self-reliant teenager can be a wonderful companion on a business trip you would otherwise take alone. He can visit museums or take a tour while you are in meetings, then you can share the evening together.

7. Planning a family vacation to tie in with your own or your spouse's professional meetings can be rewarding, especially if the location is attractive. Hotel and travel rates are often discounted, and during the meeting you will be seeing other people you know and can get together with other families attending. Some professional meetings offer interesting activities for members' spouses and children.

8. Family travel brings family members together, away from the distractions of work, school, telephone calls, and meetings, and the busy schedules that pull parents and children apart. It gives time to share thoughts, to read together, to play silly games, to get acquainted in new ways, to make memories that will become treasured parts of your family history.

The Cons

1. You will have less time to stroll through museums, take in the nightlife, and eat at elegant restaurants. Small children are apt to get restless during guided tours.

2. Getting small children to sleep in unfamiliar surroundings, particularly when the whole family is sharing one hotel room, can be tedious.

3. A restful, carefree vacation is unlikely if you have small children who respond to the stimulus of new surroundings by waking early. (Taking along an energetic teenager to help look after them may solve this problem.)

4. If your trip requires long hours of travel with close connections and a full schedule of adult-oriented events at the other end, children will probably feel rushed and left out.

5. If what you and your husband really want and need is a second honeymoon together, it's fairer to both the children and yourselves to leave them home. Or give them their own trip to visit friends or relatives or a summer camp.

6. Forcing family vacations on an unwilling teenager can be disastrous. Bringing along the friend he can't bear to be apart from may save the day; or make arrangements for him to stay with another family while you are away.

R FOR AMUSEMENT PARK FUN

Amusement parks should be fun. But how often they become an ordeal: harried parents pulled this way and that by overexcited kids, one pleading for another ride on the bumper cars, a second whining for a soda pop, and a third needing a rest room; long lines in the hot sun; traffic jams; and all for more money than you were prepared to spend. Making a family outing at an amusement park a success—whether it is a week at Disney World or a day trip to a nearby theme park—takes the same kind of forethought and planning any family travel does. Here are some tips for a tip-top time:

- Write or phone ahead to ask for information about hours, attractions, prices, recommended ages for the activities provided, food facilities, whether picnics are allowed, whether there are indoor as well as outdoor activities, and the least crowded days and hours. Some parks, such as Disney World in Orlando, Florida, will mail you a brochure with advice to help you plan your visit.
- Plan your outing for the less crowded times. If you cannot go during the week, at least try to avoid major holidays and get there early. Arriving at opening time is usually a good idea.
- Don't pick the hottest day of the year. Amusement parks can be just as much fun on cloudy days as on sunny ones.
- Prepare your children by letting them look at a brochure and telling them about the attractions. If your child is terrified of alligators or Ferris wheels and these are major attractions, perhaps he isn't ready for this particular outing.
- Few amusement parks are really appropriate for very small children. You and your older kids will probably have a better time without a tired, cranky toddler to tend, even if he does enjoy some of it and does get in free.
- Don't take too many kids. Letting each child bring a friend can be fun, but it can double the difficulty of pleasing and keeping track of them. Be sure those you do invite along will mind you.
- Providing your own food, snacks, milk, and fruit juice has several advantages—they're cheaper and healthier, and you don't have to stand in lines for them. Pack them in disposable containers so your load will lighten as the kids eat. A backpack or shoulder bag is easiest to tote.
- Before leaving home, make it clear just how much and what kinds of candy and junk food will be purchased—if at all. Ditto for balloons and souvenirs.
- If there are separate charges for the various rides and attractions, set reasonable limits on how much each child will be allowed to spend.
- Any restrictions on rides you consider unsafe should also be decided beforehand.
- Get a map ahead of time or on arrival, and plan your route together. Aim for a balance of active and passive experiences—a romp in the ball pool, say, then a film. Note where rest rooms are, and make stops when you are nearby, before the situation is desperate.
- Join in the fun yourself. When did you last ride a roller coaster?
- Don't try to squeeze in too much. Take a break before the kids get tired. Sitting in the shade with a lemonade or an ice cream cone will stoke everyone's energy. And leave early while cheerful moods still prevail: You'll avoid traffic congestion, and the kids will have a chance to wind down before bedtime.

Surviving Long Car Trips

A long car trip with kids can be agony—but it doesn't have to be if you plan well in advance and make sure the car is well stocked with activities, amusements, and food to help while away the miles. Here are some ideas to consider:

THE TOY BOX

A tote bag can become a handy toy chest. Fill it with things your children like to do—toys and games, reading and listening materials, paper and pencils.

Some good toys to take along are wind-up music boxes with pictures, viewers with animal slides, a kaleidoscope, small plastic mazes and pinball games, Bristle Blocks, a magic slate, portable computer games, sewing cards, toy cars and trucks. It's a good idea to set aside toys for the trip a week or more before leaving, or even better, provide toys that are used only in the car, never at home; they'll seem like new. Some could even be wrapped and put in a drawstring "grab bag" for the child to reach into for a "surprise" when boredom sets in.

For reading, small books are handy, as are new issues of children's magazines, a paperback with a selection of stories for you to read aloud, and a song book with pictures.

A portable tape recorder and a selection of cassettes will hold a child's attention for long stretches. Make your own tapes ahead of time from records borrowed from the library, or buy cassettes of popular children's stories and songs. Some cassettes come with books to look at or draw in while listening.

The car is a fine place for artwork, too: Provide a blank book made out of stapled construction paper and a package of markers; paint-with-water books and a bag of wet cotton swabs; and stickers for collages.

THE FOOD STASH

A tote bag full of healthy snacks helps everyone's mood. Bring fruit juice in paper packs with straws, unsalted nuts and raisins, apples, small peanut-butter-and-honey sandwiches, granola bars, raw vegetables (carrot sticks, celery, peas, string beans). Avoid overly sweet or salty foods (they will deplete your juice supply and increase your bathroom stops) and foods that don't travel well—you don't want to end the trip with a bag of brown bananas, bruised pears, and crumbled cookies. Your bag should also have a roll of paper towels, a plastic bottle of water, a Swiss Army knife, and a bottle opener.

One note of caution: Children with a tendency to motion sickness travel best on empty stomachs and should not eat in a moving vehicle. If your child is easily carsick, ask your pediatrician for medication to give the child before the trip and be sure the car is well ventilated. Any meal eaten before or during the trip should be small and bland. Bring along a motion sickness bag just in case.

PIT STOPS

Stops will be necessary on any trip longer than one and a half hours, especially with very young children. Make sure everyone "tries" the bathroom whether he thinks he needs to or not, then let off some steam with five minutes or so of jumping jacks and races. A lunch stop at a picnic area gives a chance for more exercise.

On a very long car trip, don't make unnecessary stops or stops longer than thirty minutes, as it will only make the travel time seem that much longer. If you want to visit an interesting attraction en route, be sure it will be worth the time lost.

Be prepared for emergency stops with plenty of pre-moistened paper towels. And plan a "treat" stop near the end of the trip to reward weary travelers—an ice-cream cone is always welcome.

SLEEPY TIME

Some children are lulled to sleep by the motion of the car. A pillow, a small blanket, such as a receiving blanket, and a favorite cuddly toy, maybe one with a music box, will give comfort to sleepyheads. If your children do sleep well in a car, you may want to plan to take longer car trips at night.

GAMES TO PLAY

Car trips are a good time for family games and singing. Practice your story-telling skills, teach your children all the songs that were popular when you were a teenager, and let them teach you songs they've learned at school. Play Twenty Questions—you think of something, and your children can ask twenty questions to figure out what it is—or I Spy—one player says "I spy a _____." The other players then have to guess what it is. Another fun game is Suitcase. The first player starts with: "I'm going on a trip and taking a nightgown in my suitcase." The second counters with the same but adds something of his own. Each player adds an item but must repeat all of the previous items mentioned.

You can also try License Plate: Have everyone choose a number and then see if the license plate of the next car that passes you has those numbers. Compose silly poems: The first player makes up a line, the next adds a line that rhymes with it, and so on. Get in a few stretches by playing Simon Says.

GETTING KIDS READY FOR CAMP

A working mom's dream: two whole childless months, while your kid enjoys fresh air, sunshine, and active sports and learns the responsibilities and discipline of group living. He gets the healthy outdoor life, the camp-fire songs, marshmallows, and close friendships; you get the freedom to focus on career and husband, your friends and interests. Here's how to make this wonderful deal work:

1. Wait until your child is ready. Patience will pay off. If you push the idea too soon, you may turn him off entirely. A summer is a long time to a youngster: The thought of spending it away from home in new, unfamiliar surroundings is pretty scary. Don't be surprised if your seven- or eight-year-old isn't ready. Prepare him with shorter stays away from home, gradually lengthening the time spent away: sleepovers with friends, a weekend with another family, a week with relatives in a different town. As he gets used to longer separations, and as he gets older, he'll overcome his anxiety. If he has been fearful, it might be a good idea to make his first camp experience shorter—one month, say, instead of two.

2. Get him used to camping experiences. Almost as scary as the length of time involved is the strangeness of group living. Day-camp experience is helpful. Some day camps have the added bonus of one- or two-night sleepovers as part of their program, or your son's scout troop or some other club may organize a weekend trip: Take advantage of opportunities like these. Camping trips with another family or even "pretend" camping at home can introduce some camping routines that may be unfamiliar and let him know how enjoyable camp can be.

3. Choose the camp carefully—and together. Camps vary a lot in size and philosophy: Some are highly structured and competitive, others more easygoing and nurturing. The camp his father or his cousin went to may not be the right one for your child. Look for a camp geared to his interests and personality. The American Camping Association offers a free camp referral service to help parents match kids and camps. When you write to a camp for information, ask for the names of campers in your area who can tell you and your child about their experiences.

4. Provide whatever support you can. Having a friend or sibling at the camp will reassure a first-time camper a lot; but if this isn't the case, you can still help by getting him together beforehand with a child who already knows the camp and can tell him about the fun he's had there. Keep a positive outlook yourself—don't undermine the whole project by being overprotective or by talking about how much you will miss him.

5. Once he's there, give him a chance to adjust to his new environment. Don't overreact to homesick letters telling you how miserable he is; don't phone him; and don't write letters telling him how sad the dog is without him or about the super outings he's missing. Do write regularly about what's going on at home; do send a "care package" of goodies (if the camp permits them) or small toys; do come to parents' day to admire all his new skills and achievements.

Helpful Books

Summer Camps & Programs by Adrienne Lansing and Alice Goldsmith (Harmony Books)

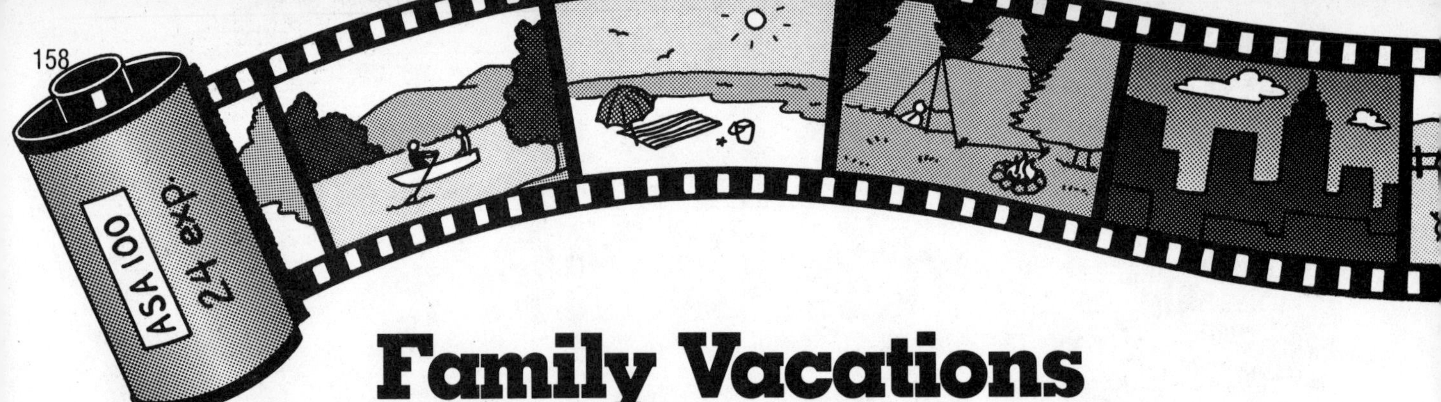

Family Vacations That Won't Break the Bank

If you've been thinking of getting away for a week or two with your family but are discouraged by the high cost of travel when you see the ads, don't give up! There *are* ways to get around the money obstacle. Here are some ideas priced moderately enough to allow the entire family to go away together and have some fun.

College and University Accommodations

Many colleges open up their dormitory space to travelers in the summer months at unbelievably inexpensive rates. Approximately three hundred colleges around the country participate in such a program. Some are located near vacation spots, others require only a short drive to get to resort and sightseeing areas. The average cost for accommodations is $6 to $20 a night. For a complete listing, write Campus Travel Service, 1303 East Balboa Drive, Newport Beach, CA 92661 for their *Travel Accommodations Guide*. Here is a sampling of what is available.

Northeast

Bentley College Beaver and Forest Streets
Waltham, Massachusetts 02254
617-891-2148

Temple University Jones Hall
Park Avenue and Ontario Streets
Philadelphia, Pennsylvania 19140
215-221-3739

South

Tulane University 27 McAllister Drive
New Orleans, Louisiana 70118
504-865-4436

Midwest

University of Detroit 3939 Florence Avenue
Detroit, Michigan 48221
313-927-1230

College of St. Catherine 2004 Rudolph Avenue
St. Paul, Minnesota 55105
612-690-6703

House Exchange

Another way to save on the cost of accommodations, especially if you plan a longer vacation, is to exchange homes with someone who lives where you'd like to vacation. The easiest way to find available houses is to subscribe to a service that publishes a directory of people who are looking to swap. You can also scan the classified section of out-of-town newspapers for someone interested in home swapping. Here's a list of several home exchange services. Fees vary.

Vacation Exchange Club 12006 111 Avenue,
Unit 12, Youngtown, Arizona 85363

International Home Exchange Service
P.O. Box 3975, San Francisco, California 94119

Travelers Home Exchange Club, Inc.
P.O. Box 825, Parker, Colorado 80134

Family Plans

A number of hotels in summer vacation spots offer budget packages for families. Here is a sampling of what you can expect to find, but

consult your travel agent or newspaper to learn more about such package deals and how much money they can save you.

Golden Acres Farm and Ranch
Gilboa, New York (Near Cooperstown, Howe Caverns, Catskill Game Farm)

Based on the concept of a family farm resort, this ranch offers children the opportunity to feed farm animals. There are teen and children's programs, horseback rides, hay rides, bonfires, a lake for boating, square and folk dancing, and tennis. Other features include an indoor pool, sauna, and hot tub.

If you stay eight days and seven nights, you get a discount of 25 percent. If you use the European plan (no meals), you get a discount of 33 percent. And if you and your family stay in an apartment and do your own cooking, you can save 50 percent.

Call toll-free: 800-252-7787 or 800-847-2151

Hershey Park Hershey, Pennsylvania

No child would turn down a trip to the place where Hershey candy bars are made. And the Hershey company makes it easy for you to afford a summer visit. In addition to taking a tour of the candy factory, you can visit the park, which offers rides and attractions, live shows in three theaters, a zoo, a pioneer frontier theme area, and more.

Rates at Hershey Lodge are reasonable, and special children's rates are available. Price includes hotel room, admission to Hershey Park and the zoo, and choice of two Hershey attractions: Hershey Gardens, the Hershey Museum of American Life, or the Hershey Lodge Cinema. Rates are lower if you stay two or three nights. Family camping is available at Hershey Highmeadow Camp nearby.

Call toll-free: 800-533-3131

Washington, D.C.

If you've always wanted to take the family to historical Washington, D.C., the nation's capital, summer is the perfect time to do it. A number of hotels offer good rates, and some allow children to stay in the room with their parents for free.

Sheraton Hotel Washington, N.E.
8500 Annapolis Road
New Carrollton, Maryland 20784

The weekend rate is a real bargain, based on double occupancy, and kids stay for free in the same room with parents. Rate includes in-room movies, pool, parking, limo to the Metro (subway), and discount coupons for tourist attractions.

Call toll-free: 800-325-3535

The Potomac Hotel Group offers a choice of five hotels with reasonable rates based on double occupancy and a three-day, two-night stay. The Capitol Hill Hotel is located just across from the Capitol building. You can walk to the Smithsonian, the Air and Space Museum, the Supreme Court, and the Metro.

Call toll-free: 800-424-9165. Ask about their other hotel locations.

Florida

Florida in the summer? It may sound like a wild idea, but it's a very inexpensive way to take the family on vacation. Try:

Hawaiian Isle Hotel, 176th Street and
Collins Avenue
North Miami Beach, Florida 33160

Kids stay free in the same room with parents. Rates are in effect until December 20th in 30 of the hotel's 210 rooms, so make plans early. Bonus: The seventh night is free. Amenities include two heated pools, 400 feet of beach, free tennis and parking, refrigerators in all rooms, and play room with counselor. AAA recommended.

If you're going to Florida, you might prefer to see one of the state's most popular tourist attractions, Walt Disney World and Epcot Center near Orlando. The Travel Lodge Kissimmee Flags is an eight-minute drive away from the theme park and offers special rates for families. The hotel has air-conditioned rooms, swimming pool, playground, on-site restaurant, and guest laundry room, and is adjacent to a shopping center. This offer is valid between June and September.

Call toll-free: 800-327-3227